Ethnographic
Atlas

Ethnographic Atlas

George Peter Murdock

University of Pittsburgh Press

Contents

Introduction   1

Uses of the Atlas   3

Classification by Clusters   7

Codes   46

Tables   62

Additional Bibliography   126

Ethnographic
Atlas

Introduction

This Atlas was initiated in 1962 as a regular feature of the journal *Ethnology,* in which it has been presented in 21 installments. Experience has shown that these scattered materials are increasingly difficult to use efficiently, especially since they include numerous corrigenda, and a widespread demand has been expressed for collating and summarizing them in a single volume. Although this summary also appears in the pages of *Ethnology,* its potential usefulness as a reference work warrants its separate publication in a hardcover reference edition.

It has not been considered necessary to reproduce all the material as it appeared in *Ethnology.* Thus the bibliographical references, which consumed about half the space of each installment, are omitted, though with an indication of where they originally appeared. Likewise, societies are omitted from the tables in all cases where the ethnographic sources are substantially less adequate, or the assessment of data from them substantially less complete, than for included societies with closely similar cultures. They are nevertheless listed by their identification numbers in the "Classification by Clusters" below, so that readers who wish to use the material on them for any purpose can readily locate it in back issues of *Ethnology.* Also omitted are the synonymies and such comments in the original "Notes" as are not essential for interpreting the symbols in the tables. The total number of societies included in this summary is 862, distributed regionally as follows:

Africa (sub-Saharan)	239
Circum-Mediterranean	95
East Eurasia	93
Insular Pacific	128
North America	218
South and Central America	89

The unequal geographical distribution calls for comment. Practically the entire ethnographic literature has been surveyed for three of the six regions —Africa (Aa to Aj), North America (Na to Nj), and South America (Sa to Sj)—and, with relatively few exceptions, all the societies with adequate ethnographic coverage in these regions have been included. The smaller number listed for South America merely reflects the relative paucity of satisfactory data for this continent. Comparable completeness has been achieved for particular areas in the other regions, notably North Africa (Ca to Cd), the Semitic Near East (Cj), Assam and Burma (Ei), Micronesia (If), and Polynesia (Ii to Ij). For most of East Eurasia and the Insular Pacific, however, only a reasonably wide and representative selection of societies has been assessed, and scores of adequately described societies have not been covered. Were these included, the total number of societies in these regions would probably approximate those for Africa and North America.

The case is still different for Europe (Ce to Ch), an area for which ethnographic responsibility rests primarily with sociologists and historians rather than anthropologists. The author acknowledges no special competence in this area and has included only a small and unrepresentative fraction of the many adequately described societies—and these only because of his conviction that the exclusion of the Western peoples and their cultures from the ethnographic universe is totally unwarranted. He makes no pretense that his selection is other than arbitrary or that the ethnographic sources utilized for them are other than highly incomplete.

Within the above limits, the selection of societies has probably not been seriously affected by adventitious factors, such as the language barrier. The author reads fluently the four principal ethnographic languages—English, French, German, and Spanish—and he can use with varying degrees of difficulty three lesser ones—Dutch, Italian, and Portuguese. For the rest, he has received occasional help from translations or translators.

Appreciation is due to the many colleagues, correspondents, and students who have supplied new or corrected ratings on the basis of their own field work or, in some instances, library research. At least 90 per cent of the entries, however, are the product of the author's own assessment of the ethnographic sources. During the present revision he has checked a substantial proportion of these against other sources at his disposal, including the Human Relations Area Files. The societies not so checked, usually identifiable as those with an unusual number of dots in the first six columns of Table C, are mainly those assessed when the author was compiling his *Africa* (1959) and his "World Ethnographic Sample" (*American Anthropologist* 59: 664-687, 1957) and for which the pertinent literature has not since been readily available. Graduate students have independently checked the entries for about 200 of the societies, and Harold Driver and John Whiting have compared the entries for several columns with their own independent ratings and generously made available their reconciliations of discrepancies.

Uses of the Atlas

This Atlas lends itself to a wide variety of professional uses. The reader may employ it to obtain a quick and approximate answer to specific questions about the content of any included culture, e.g., what is the level of its subsistence economy, the general character of its social organization, or its degree of political integration. He can rapidly survey variations in culture within any geographical area, and if he desires to go further, e.g., to prepare an area course, he can utilize the bibliographical references to lead him to the ethnographic sources that are likely to prove the most helpful. By simple counting he can ascertain the approximate incidence and distribution, either for the world as a whole or for any particular region, of social or cultural phenomena in which he may have a special interest, e.g., avunculocal residence, ambilineal descent, circumcision, games of strategy, or endogamous castes. If he wishes to undertake field work in an area which is relatively untouched ethnographically, he can readily ascertain by elimination the most promising possibilities, e.g., Wadai in Africa, eastern Turkey, the Bismarck Archipelago, or the Montaña in South America.

Other potential uses are legion. But the particular one which the author has had in mind from the outset, and which has largely guided his efforts, is the facilitation of comparative research, especially of cross-cultural studies of a quantitative nature which require a sample of the world's cultures. Although such studies have been appearing of late at a geometrically increasing rate, all of them have exhibited one or more of five serious methodological errors, any one of which is sufficient to call into question the validity of the results. The primary objective of this revision of the Atlas is to provide both a method and the means for avoiding these errors.

The first error consists in including in a sample two or more societies whose cultures are very similar in consequence of derivation from a recent common source. Numerous examples may be found in the author's *Social Structure* (1949), e.g., the inclusion of three closely related Nguni peoples from southeast Africa (Swazi, Xhosa, and Zulu), of five kindred Naga tribes from Assam (Angami, Ao, Lhota, Rengma, and Sema), and of five Western Polynesian groups (Futunans, Pukapukans, Samoans, Tokelau, and Tongans). [Here and below, to avoid invidious comparisons, examples of errors will be cited only from the author's own earlier work.] Such a procedure leads to the plural representation of what are really only variant instances of a single case and thereby obviously distorts all ensuing statistical computations. The solution consists in isolating groups of societies, herewith called "clusters," whose cultures are genetically closely related and hence merit at most but a single representative in any world sample. Only anthropologists possess the knowledge required to identify such clusters, and it is incumbent upon them to make this knowledge available to scholars from other disciplines who may wish to undertake comparative ethnographic research. The principle involved may be stated as follows: *The universe from which a world sample should be drawn consists, not of the total-*

ity of the world's culture-bearing units, but of clusters of such characterized by close genetic relationships.

Under "Classification by Clusters" below the societies of the world are grouped into 412 such clusters. The fundamental criterion for the establishment of clusters is the assumption that at least 1,000 years of separation and divergent evolution are necessary before two societies derived from a common ancestor are likely to develop sufficient differences to be treated as independent cases for comparative purposes. For this reason, societies known historically to have been separated for less than 1,000 years, such as the Bedouin Arabs of North Africa and Arabia or the former colonial peoples of the New World and their cousins of kindred speech in Europe, are not assigned to different clusters. For peoples without written records, the evidence of ethnology and especially of linguistics is drawn upon to estimate a comparable time depth since separation. Occasionally a slightly shorter time span, if accompanied by isolation in a radically different natural environment, is deemed sufficient, e.g., in the case of the Maori of New Zealand as compared with the other Eastern Polynesian peoples. By contrast, the separation of the Bantu peoples of Africa into a number of clusters is consistent with the linguistic evidence (cf. Olmsted in *American Anthropologist* 59: 839-842, 1957) that they have been differentiating for between 20 and 30 centuries.

A second error consists in including in a sample societies which are closely adjacent geographically, even though linguistic evidence does not suggest a genetic relationship between them. Ethnographic evidence is overwhelming that neighboring societies ordinarily borrow cultural elements freely from one another, so that their cultures cannot be regarded as independent units any more than can those of societies derived from a proximate common ancestor. The principle involved may be expressed as follows: *No world sample should include any two societies located geographically so close to one another that diffusion is likely to have jeopardized the essential independence of their cultures.*

Various practical suggestions have been proposed, especially by Naroll, to guard against this danger, and the present writer has adopted (see *Ethnology* 5: 112:113, 1966) a compromise which may be called the "three degree rule." This assumes that a distance of 200 miles between the geographical centers of two societies belonging to different clusters will ordinarily be sufficient to assure a degree of independence comparable to that achievable by genetically related societies over a time span of 1,000 years. Since 200 miles is approximately equal to 3 degrees of latitude in any part of the world and to 3 degrees of longitude in the tropics, it can be estimated readily from the geographical coordinates listed in the "Classification by Clusters." The rule is applied as follows. If any two societies belonging to different clusters are separated by 3 or more degrees of latitude or by 3 or more degrees of longitude (in the tropical zone; 4° or 5° in the temperate zone, depending upon a distance of less or more than 35° from the Equator; 6° in the frigid zone), they may be included in the same world sample; otherwise not. In some instances, for convenience, adjacent societies with different languages but clearly related cultures have been assigned to the same cluster, since plural representation would in any case be impossible.

A third error is the inclusion of societies for which the ethnographic information is exceedingly scanty. Thus, *Social Structure* erred in using, for example, the Daka, Getmatta, and Mikir. It is impossible, of course, to include societies whose cultures are completely undescribed or whose descriptions lie undiscovered in archives or unavailable in manuscript form. And the use of societies whose cultures are inadequately described involves a double risk: (1) that the data are undependable as well as incomplete and (2) that the utilization of alternative societies in the same cluster with more satisfactory source materials is thereby prevented. The only admissible exceptions are instances, like the Chibcha, Guanche, and Tasmanians, where a culture is known to be highly distinctive, where its description, though inadequate, contains at least a fair amount of potentially usable information, and where the cluster offers no acceptable alternative. The principle involved may be phrased as follows: *The universe from which a world sample may appropriately be drawn consists, not of all the societies or clusters which are known to exist or to have existed, but only of those whose cultures have been adequately described in sources that are generally available.* In accordance with this principle, some 300 societies which were included in *Ethnology* installments have been excluded here.

A fourth error is to exclude from a sample for any reason, or to underrepresent in it, any category of known and adequately described societies. *Social Structure,* for example, included none of the civilizations of antiquity known from historical sources, no society in Indonesia described in the Dutch language, and only three Indo-European-speaking societies from Europe and the New World. A serious attempt has been made to correct such deficiencies in the present summary. The principle involved is, of course, that *the universe from which a world sample is properly drawn should consist of all societies and clusters whose cultures have been adequately described without arbitrary limitations of time, area, or the languages in which the ethnographic accounts have been written.* An incomplete roster of adequately described societies within a cluster is far less serious than an incomplete list of clusters, for the members of a cluster are in a sense interchangeable whereas the omission of a cluster distorts the universe.

A fifth error is to depart in any respect from chance, i.e., from randomizing methods, in the selection of a sample. It is improper, for example, to include a society because the investigator happens to know its culture at first hand, as did the author when he used, in *Social Structure,* the culture in which he was reared (Yankees of Connecticut) and all three of the cultures which he had personally studied in the field (Haida, Tenino, and Trukese). The principle may be formulated as follows: *Any known and adequately described society must have an unimpeded chance of being drawn in any world sample, and all clusters must enjoy an essentially equal chance of being represented.* Unless this ideal is at least approximately achieved, it is in theory illegitimate to employ probability statistics to validate discovered associations or "adhesions," as has been done in most cross-cultural studies to date. It is a primary objective of this summary to provide a theoretical justification for the use of statistics in comparative research.

Observing all the foregoing principles and precautions, any reader may test any hypothesis for which the data in the tables are relevant with a sample of maximal size by adhering to the following procedure:

1. Formulate an hypothesis according to which two sets of tabulated data should be expected to reveal a positive or negative association.
2. Rearrange the 412 clusters in a new rank order by some method of pure chance, e.g., a table of random numbers.
3. For each cluster containing more than one society, select by chance, e.g., by a cast of dice, a particular society to represent it.
4. Discard any selected society for which the tables do not contain the needed data, and select by chance a substitute from the same cluster. Eliminate entirely any cluster for which information is lacking on all member societies.
5. Check the geographical coordinates for all the remaining societies, and eliminate the second ranking one of every pair which violates the "three degree rule." Substitute, if possible, another society of the same cluster which does not violate the rule; if there are none, eliminate the cluster.
6. When all necessary eliminations have been made, tabulate the results and employ any suitable statistical technique to assess the bearing of the results on the hypothesis.

If desired, the probability that the results reflect pure chance may be calculated, but it should be remembered that the test has exhausted the entire universe of cultural clusters and that the only possibility of refining the results is by redoing the entire study with another set of random selections.

A similar procedure may be used with smaller samples, especially if the researcher produces an independent series of ratings on new data and wishes to correlate them with information in the Atlas.

Classification by Clusters

The 862 societies included in the tables are classified below into the 412 proposed clusters which comprise them. The total number of clusters, by region, is as follows:

Africa	85
Circum-Mediterranean	55
East Eurasia	66
Insular Pacific	70
North America	69
South America	67

The author has reason to predict that a completely exhaustive survey of the literature would reveal further adequately described societies and additional clusters in approximately the following numbers:

In Africa, a few new societies but probably no additional clusters.

In the Circum-Mediterranean, more than 100 new societies, nearly all from Europe (Ce to Ch), and one or two new clusters, of which the Gypsies would certainly be one.

In East Eurasia, about 50 new societies and perhaps six additional clusters—at least two in India (Ef to Eg) and the rest scattered.

In the Insular Pacific, at least 50 new societies and about ten additional clusters, mainly in Melanesia (Ig to Ih) and in Indonesia (Ib to Ic), where the ethnographic literature in Dutch has as yet been only partially assessed.

In North America, a handful of new societies and probably no additional clusters.

In South America, at least a dozen new societies and perhaps two or three additional clusters, of which one would certainly be the Caribbean Negroes, the peoples who have combined European and African cultural elements in a new creative synthesis characterized, amongst other special features, by the so-called "matrifocal family."

The incorporation of such additional data would bring the total number of relatively independent clusters in the world to approximately 430 and would complete the identification and "stratification" of the known cultural universe. Future ethnographic, historical, and sociological research will, of course, add substantially to the number of adequately described societies and will occasionally bring to light an additional cluster.

Conscientious users of this survey may wish to include the probable additional clusters in the list to be rearranged and drawn from, and to search out for themselves adequately described cultures from the clusters selected for representation. Any ratings they obtain would be particularly welcome for publication in future installments of the Atlas.

Under each of the clusters below the individual societies are listed in ap-

7

proximately the order of the number of columns in the tables containing codified information on them. The name of each society is followed by its identifying number (in parentheses), its geographical location (L) in degrees of latitude and longitude, the approximate time level (T) to which the ethnographic data pertain, an estimate of its population (P), references (B) to the volumes and pages in *Ethnology* where bibliographical sources are cited, and comments explanatory of entries in the tables marked by asterisks.

1: Pygmies
>   Mbuti (Aa5), with special reference to those of Efulu. L: 2N, 28E. T: 1930. P: 10,000. B: I, 393; III, 331; V, 122; V, 444. Comment—Column 64: NcB in some groups.

2: Bushmen
>   Kung (Aa1), with special reference to those of Nyae Nyae. L: 20S, 21E. T: 1950. P: 3,500 in 1953. B: I, 124; I, 537; V, 122.
>   Naron (Aa7). L: 20S, 24E. T: 1910. P: A few hundred. B: IV, 118.
>   Others: Xam (Aa8).

3: Hottentot
>   Nama (Aa3). L: 26S, 18E. T: 1840. P: 24,000 in 1946. B: I, 275. Comment—Column 37: But early sources report the excision of one testicle at the age of nine or ten.
>   Others: Bergdama (Aa4).

4: Nguni
>   Swazi (Ab2). L: 27S, 32E. T: 1880. P: 180,000 in 1946. B: I, 124; V, 122.
>   Zulu (Ab12). L: 29S, 31S. T: 1830. P: 250,000 in 1921. B: II, 260; IV, 451.
>   Mpezeni Ngoni (Ac9). L: 12S, 33E. T: 1940. P: 85,000 in 1950. B: II, 124. Comment—Column 24: There are vestigial patrisibs; Column 37: But circumcision was formerly practiced.
>   Ndebele (Ab9). L: 20S, 28E. T: 1870. P: 300,000 in 1948. B: II, 259.
>   Pondo (Ab10). L: 31S, 30E. P: 260,000 in 1936. B: II, 260.
>   Others: Xhosa (Ab11).

5: Sotho
>   Tswana (Ab13), with special reference to the Kgatla. L: 24S, 27E. T: 1880. P: 580,000 in 1946. B: II, 260. Comment—Columns 20 and 22: Quasi-lineages inferred from the patrilocal but basically territorial ward organization and from vestigial patrisibs.
>   Venda (Ab6). L: 23S, 30E. T: 1900. P: 150,000 in 1930. B: I, 393. Comment—Column 37: But only recently adopted; Columns 42 and 44: But no longer practiced; Column 78: But without actual penetration.
>   Sotho (Ab8). L: 29S, 28E. T: 1860. P: 900,000 in 1953. B: I, 538.
>   Others: Pedi (Ab15).

6: Shona-Thonga
>   Thonga (Ab4). L: 24S, 32E. T: 1920. P: More than 1,000,000. B: I, 275.
>   Shona (Ab17), with special reference to the Zezuru. L: 19S, 31E. T: 1920. P: 700,000 in 1931. B: II, 260. Comment—Column 12: St with uxorilocal residence a patterned alternative.
>   Lovedu (Ab14). L: 24S, 31E. T: 1930. P: 40,000. B: II, 260. Comment—Column 42: Formerly though not recently.
>   Lenge (Ab16). L: 25S, 34E. T: 1930. B: II, 260.
>   Others: Ndau (Ab17).

7: Ila-Tonga
>   Ila (Ac1). L: 16S, 27E. T: 1920. P: 22,000 in 1957. B: I, 124.
>   Plateau Tonga (Ac30). L: 18S, 28E. T: 1940. P: 90,000 in 1948. B: V, 124. Comment—Column 25: But formerly Cc.

8: Barotseland
Lozi (Ab3). L: 15S, 23E. T: 1890. P: 67,000 in 1934. B: I, 275.
9: Southwestern Bantu
Herero (Ab2). L: 21S, 16E. T: 1900. P: 100,000 in 1930. B: I, 124.
Ambo (Ab19), with special reference to the Kuanyama. L: 17S, 16E. T: 1910. P: 60,000 Kuanyama in 1948. B: II, 260. Comment—Column 35: Formerly Cp.
Nyaneka (Ab7). L: 15S, 14E. T: 1920. P: 40,000 in 1920. B: I, 538.
Others: Ngumbi (Ab20).
10: Western Angola
Mbundu (Ab5). L: 12S, 16E. T: 1930. P: 1,200,000 in 1940. B: I, 393.
Others: Kisama (Ab21).
11: Lower Congo
Suku (Ac17). L: 6S, 18E. T: 1910. P: 80,000 in 1949. B: V, 123.
Yombe (Ac8). L: 5S, 13E. T: 1930. P: 170,000 in 1933. B: I, 538.
Pende (Ac2). L: 6S, 20E. T: 1920. P: 27,000 in 1955. B: I, 124. Comment—Column 27: But I for all cross-cousins except FaSiSo (ms) and MoBrDa (ws).
Sundi (Ac18). L: 5S, 14E. T: 1910. P: 65,000 in 1953. B: V, 123.
Kongo (Ac14). L: 7S, 15E. T: 1900. B: V, 123. Comment—Column 32: Formerly 33.
Others: Mbala (Ac15), Shogo (Ac16), Teke (Ac19), Yaka (Ac20).
12: Kasai
Kuba (Ac4). L: 5S, 22E. T: 1910. P: 73,000 in 1947. B: I, 275. Comment—Column 12: A patterned alternative is T, with alternating U and A residence.
Lele (Ac23). L: 5S, 21E. T: 1950. P: 10,000 in 1947. B: V, 124; V, 444. Comment—Column 25: The preferred marriage is with a MoBrDaDa; Column 69: Dependent Pygmies.
Dzing (Ac22). L: 4S, 20E. T: 1930. B: V, 124.
Bunda (Ac21). L: 4S, 19E. T: 1910. B: V, 123. Comment—Column 25: But the most highly preferred marriage is with a MoBrDaDa.
Songo (Ac25), with reference to the tribe of this name on the Luniunga and Gobari rivers. L: 5S, 18E. T: 1930.
Others: Sakata (Ac24), Yanzi (Ac26).
13: Lunda
Luvale (Ac11). L: 12S, 22E. T: 1930. P: 90,000 in 1940. B: IV, 248.
Ndembu (Ac6). L: 11S, 26E. T: 1930. P: 63,000. B: I, 393.
Chokwe (Ac12). L: 10S, 21E. T: 1920. P: 600,000 in 1940. B: IV, 346.
Luimbe (Ac28). L: 12S, 18E. T: 1930. P: 40,000 in 1950. B: V, 124.
Others: Luchazi (Ac27), Luwa (Ac29).
14: Bemba-Lamba
Bemba (Ac3). L: 11S, 31E. T: 1900. P: 150,000 in 1951. B: I, 275.
Lamba (Ac5). L: 13S, 28E. T: 1920. P: 70,000. B: I, 393.
Luapula (Ac34). L: 10S, 29E. T: 1940. P: 100,000. B: V, 125. Comment—Column 44: Formerly P.
Tumbuka (Ac36). L: 12S, 34E. T: 1920. P: 115,000 in 1945. B: V, 125. Comment—Column 12: Formerly St; Column 16: Formerly uAu; Column 20: Formerly O; Column 22: Formerly 5; Column 32: Formerly, but more recently subject to the Ngoni; Column 39: But cattle were formerly kept; Column 73: Formerly matrilineal.
Lala (Ac33). L: 15S, 31E. T: 1940. P: 60,000 in 1950. B: V, 125. Comment—Column 42: Formerly Mc.
Others: Buye (Ac31), Kaonde (Ac32), Shila (Ac35).
15: Maravi
Chewa (Ac10). L: 14S, 33E. T: 1920. P: 750,000 in 1955. B: IV, 118.
Nyanja (Ac38). L: 16S, 36E. T: 1910. P: 575,000 in 1945. B: V, 125.
Lakeshore Tonga (Ac13). L: 12S, 34E. T: 1950. P: 50,000 in 1953. B: IV, 451.
Others: Kunda (Ac37), Sena (Ac40).

16: Yao-Makonde
Yao (Ac7). L: 13S, 36E. T: 1920. P: 360,000 in 1945, exclusive of a large number in Mozambique. B: I, 538.
Others: Makonde (Ac41), Makua (Ac42).

17: Ngonde
Nyakyusa (Ad6). L: 9S, 34E. T: 1930. P: 163,000 in 1931. B: I, 393. Comment
—Column 36: Coitus interruptus is practiced from "very soon" after childbirth until the child is able to walk.
Ngonde (Ad16). L: 10S, 34E. T: 1920. P: 60,000 in 1945. B: V, 126.

18: Rukwa
Fipa (Ad19). L: 8S, 31E. T: 1910. P: 85,000 in 1957. B: V, 126; V, 445. Comment—Column 39: But So in some districts.
Iwa (Ad15). L: 10S, 32E. T: 1900. P:12,000 in 1953. B: V, 126; V, 445.
Pimbwe (Ad31). L: 7S, 31E. T: 1930. P: 11,000 in 1957. B: V, 126; V, 445.
Comment—Columns 20 and 22: "A man belongs to the kin group (*uluko*) of his father's father or his son's son, but not to that of his father or of his son (who both belong to another *uluko*). There is thus a perpetual alternation of two *uluko*-names in each patrilineage."
Safwa (Ad17). L: 8S, 33E. T: 1920. P: 45,000 in 1950. B: V, 126.
Others: Mambwe (Ac43).

19: Nyamwezi
Sukuma (As22). L: 3S, 34E. T: 1950. P: 1,000,000 in 1948. B: V, 127. Comment—Column 12; Alternatively O, in which case children are affiliated with the mother's kin group; Column 76: Patrilineal, but matrilineal if no bride-price was paid for mother.
Nyamwezi (Ad20). L: 5S, 33E. T: 1920. B: V, 126. Comment—Column 12: Alternatively Ts, in which case children are affiliated with the mother's kin group; Columns 73, 74, and 75: Mixed P and M succession and inheritance.
Others: Bende (Ad18), Sumbwa (Ad47).

20: Hatsa
Hatsa (Aa9), previously called Kindiga. L: 3S, 35E. T: 1910. P: 600. B: V, 122.

21: Rift
Gogo (Ad24). L: 7S, 36E. T: 1910. P: Over 100,000 in 1910. B: V, 127.
Turu (Ad26). L: 5S, 34E. T: 1910. P: 145,000 in 1949. B: V, 127.
Sandawe (Aa6). L: 5S, 36E. T: 1920. P: 23,000 in 1948. B: I, 537. Comment—Column 27: Special terms for MoBrCh, but sibling terms for other cousins.
Others: Mbugwe (Ad5), Rangi (Ad25).

22: Rufiji
Hehe (Ad8), with special reference to the Iringa. L: 8S, 35E. T: 1910. P: 85,000 in 1930. B: I, 539.
Bena (Ad11). L: 9S, 36E. T: 1930. P: 16,000 in 1931. B: IV, 118
Others: Sangu (Ad23).

23: Luguru-Zigula
Luguru (Ad14). L: 8S, 38E. T: 1930. P: 200,000 in 1960. B: IV, 451
Others: Kwere (Ad27), Zigula (Ad28).

24: Swahili
Bajun (Ad1). L: 2S, 41E. T: 1950. P: 2,000 in 1950. B: I, 124. Comment—Columns 42, 46, and 48: Despised as slave occupations.
Hadimu (Ad29). L: 6S, 40E. T: 1930. P: 100,000 in 1924. B: V, 127. Comment—Column 24: But with a patrilineal bias; Column 44: Formerly P; Column 48: Formerly.

25: Nyika
Pokomo (Ad33). L: 1S, 40E. T: 1900. P: 20,000 in 1948. B: V, 127.
Digo (Ad30). L: 4S, 39E. T: 1890. P: 112,000 in 1948. B: V, 127.
Giriama (Ad32). L: 3S, 40E. T: 1900. P: 120,000 in 1948. B: V, 127.
Others: Duruma (Ad31).

26: Kenya Highlands

Kikuyu (Ad4). L: 1S, 37E. T: 1930. P: 1,000,000 in 1948. B: I, 275.
Chagga (Ad3). L: 3S, 37E. T: 1910. P: 235,000 in 1948. B: I, 275.
Meru (Ad35). L: Equator, 35E. T: 1940. P: 255,000 in 1948. B: V, 128.
Shambala (Ad10). L: 5S, 38E. T: 1910. P: 220,000 in 1948. B: III, 422.
Others: Kamba (Ad34), Pare (Ad10), Teita (Ad37).

27: East Nyanza
Gisu (Ad9). L: 1N, 34E. T: 1900. P: 250,000. B: II, 124. Comment—Column
 78: But without penetration.
Sonjo (Ad39). L: 3S, 36E. T: 1950. P: 4,500 in 1957. B: V, 128.
Vugusu (Ad41). L: 1N, 35E. T: 1930. P: 50,000 in 1937. B: V, 128.
Others: Gusii (Ad12), Kara (Ad38), Tiriki (Ad40).

28: East Lacustrine Bantu
Ganda (Ad7). L: 1N, 32E. T: 1880. P: 800,000 in 1948. B: I, 538.
Nyoro (Ad2). L: 2N, 32E. T: 1950. P: 110,000 in 1957. B: I, 125; I, 538.
Haya (Ad42). L: 1S, 32E. T: 1900. P: 325,000 in 1957. B: V, 129.
Soga (Ad46). L: 1N, 33E. T: 1950. P: 425,000 in 1948. B: V, 129.
Others: Kerewe (Ad43), Zinza (Ad49).

29: West Lacustrine Bantu
Rundi (Ae8). L: 3S, 30E. T: 1910. P: 2,000,000. B: I, 539; V, 129. Comment—
 Column 67: Ethnic classes or castes of herders, tillers, and hunters.
Ruanda (Ae10). L: 2S, 30E. T: 1910. P: 2,130,000 in 1952. B: IV, 118; V, 129.
 Comment—Column 67: Ethnic classes or castes of herders, tillers, and
 hunters.
Ha (Ae14). L: 5S, 30E. T: 1950. P: 200,000 in 1948. B: V, 130.
Chiga (Ad13). L: 3S, 30E. T: 1930. P: 100,000 in 1940. B: IV, 248.
Nyankole (Ad45). L: Equator, 31E. T: 1920. P: 520,000 in 1959. B: V, 129.
Hunde (Ae15). L: 2S, 28E. T: 1940. B: V, 130. Comment—Column 67: Ethnic
 classes or castes of herders, tillers, and hunters.
Konjo Ad44). L: 1S, 30E. T: 1920. P: 375,000 in 1959. B: V, 129.
Others: Bashi (Ae13), Toro (Ad48).

30: Luba
Rega (Ae17). L: 3S, 28E. T: 1900. B: V, 130.
Luba (Ae6), with special reference to the Bena Kalundwe. L: 8S, 26E. T: 1930.
 B: I, 394.
Others: Lulua (Ae16), Songe (Ae18), Yeke (Ae19)

31: Mongo
Nkundo (Ae4). L: Equator, 20E. T: 1930. P: 150,000 in 1940. B: I, 276.
Kutshu (Ae22). L: 4S, 22E. T: 1900. B: V, 130.
Others: Ekonda (Ae20), Kela (Ae21), Lalia (Ae23), Mongo (Ae24), Tetela
 (Ae25), Topoke (Ae26).

32: Riverain Congo
Poto (Ae29). L: 2N, 22E. T: 1900. B: V, 131.
Ngala (Ae28). L: 1N, 18E. T: 1900. P: 125,000 in 1950. B: V, 131.
Songola (Ae11). L: 4S, 26E. T: 1900. P: Over 100,000. B: IV, 248.
Others: Lokele (Ae27).

33: Babwa-Bira
Amba (Ae1), with special reference to those of Bwamba in Uganda. L: 1N, 30E.
 T: 1950. P: 18,000 in Bwamba in 1948. B: I, 125; IV, 451. Comment—Col-
 umn 37: But circumcision was practiced until 1933.
Babwa (Ae7). L: 3N, 25E. T: 1910. P: 16,000 in 1924. B: I, 539.
Others: Bira (Ae30), Budu (Ae31), Kumu (Ae32), Ndaka (Ae33), Plains Bira
 (Ae34), Rumbi (Ae35).

34: Ngombe
Ngombe (Ae39). L: 2N, 20E. T: 1920. B: V, 132. Comment—Column 27: Sib-
 ling terms extended to FaBrCh, but a special term for all other cousins.
Ndoko (Ae38). L: 2N, 21E. T: 1920. B: V, 132.
Others: Bombesa (Ae36), Budja (Ae37).

35: Fang-Dzem
  Fang (Ae3). L: 1N, 11E. T: 1910. P: 850,000 in 1950. B: I, 276. Comment—
    Column 35: But S in consequence of recent borrowing.
  Kota (Ae41). L: 1N, 14E. T: 1940. B: V, 132. Comment—Column 69: De-
    pendent Pygmies.
  Others: Dzem (Ae40), Ngumba (Ae42), Sanga (Ae43).
36: Biafra Coast
  Kpe (Ae2). L: 4N, 9E. T: 1950. P: 38,000 in 1953. B: I, 125. Comment—Col-
    umn 37: Formerly 6; Column 42: Formerly.
  Duala (Ae12). L: 4N, 10E. T: 1940. P: 40,000 in 1947. B: Iv, 346. Comment—
    Column 22: Matrilineal descent was formerly recognized; Column 38: For-
    merly T: Column 42: Formerly.
  Others: Bubi (Ae44), Kundu (Ae45), Mpongwe (Ae46), Puku (Ae47).
37: Middle Cameroon
  Banen (Ae51). L: 5N, 11E. T: 1940. P: 25,000 in 1949. B: V, 133.
  Bafia (Ae48). L: 5N, 11E. T: 1930. P: 12,000 in 1949. B: V, 133. Comment—
    Column 12: Usually after capture.
38: Cameroon Highlands
  Bamileke (Ae5). L: 5N, 10E. T: 1910. P: 455,000 in 1951. B: I, 393.
  Bamum (Ae50). L: 6N, 11E. T: 1920. P: 80,000 in 1951. B: V, 133.
  Fut (Ae9). L: 6N, 10E. T: 1950. P: 34,000 in 1953. B: IV, 118.
  Ndob (Ae55). L: 6N, 10E. T: 1950. P: 44,000 in 1953. B: V, 134.
  Nsaw (Ae56). L: 6N, 11E. T: 1950. P: 60,000 in 1953. B: V, 134.
  Others: Bali (Ae49), Fungom (Ae52), Kom (Ae54), Nsungli (Ae57), Tikar
    (Ae58), Widekum (Ae59).
39: Cross River
  Yako (Af4). L: 6N, 8E. T: 1930. P: 20,000. B: I, 276.
  Others: Banyang (Af16), Boki (Af17), Ekoi (Af18).
40: Coastal Nigeria
  Ibibio (Af20). L: 5N, 8E. T: 1910. P: 1,000,000. B: V, 329.
  Itsekiri (Af22). L: 6N, 5E. T: 1940. P: 33,000 in 1952. B: V, 329. Comment—
    Column 62: Performed almost exclusively by slaves.
  Efik (Af19). L: 5N, 8E. T: 1950. P: 30,000 in 1945. B: V, 329.
  Others: Ijaw (Af21).
41: Ibo-Edo
  Ibo (Af10). L: 6N, 7E. T: 1930. P: 3,500,000 in 1950. B: IV, 119. Comment—
    Column 36: "The period of lactation lasts about two years."
  Edo (Af24). L: 6N, 6E. T: 1900. P: 200,000 in 1952. B: V, 329.
  Afikpo Ibo (Af23). L: 6N, 8E. T: 1950. B: V, 329; I, 455. Comment—Columns
    74 and 76: Mixed but with a matrilineal emphasis.
  Isoko (Af25). L: 5N, 6E. T: 1930. P: 435,000 in 1952. B: V, 329. Comment—
    Column 42: But smiths are aliens of the Ibo tribe.
  Others: Kukuruku (Af26).
42: Nupe-Idoma
  Nupe (Af8). L: 9N, 6E. T: 1930. P: 360,000 in 1955. B: I, 539.
  Igbira (Af13). L: 8N, 7E. T: 1920. P: 150,000 in 1952. B: IV, 248.
  Gbari (Af28). L: 10N, 7E. T: 1910. P: 200,000 in 1960. B: V, 330. Comment—
    Column 37: But circumcision occurs sporadically; Columns 74-76: Patri-
    lineal with local variations regarding participation of brothers and sons.
  Others: Afo (Af27), Idoma (Af29), Igala (Af30), Koro (Af31).
43: Yoruba
  Oyo Yoruba (Af6). L: 8N, 4E. T: 1950. P: 220,000 in 1931. B: I, 394; V, 328.
    Comment—Columns 74 and 76: But Pe for property acquired rather than
    inherited by deceased.
  Ekiti (Af32). L: 8N, 5E. T: 1950. P: 220,000. B: V, 330. Comment—Columns
    74-76: But Pe for property acquired rather than inherited by deceased.
  Egba (Af32). L: 7N, 3E. T: 1920. P: 500,000. B: V, 330.
  Others: Ife (Af34).

44: Ewe-Fon
    Fon (Af1). L: 7N, 2E. T: 1890. P: 250,000. B: I, 125; II, 403.
    Ewe (Af36), with special reference to the Glidyi. L: 7N, 1E. T: 1900. P: 700,000
        in 1948. B: V, 331.
    Others: Adangme (Af35), Buem (Af37).
45: Akan
    Ashanti (Af3). L: 7N, 2W. T: 1900. P: 800,000 in 1948. B: I, 276. Comment—
        Column 38: But A for about 50 per cent of boys.
    Fanti (Af42). L: 6N, 1W. T: 1900. P: 200,000 in 1950. B: V, 331. Comment—
        Column 76: But sons inherit some property.
    Baule (Af9). L: 8N, 5W. T: 1900. P: 385,000 in 1950. B: IV, 118.
    Ga (Af43). L: 6N, longitude of Greenwich. T: 1930. B: V, 332. Comment—
        Column 22: But Daniell reports E.
    Others: Abron (Af38), Akyem (Af12), Alagya (Af44), Anyi (Af39), Assini
        (Af40), Attie (Af41), Avikam (Af45).
46: Kru
    Sapo (Af49). L: 6N, 9W. T: 1940. B: V, 332.
    Bete (Af7). L: 6N, 7W. T: 1950. P: 150,000 in 1956. B: I, 539.
    Others: Bakwe (Af46), Kran (Ac47), Kru (Af48).
47: Southern Mande
    Ngere (Af56), with special reference to the Gio. L: 7N, 8W. T: 1930. P: 70,000
        in 1950. B: V, 333. Comment—Column 52: Rude rafts only.
    Gagu (Af51). L: 7N, 6W. T: 1920. P: 13,000 in 1950. B: V, 332.
    Guro (Af51). L: 7N, 6W. T: 1920. P: 13,000 in 1950. B: V, 332.
    Others: Dan (Af50), Tura (Af53).
48: Mende-Temne
    Mende (Af5). L: 8N, 11W. T: 1930. P: 580,000 in 1931. B: I, 394. Comment—
        Column 38: But only temporarily.
    Kissi (Af2). L: 9N, 10W. T: 1950. P: 200,000 in 1954. B: I, 125.
    Kpelle (Af15). L: 7N, 9W. T: 1920. P: 175,000 in 1950. B: IV, 451; V, 328.
    Gbande (Af54). L: 8N, 10W. T: 1930. P: 25,000 in 1930. B: V, 332.
    Toma (Af11). L: 11N, 9W. P: 150,000 in 1950. B: IV, 119; V, 328.
    Temne (Af57). L: 8N, 13W. T: 1910. P: 525,000 in 1948. B: V, 333. Comment—
        Columns 42 and 46: But these specialists are aliens of the Yalunka tribe.
    Sherbro (Af14). L: 7N, 13W. T: 1930. P: 100,000 in 1948. B:IV, 346. Comment
        —Columns 22 and 24: From a recent report, matrilineages have apparently
        become converted into ambilineal ramages; Columns 74 and 76: For-
        merly M.
    Others: Gola (Af55), Vai (Af58)
49: Guinea
    Banyun (Ag16). L: 12N, 16W. T: 1930. P: 7,500 in 1950. B: V, 333.
    Bijogo (Ag18). L: 11N, 16W. T: 1930. P: 20,000 in 1945. B: V, 333.
    Diola (Ag19), with special reference to the Felup. L: 12N, 17W. T: 1930. P:
        50,000 Felup in 1950. B: V, 333.
    Others: Baga (Ag14), Balante (Ag15), Biafada (Ag17), Pepel (Ag20)
50: Tenda
    Coniagui (Ag8). L: 13N, 13W. T: 1910. P: 11,000 in 1945. B: I, 539.
    Bassari (Ag21). L: 12N, 13W. T: 1910. P: 7,600 in 1945. B: V, 334.
51: Senegal
    Wolof (Cb2). L: 15N, 17W. T: 1950. P: 850,000. B: I, 126. Comment—Column
        31: But 3 if Dakar is not considered an indigenous city.
    Serer (Ag22), with special reference to those of Sine. L: 14N, 17W. T: 1920. P:
        300,000 in 1950. B: V, 334. Comment—Column 76: But matrilineal until
        recently.
52: Sedentary Fulani
    Futajalonke (Ag6). L: 11N, 13W. T: 1890. P: 720,000 in 1940. B: I, 394.
    Tukulor (Cb23). L: 17N, 14W. T: 1930. P: 275,000 in 1950. B: V, 344.
    Others: Liptako (Cb22).

53: Nuclear Mande
> Bambara (Ag1). L: 13N, 7W. T: 1920. P: 1,000,000 in 1954. B: I, 125. Comment—Column 25: But O or C in some districts; Column 32: Formerly 43.
> Malinke (Ag9). L: 11N, 9W. T: 1930. P: 830,000 in 1950. B: IV, 119.
> Soninke (Ag25). L: 15N, 10W. T: 1900. P: 360,000 in 1950. B: V, 334. Comment—Column 60: Cattle are herded and milked exclusively by Fulani.
> Susu (Ag26). L: 15N, 13W. T: 1930. P: 300,000 in 1950. B: V, 334.
> Others: Kasonke (Ag23), Koranko (Ag24).

54: Marka
> Diula (Ag27). L: 9N, 4W. T: 1910. P: 160,000 in 1950. B: V, 334. Comment—Column 7: But the economy is primarily mercantile.
> Others: Nono (Ag28), Samo (Ag29).

55: Niger Fishermen
> Bozo (Ag7). L: 14N, 5W. T: 1930. P: 29,000 in 1942. B: I, 539.

56: Habe
> Dogon (Ag3). L: 15N, 3W. T: 1930. P: 225,000 in 1957. B: I, 276. Comment—Column 25: Formerly M.
> Bobo (Ag30). L: 13N, 4W. T: 1910. P: 240,000 in 1952. B: V, 334.

57: Senufo
> Senufo (Ag32). L: 10N, 6W. T: 1900. P: 540,000 in 1948. B: V, 335.
> Minianka (Ag31). L: 12N, 6W. T: 1910. P: 150,000 in 1942. B: V, 335.

58: Lobi
> Birifor (Ag5). L: 10N, 3W. T: 1930. P: 85,000. B: I, 394.
> Lobi (Ag11). L: 10N, 4W. T: 1910. P: 100,000. B: IV, 248.
> Others: Dian (Ag33), Dorosie (Ag34), Kulango (Af35), Lowiili (Ag36).

59: Grusi
> Tallensi (Ag4). L: 11N, 1W. T: 1930. P: 35,000 in 1931. B: I, 276. Comment—Columns 74 and 76: But Pe for property acquired rather than inherited by deceased.
> Nankanse (Ag12). L: 10N, 1W. T: 1910. P: 70,000 in 1948. B: IV, 249.
> Kusasi (Ag41). L: 11N, longitude of Greenwich. T: 1920. P: 93,000 in 1948. B: V, 335. Comment—Columns 74 and 76: Brothers and sons share in inheritance.
> Kasena (Ag13). L: 11N, 1W. T: 1910. P: 40,000 in 1948. B: IV, 451.
> Others: Awuna (Ag37), Builsa (Ag38), Dagari (Ag39), Isala (Ag40), Nunuma (Ag42), Vagala (Ag43).

60: Mole
> Yatenga Mossi (Ag2). L: 13N, 2W. T: 1950. P: 400,000 in 1950. B: I, 125; IV, 248.
> Mossi (Ag47), with special reference to those of Ougadougou. L: 12N, 2W. T: 1900. P: 1,300,000 in 1950. B: V, 336.
> Others: Dagomba (Ag44), Gurma (Ag45), Mamprusi (Ag46).

61: Borgu-Mango
> Konkomba (Ag10). L: 10N, longitude of Greenwich. T: 1940. P: 60,000 in 1948. B: IV, 248; IV, 451; V, 333. Comment—Column 27: For female cross-cousins, but O for male cross-cousins.
> Kabre (Ag49). L: 10N, 2E. T: 1930. P: 160,000 in 1950. B: V, 336.
> Basari (Ag48). L: 9N, 1E. T: 1890. P: 40,000 in 1950. B: V, 336.
> Others: Moba (Ag50), Somba (Ag51), Tem (Ag52).

62: Middle Niger
> Kamuku (Ah14). L: 11N, 6E. T: 1920. P: 22,000 in 1949. B: V, 337.
> Reshe (Ah15). L: 11N, 5E. T: 1920. P: 20,000 in 1931. B: V, 337.
> Basa (Ah11). L: 8N, 8E. T: 1950. P: 70,000 in 1960. B: V, 337.
> Others: Basakomo (Ah12), Dakakari (Ah13).

63: Jos Plateau
> Katab (Ah1). L: 10N, 8E. T: 1930. P: 18,000 in 1949. B: I, 125; II, 540.
> Anaguta (Ah9). L: 10N, 9E. T: 1920. P: 5,700 in 1934. B: III, 331.
> Kagoro (Ah20). L: 10N, 8E. T: 1920. P: 10,500 in 1950. B: V, 337.

Kadara (Ah19). L: 10N, 7E. T: 1920. P: 10,000 in 1921. B: V, 337.
Others: Angas (Ah16), Birom (Ah17), Borrom (Ah18), Chawai (Ah10), Gure (Ah6), Kurama (Ah21), Yergum (Ah22).

64: Tiv-Jukun
Tiv (Ah3). L: 7N, 9E. T: 1920. P: 700,000 in 1952. B: I, 277; IV, 451. Comment —Column 12: Alternatively T, involving avunculocal residence and affilia tion with the mother's kin group; Column 50: Crude rafts only.
Mambila (Ah4). L: 7N, 12E. T: 1920. P: 18,000 in 1931. B: I, 394. Comment— Column 76: But Me if deceased was married by a token bride-price rather than by an exchange of sisters.
Jukun (Ah2). L: 8N, 10E. T: 1920. P: 25,000 in 1931. B: I, 277.
Others: Jibu (Ah23), Kentu (Ah24), Tigon (Ah25), Zuande (Ah27).

65: Wute
Wute (Ah8). L: 6N, 12E. T: 1910. P: 30,000. B: II, 125; V, 337.

66: Chamba-Yungur
Mumuye (Ah31). L: 9N, 12E. T: 1910. P: 65,000 in 1932. B: V, 338.
Yungur (Ah33). L: 10N, 12E. T: 1920. P: 9,000 in 1921. B: V, 338.
Longuda (Ah30). L: 10N, 12E. T: 1920. P: 12,000 in 1921. B: V, 338.
Others: Chamba (Ah28), Daka (Ah29), Ndoro (Nh26), Vere (Nh32).

67: Mandara Highlands
Matakam (Ah7). L: 11N, 14E. T: 1940. P: 100,000 in 1958. B: I, 540; V, 337. Comment—Column 36: Mention of a "fairly long delay" before resumption of sex relations.
Podokwo (Ah39). L: 11N, 14E. T: 1950. P: 10,000 in 1950. B: V, 339.
Kapsiki (Ah38). L: 11N, 14E. T: 1930. P: 25,000 in 1950. B: V, 329.
Gude (Ah36). L: 10N, 13E. T: 1920. P: 30,000 in 1958. B: V, 339.
Others: Bata (Ah34), Bura (Ah35), Hona (Ah37), Margi (Ah5).

68: Adamawa
Mundang (Ai15). L: 10N, 14E. T: 1900. P: 90,000 in 1960. B: V, 339.
Fali (Ai12). L: 10N, 14E. T: 1950. P: 20,000 in 1952. B: V, 339.
Mbum (Ai14). L: 7N, 14E. T: 1920. P: 25,000 in 1960. B: V, 339.
Others: Laka (Ai13), Namshi (Ai16).

69: Logone
Masa (Ai9). L: 10N, 16E. T: 1910. P: 125,000 in 1957. B: IV, 119; V, 339; New.
Others: Gisiga (Ai17), Kotoko (Ai18), Musgu (Ai19), Tuburi (Ai20).

70: Bagirmi-Sara
Bagirmi (Ai21). L: 11N, 17E. T: 1880. P: 26,000 in 1954. B: V, 340. Comment —Column 20: Inferential.
Sara (Ai22). L: 9N, 18E. T: 1890. B: V, 340.

71: Banda-Baya
Bwaka (Ai23). L: 3N, 19E. T: 1920. P: 180,000 in 1940. B: V, 340.
Banda (Ai1). L: 7N, 22E. T: 1920. B: I, 125.
Ngbandi (Ai26). L: 4N, 22E. T: 1920. P: 115,000 in 1958. B: V, 340.
Baya (Ai7). L: 6N, 16E. T: 1910. P: 200,000 in 1930. B: I, 540.
Others: Mandja (Ai24), Mbandja (Ai25).

72: Azande
Azande (Ai3). L: 5N, 27E. T: 1920. P: 750,000 in 1949. B: I, 277; I, 540.
Others: Abarambo (Ai27).

73: Mangbetu
Mangbetu (Ai11). L: 3N, 28E. T: 1900. P: 500,000. B: IV, 347.
Popoi (Ai28). L: 2N, 26E. T: 1910. P: 5,500 in 1912. B: V, 340.

74: Moru-Madi
Lendu (Ai29). L: 2N, 30E. T: 1920. P: 150,000. B: V, 340.
Lese (Ai30). L: 2N, 29E. T: 1920. P: 19,000 in 1949. B: V, 341. Comment— Column 58: Mainly by Pygmies; Column 69: Dependent Pygmies.
Mamvu (Ai5). L: 3N, 29E. T: 1920. P: 33,000 in 1949. B: I, 394.
Bongo (Ai35). L: 7N, 29E. T: 1870. P: 5,000 in 1929. B: V, 341.

Madi (Ai33). L: 4N, 32E. T: 1940. P: 66,000 in 1948. B: V, 341.
Lugbara (Ai32). L: 3N, 32E. T: 1920. P: 240,000 in 1948. B: V, 341.
Others: Logo (Ai31), Moru (Ai34).

75: *Nuba*

Otoro (Ai10). L: 12N, 31E. T: 1940. P: 40,000 in 1947. B: IV, 119.
Tullishi (Ai42). L: 12N, 29E. P: 3,500 in 1947. B: V, 342. Comment—Column 27: But D for MoBrDa; Column 74: Mixed patrilineal and matrilineal.
Mesakin (Ai39). L: 11N, 30E. T: 1940. P: 6,000 in 1947. B: V, 341. Comment— Columns 74 and 76: Mixed matrilineal and patrilineal.
Moro (Ai40). L: 11N, 30E. T: 1940. P: 20,000 in 1947. B: V, 341.
Tira (Ai41). L: 11N, 30E. T: 1930. P: 8,000 in 1947. B: V, 341.
Korongo (Ai38). L: 10N, 30E. T: 1930. P: 14,000 in 1947. B: V, 341. Comment —Columns 74 and 76: Mixed Me and Pe.
Others: Koalib (Ai37), Nyaro (Ai2).

76: *Fung*

Shilluk (Ai6). L: 10N, 32E. T: 1900. P: 110.000 in 1948. B: I, 394.
Anuak (Ai44). L: 8N, 34E. T: 1920. P: 35,000 in 1957. B: V, 342.
Others: Ingassana (Ai4), Meban (Ai45).

77: *Koma*

Mao (Ai47), with special reference to the northern Mao. L: 9N, 35E. T: 1930. P: 6,000 northern Mao in 1939. B: V, 342.
Koma (Ai46). L: 9N, 35E. T: 1930. P: 3,000 in 1938. B: V, 342.

78: *Northern Nilotes*

Nuer (Aj3). L: 8N, 32E. T: 1930. P: 430,000 in 1931. B: I, 277.
Dinka (Aj11). L: 9N, 29E. T: 1900. P: 500,000 in 1952. B: IV, 249; IV, 451; V, 342.
Jur (Ai36). L: 8N, 28E. T: 1920. B: V, 341; VI, 100. Comment—Columns 74 and 76: But Pe for property acquired rather than inherited by deceased.

79: *Bari-Lotuko*

Bari (Aj8). L: 5N, 32E. T: 1920. P: 35,000 in 1952. B: II, 125.
Lotuko (Aj12). L: 4N, 33E. T: 1920. P: 60,000 in 1940. B: IV, 249. Comment— Column 27: But half-sibling terms are applied to FaBrCh.
Kuku (Aj15). L: 4N, 32E. T: 1900. P: 26,000 in 1952. B: V, 342. Comment— Column 44: Aprons only.
Mondari (Aj16), with special reference to the Riverain Mondari. L: 6N, 31E. T: 1930. P: 22,000 in 1962. B: V, 343.
Others: Fajulu (Aj13), Kakwa (Aj14)

80: *Southern Nilotes*

Lango (Aj4). L: 2N, 33E. T: 1920. P: 275,000 in 1947. B: I, 395.
Luo (Aj6). L: 1S, 34E. T: 1940. P: 800,000 in 1947. B: I, 540. Comment—Column 27: But O for MoBrDa; Column 78: But without actual penetration.
Alur (Aj17). L: 2N, 31E. T: 1890. P: Over 200,000. B: V, 343.
Others: Acholi (Aj10).

81: *Beir-Didinga*

Didinga (Aj19). L: 4N, 34E. T: 1920. P: 25,000 in 1920. B: V, 343.
Bodi (Aj18). L: 5N, 35E. T: 1950. P: 2,600 in 1950. B: V, 343.
Suri (Aj20). L: 6N, 35E. T: 1940. P: 4,000 in 1947. B: V, 343.

82: *Karamojong*

Plains Suk (Aj23). L: 1N, 36E. T: 1950. P: 42,000 in 1948. B: V, 343.
Turkana (Aj5). L: 4N, 35E. T: 1920. P: 80,000 in 1951. B: I, 395.
Jie (Aj21). L: 3N, 34E. T: 1930. P: 18,000 in 1948. B: V, 343.
Teso (Aj1). L: 2N, 34E. T: 1950. P: 560,000 in 1948. B: I, 125.
Topotha (Aj24). L: 5N, 34E. T: 1930. P: 34,000 in 1948. B: V, 343.
Others: Labwor (Aj22).

83: *Nandi*

Nandi (Aj7). L: Equator, 35E. T: 1910. P: 113,000 in 1948. B: I, 541. Comment —Column 69: Entry follows Huntingford, contra earlier reports of D.
Kipsigis (Aj9). L: 1S, 36E. T: 1920. B: IV, 119.

Hill Suk (Aj26). L: 1N, 36E. T: 1910. P: 20,000 in 1948. B: V, 344. Comment—
Column 27: But with certain O features.
Others: Keyu (Aj25), Sapei (Aj27).

84: Dorobo
Dorobo (Aa2), with special reference to the Central Dorobo. L: Equator, 36E.
T: 1920. P: 221 Central Dorobo in 1942. B: I, 275.

85: Masai
Masai (Aj2). L: 2S, 36E. T: 1900. P: 187,000 in 1948. B: I, 277. Comment—
Column 78: But without actual penetration.
Others: Samburu (Aj29), Tatoga (Aj28).

86: Southern Cushites
Iraqw (Ca4). L: 4S, 35E. T: 1950. P: 100,000 in 1948. B: I, 395; V, 223. Comment—Column 22: Matrilineages are unnamed, unimportant, and not specifically reported to be exogamous.
Others: Goroa (Ca9).

87: Afar-Somali
Somali (Ca2), with special reference to the more nomadic groups. L: 8N, 48E.
T: 1950. P: Over 3,000,000. B: I, 126; V, 344. Comment—Column 27: Per-
formed by slaves.
Afar (Ca6). L: 12N, 42E. T: 1880. P: 110,000 in 1950. B: IV, 119. Comment—
Column 25: But forbidden with a MoSiDa; Column 62: Performed only by
serfs.
Others: Esa (Ca10).

88: Galla
Arusi (Ca11). L: 8N, 40E. T: 1890. B: V, 224.
Jimma (Ca39). L: 8N, 37E. T: 1930. P: 300,000 in 1936. B: V, 445. Comment—
Column 27: But sibling terms are applied to FaBrCh.
Gibe (Ca12). L: 8N, 37E. T: 1880. B: V, 224.
Macha (Ca13). L: 9N, 37E. T: 1950. B: V, 224. Comment—Column 32: Incor-
porated in the Ethiopian state.

89: Sidamo
Sidamo (Ca16). L: 7N, 38E. T: 1930. B: V, 224.
Burji (Ca14). L: 5N, 38E. T: 1950. B: V, 224.
Darasa (Ca15). L: 6N, 38E. T: 1930. B: V, 224.
Gurage (Ca8). L: 8N, 38E. T: 1940. P: 350,000 in 1960. B: IV, 452.

90: Konso
Konso (Ca1). L: 6N, 37E. T: 1930. B: I, 126.
Tsamai (Ca17). L: 5N, 37E. T: 1950. P: 1,000 in 1951. B: V, 224.

91: North Rudolf
Banna (Ca19). L: 6N, 36E. T: 1950. P: Over 5,000 in 1950. B: V, 224.
Others: Arbore (Ca18), Galab (Ca20), Hammar (Ca21), Male (Ca22).

92: Western Cushites
Kafa (Ca30). L: 7N, 36E. T: 1890. P: Estimated at 500,000 in 1905. B: V, 225.
Comment—Column 27: If Bieber is correct in reporting one term for "male
cousin" and another for "female cousin"; Column 58: By an outcaste group.
Bako (Ca23). L: 6N, 37E. T: 1950. B: V, 224.
Basketo (Ca28). L: 6N, 37E. T: 1950. P: 5,000 in 1951. B: V, 225.
Janjero (Ca29). L: 8N, 38E. T: 1920. B: V, 225.
Others: Anfillo (Ca27), Dime (Ca24), Shangama (Ca25), Ubamer (Ca26).

93: Central Ethiopia
Amhara (Ca7), with special reference to those of Gondar. L: 13N, 38E. T: 1950.
P: 2,000,000. B: IV, 249. Comment—Column 27: But separate terms for an
uncle's child and an aunt's child; Column 36: From report of a "two-year
breast-feeding period."
Tigrinya (Ca3). L: 14N, 39E. T: 1950. P: Over 1,000,000. B: I, 277.
Falasha (Ca31). L: 12N, 37E. T: 1860. P: 20,000. B: V, 225.

94: Barea-Kunama

Kunama (Ca33). L: 15N, 37E. T: 1860. P: 17,000 in 1937. B: V, 225.
Barea (Ca32). L: 16N, 38E. T: 1860. P: 9,500 in 1937. B: V, 225.
95: *Beja*
Bisharin (Ca5). L: 20N, 35E. T: 1930. P: 15,000 in 1933. B: I, 541.
Others: Ababda (Ca34), Amarar (Ca35), Beni Amer (Ca36), Bogo (Ca37), Tigre (Ca38).
96: *Nubians*
Barabra (Cd1), with special reference to the Kenuzi. L: 23N, 33E. T: 1920. B: I, 126; V, 229. Comment—Column 32: Integrated into the Egyptian state.
Nyima (Ai43). L: 12N, 29E. T: 1930. P: 37,000 in 1947. B: V, 342.
Dilling (Ai8). L: 12N, 30E. T: 1930. P: 8,000. B: I, 540.
Others: Midobi (Cb11).
97: *Baggara*
Hasania (Cb4). L: 14N, 32E. T: 1920. B: I, 395.
Others: Gimma (Cb12), Habbania (Cb13), Hemat (Cb14), Messiria (Cb15), Shuwa (Cb16).
98: *Darfur*
Fur (Cb17). L: 12N, 24E. T: 1880. P: Over 120,000 in 1937. B: I, 226. Comment—Column 16: Husbands live in separate houses from their wives and eat at a special men's mess; Column 78: Entry follows Felkin, but Beaton reports V.
99: *Lake Chad*
Buduma (Cb5). L: 13N, 15E. T: 1910. P: 16,000 in 1937. B: I, 541; V, 344.
100: *Bornu*
Kanuri (Cb19). L: 12N, 13E. T: 1870. B: V, 227. Comment—Columns 20 and 24: Descent, though patrilineal prior to 1850, is now "bilateral with an agnatic bias"; Column 25: Marriage is forbidden with a MoSiDa.
Kanembu (Cb18). L: 14N, 14E. T: 1930. P: 30,000 in 1937. B: V, 226.
101: *Bolewa-Tera*
Bolewa (Cb7). L: 11N, 11E. T: 1920. P: 33,000 in 1933. B: IV, 249. Comment—Column 27: For cross-cousins of opposite sex, but H for those of same sex.
Tera (Cb6). L: 11N, 12E. T: 1920. P: 38,000 in 1948. B: II, 126.
Others: Bachama (Cb27), Dera (Cb28), Karekare (Cb10), Ngizim (Cb29).
102: *Hausa*
Zazzagawa (Cb26). L: 11N, 8E. T: 1950. P: 260,000 in 1948. B: V, 344. Comment—Column 27: Alternatively H; Column 39: But cattle are tended mainly by Fulani.
Kanawa (Cb9). L: 12N, 9E. T: 1940. P: 1,000,000. B: IV, 249. Comment— Column 39: Milking is done exclusively by Fulani.
Others: Mazugawa (Cb1), Tazarawa (Cb25).
103: *Pastoral Fulani*
Bororo Fulani (Cb8). L: 13N, 5E. T: 1920. P: 450,000. B: IV, 249.
Djafun (Cb21). L: 8N, 13E. T: 1930. B: V, 344.
Wodaabe Fulani (Cb24). L: 12N, 12E. T: 1950. B: V, 344.
104: *Songhai*
Songhai (Cb3). L: 17N, 1W. T: 1940. P: 400,000 in 1953. B: I, 277.
Others: Zerma (Cb20).
105: *Tuareg*
Ahaggaren (Cc9). L: 23N, 6E. T: 1920. P: 4,400 in 1950, exclusive of 3,500 serfs and 4,000 slaves. Comment—Column 30: But serfs are sedentary; Column 62: Performed exclusively by serfs and slaves.
Antessar (Cc5). L: 18N, 3W. T: 1910. P: 10,000 in 1941. B: IV, 119; V, 227. Comment—Column 62: Performed exclusively by sedentary serfs.
Asben (Cc10). L: 18N, 8E. T: 1900. P: 28,000 in 1944. B: V, 227. Comment—Column 30: But serfs are sedentary; Column 62: Performed by serfs and slaves.
Others: Aulliminden (Cc8), Azjer (Cc11), Ifora (Cc12), Udalan (Cc13).

106: Teda
Teda (Cc2), with special reference to those of Tibesti. L: 21N, 17E. T: 1950. P: 25,000 in Tibesti. B: I, 126; V, 227.
Others: Daza (Cc14)
107: Oasis Berbers
Siwans (Cc3). L: 29N, 26E. T: 1920. P: 3,000 in 1937. B: I, 278. Comment—Column 42: Alien itinerant smiths only.
Mzab (Cc4). L: 33N, 4E. T: 1920. P: 32,000 in 1939. B: I, 395.
Others: Drawa (Cc15).
108: Bedouin Arabs (of both North Africa and the Arabian Peninsula)
Rwala (Cj2). L: 33N, 37E. T: 1920. P: 35,000 in 1920. B: I, 279.
Regeibat (Cc1). L: 22N, 13W. T: 1950. P: 35,000 in 1950. B: I, 126; V, 227.
Chaamba (Cc16). L: 32N, 3E. T: 1930. P: 20,000 in 1936. B: V, 228. Comment —Column 62: Performed exclusively by serfs and slaves.
Mutair (Cj5). L: 28N, 47E. T: 1930. B: II, 261.
Delim (Cc17). L: 22N, 15W. T: 1930. P: 6,000 in 1915. B: V, 228.
Zenaga (Cc20), with special reference to the more nomadic northern groups. L: 18N, 8W. T: 1910. B: V, 229. Comment—Column 80: Tents.
Others: Berabish (Cc7), Hamama (Cd13), Hamyan (Cd14), Kababish (Cc6), Kunta (Cc18), Saadi (Cd18), Sanusi (Cd20), Trarza (Cc19), Ulad Nail (Cd17).
109: Moroccan Berbers
Riffians (Cd3). L: 35N, 4W. T: 1920. P: Nearly 400,000 in 1921. B: I, 278.
Shluh (Cd5), with special reference to those of the Grand Atlas Mountains. L: 30N, 9W. T: 1920. P: 600,000 in 1921. B: I, 541. Comment—Columns 67- 71: But class and caste distinctions and slavery are well developed among the lowland Shluh.
Others: Beraber (Cd7), Tekna (Cd9), Zekkara (Cd10).
110: Canary Islands
Guanche (Cd11). L: 28N, 16W. T: 1500. P: Extinct. B: V, 229. Comment— Certain of the entries are somewhat inferential.
111: Algerian Berbers
Kabyle (Cd4). L: 36N, 4E. T: 1890. P: 1,000,000 in 1930. B: I, 395.
Others: Shawiya (Cd8).
112: Arabs of Littoral North Africa
Egyptians (Cd2), with special reference to the town of Silwa. L: 25N, 33E. T: 1950. P: 23,000,000 in 1957. B: I, 278; I, 395.
Algerians (Cd12). L: 31N, 2E. T: 1870. B: V, 229. Comment—Column 32: Un- der French colonial administration until recently.
Others: Jebala (Cd15), Moroccans (Cd16), Sahel (Cd19), Tunisians (Cd16).
113: Ancient Egypt
Ancient Egyptians (Cd6), with special reference to the New Empire. L: 30N, 31E. T: 1400 B.C. P: Over 2,000,000. B: V, 229.
114: Greeks
Greeks (Ce7), with special reference to the village of Vasilika. L: 39N, 23E. T: 1950. B: IV, 452.
115: Albanians
Gheg (Ce1). L: 42N, 20E. T: 1900. P: 200,000 in 1930. B: I, 126.
116: Italians
Neapolitans (Ce5). L: 41N, 13E. T: 1960. B: III, 331.
Others: Romans of the Imperial period (Ce3).
117: Peoples of Spanish and Portuguese Speech
Spaniards (Ce6), with special reference to the inhabitants of Andalusia. L: 37N, 6W. T: 1950. B: IV, 119.
Brazilians (Cf4), with special reference to the village of Cruz das Almas near São Paulo. L: 43S, 47W. T: 1940. B: II, 126.
Others: Camba (Se7), Portuguese (Ce2).

118: Basques
Basques (Ce4), with special reference to those of Labourd. L: 43N, 1W. T: 1930. B: I, 385.

119: French-speaking Peoples
French Canadians (Cf5), with special reference to the parish of St. Denis. L: 47N, 72W. T: 1930. B: New.
Others: Walloons (Cg5).

120: English-speaking Peoples
New Englanders (Cf1), with special reference to central Connecticut. L: 42N, 73W. T: 1920. B: I, 126.
Tristan da Cunha Islanders (Cf3). L: 37S, 12W. T: 1930. P: 188 in 1938. B: I, 395.
Irish (Cg3), with special reference to County Clare. L: 53N, 9W. T: 1930. B: I, 278.

121: Peoples of Dutch and German Speech
Dutch (Cg1), with special reference to Anlo parish in Drente province. L: 53N, 7E. T: 1950. B: I, 126.
Others: Boers (Cf2).

122: Scandinavians
Icelanders (Cg2). L: 64N, 20W. T: 1100 A.D. B: I, 127.

123: Lapps
Lapps (Cg4), with special reference to the Könkämä Lapps of Sweden. L: 68N, 22E. T: 1950. P: 191 Könkämä Lapps in 1951. B: I, 278.

124: Finnic Peoples
Cheremis (Ch4). L: 43N, 46E. T: 1900. P: 400,000 in 1941. B: I, 541.

125: Balto-Slavs
Lithuanians (Ch9). L: 55N, 24E. T: 1930. P: 2,700 in 1950. B: New. Comment —Column 69: Jews.

126: Eastern Slavs
Ukrainians (Ch7). L: 48N, 36E. T: 1930. B: IV, 250.
Czechs (Ch3), with special reference to the Hana district of central Moravia. L: 50N, 16E. T: 1940. P: 8,800,000 Czechs in 1950. B: I, 395.
Byelorussians (Ch6). L: 55N, 28E. T: 1910. B: IV, 250.
Hutsul (Ch2). L: 49N, 24E. T: 1890. P: 60,000 in 1890. B: I, 278. Comment— Column 35: Based on a possibly incomplete list of games.

127: Hungary-Romania
Hungarians (Ch8). L: 47N, 20E. T: 1940. P: 9,400,000 in 1950. B: VI, 105.

128: South Slavs
Serbs (Ch1), with special reference to the village of Orasac. L: 44N, 20E. T: 1950. B: I, 127.
Bulgarians (Ch5), with special reference to the village of Dragelevtsy. L: 43N, 24E. T: 1940. P: 7,000,000 in 1950. B: II, 126.

129: Kipchak Turks
Kumyk (Ci3), with special reference to the Kayakent of eastern Dagestan. L: 42N, 48E. T: 1900. P: 135,000 in 1959. B: I, 278.

130: Circassians
Cherkess (Ci4). L: 44N, 42E. T: 1920. P: 250,000. B: I, 395.

131: Osset
Osset (Ci6). L: 43N, 44E. T: 1880. P: 350,000 in 1939. B: V, 230.

132: Checheno-Lesghians
Chechen (Ci7), L: 43N, 46E. T: 1900. P: 400,000 in 1939. B: V, 230.

133: Georgians
Khevsur (Ci2). L: 43N, 45E. T: 1930. P: 3,500 in 1927. B: I, 127.
Others: Georgians (Ci8), Svan (Ci9).

134: Armenians
Armenians (Ci10). L: 40N, 45E. T: 1900. P: 3,400,000 in 1952. B: V, 231.

135: Kurd

Kurd (Ci11), with special reference to those of Iraq. L: 32N, 44E. T: 1940. P: 5,000,000 in 1950. B: V, 231. Comment—Column 29: One term for FaSiCh and MoSiCh, a second for FaBrCh, and a third for MoBrCh.

136: Ottoman Turks

Turks (Ci5), with special reference to those of central Anatolia. L: 38N, 30E. T: 1950. B: IV, 120.

137: Jews

Hebrews (Cj3). L: 32N, 35E. T: 800 B.C. B: I, 396.

138: Sedentary Arabs of the Near East

Druze (Cj8), with special reference to those of Mount Carmel in Israel. L: 33N, 35E. T: 1930. P: 600 in 1930 in the Mount Carmel region. B: V, 231.

Syrians (Cj1), with special reference to the village of Tell Toqaan. L: 36N, 36E. T: 1950. B: I, 127.

Lebanese (Cj7), with special reference to the village of Munsif. L: 34N, 36E. T: 1950. P: 1,575,000 in 1956. B: II, 261. Comment—Column 14: But commonly Fm elsewhere in Lebanon; Column 25: But traditionally Qa; Column 44: Formerly F.

Others: Jordanians (Cj6), Yemeni (Cj9).

139: Marsh Arabs

Madan (Cj10), with special reference to the village of ech-Chibayish. L: 31N, 47E. T: 1950. P: 400,000. B: V, 445. Comment—Column 32: Integrated into the state of Iraq.

140: Ancient Mesopotamia

Babylonians (Cj4). L: 32N, 45E. T: 2000 B.C. B: II, 261.

141: Iranians

Iranians (Ea9), with special reference to the Teheran region. L: 36N, 52E. T: 1950. P: Over 10,000,000. B: New.

142: South Iran Nomads

Basseri (Ea6), with special reference to the nomadic population. L: 30N, 54E. T: 1950. P: 16,000 in 1957. B: II, 126.

Bakhtiari (Ea8). L: 33N, 48E. T: 1920. B: VI, 105.

143: Indus Valley

Sindhi (Ea1). L: 25N, 68E. T: 1950. P: 9,500,000 in 1961. B: I, 127.

144: Hazara

Hazara (Ea3), with special reference to the Urazgani. L: 35N, 66E. T: 1930. P: 65,000 Urazgani. B: I, 396; IV, 452. Comment—Column 64: Formerly A1M.

Moghol (Ea7). L: 34N, 63E. T: 1950. P: A few thousand. B: IV, 452. Comment —Column 27: But kin terms were obtained in Persian, not in Mongolian; Column 32: Integrated into the state of Afghanistan.

145: Pushtu

Pathan (Ea2), with special reference to the Yusufsai of Swat. L: 35N, 72E. T: 1950. P: 450,000 in Swat. B: I, 279.

146: Dard

Dard (Ee5), with special reference to the Gilgit. L: 35N, 73E. T: 1870. B: I, 541.

Kohistani (Ea4). L: 35N, 73E. T: 1950. P: 15,000. B: I, 396.

Nuri (Ea5). L: 36N, 71E. T: 1890. P: 60,000. B: I, 541. Comment—Column 34: Forcibly converted to Islam in 1896.

147: Burusho

Burusho (Ee2). L: 37N, 75E. T: 1930. P: 21,000 in 1931. B: I, 279.

148: Turkestan

Kazak (Eb1). L: 48N, 70E. T: 1910. P: More than 2,000,000. B: I, 127. Comment—Column 39: Also sheep, cattle, and camels.

Others: Turkmen (Eb5).

149: Mongols

Khalka (Eb3), with special reference to those of Narobanchin. L: 46N, 97E. T: 1940. P: 2,000 in Narobanchin. B: I, 279.

Monguor (Eb2). L: 39N, 100E. T: 1920. P: 55,000 in 1909. B: I, 127.

Kalmyk (Ci1), with special reference to the Baga Dörbed. L: 46N, 46E. T: 1920. P: 70,000 Baga Dörbed in 1939. B: I, 127.
Chahar Mongols (Eb7). L: 41N, 115E. T: 1930. P: 2,300 in 1943. B: IV, 250.
Others: Buryat (Eb6), Dagur (Eb4).

150: Samoyed
Yurak (Ec4). L: 68N, 75E. T: 1900. P: 13,000. B: I, 279; II, 127. Comment—Column 27: Or perhaps H.

151: Ostyak
Ob Ostyak (Ec10). L: 62N, 74E. T: 1880. P: 17,000 in 1897. B: VI, 105.

152: Yeniseians
Ket (Ec8). L: 62N, 90E. T: 1900. P: 1,300. B: II, 127.

153: Yakut
Yakut (Ec2). L: 65N, 125E. T: 1900. P: 245,000 in 1911. B: I, 127

154: Yukaghir
Yukaghir (Ec6). L: 70N, 145E. T: 1900. P: 1,000 in 1900. B: I, 396.

155: Paleo-Siberians
Chukchee (Ec3), with special reference to the Reindeer Chukchee. L: 66N, 177E. T: 1900. P: 12,000 Chukchee in 1900. B: I, 279.
Koryak (Ec5), with special reference to the Maritime Koryak. L: 62N, 164E. T: 1900. P: 7,500 Koryak in 1900. B: I, 396.

156: Gilyak
Gilyak (Ec1). L: 53N, 142E. T: 1920. P: 4,650 in 1897. B: I, 127

157: Ainu
Ainu (Ec7), with special reference to those of Hokkaido. L: 44N, 144E. T: 1900. P: 17,000. B: I, 541; IV, 452. Comment—Column 22: But there are patrilineal kin groups consisting of males only; Column 27: For cross-cousins, but H for parallel cousins.

158: Tungus
Goldi (Ec9). L: 47N, 132E. T: 1920. P: 100 in 1930. B: VI, 105.

159: Manchuria
Manchu (Ed3). L: 45N, 126E. T: 1920. B: I, 279. Comment—Column 32: Integrated into the Chinese state.

160: Korea
Koreans (Ed1). L: 35N, 102E. T: 1950. P: 30,000,000. B: I, 127.

161: Japan
Japanese (Ed5). L: 35N, 136E. T: 1950. P: Over 80,000,000. B: I, 396; III, 331.

162: Ryukyu Islands
Okinawans (Ed7). L: 26N, 128E. T: 1950. P: 517,000 in 1950. B: I, 541.

163: North China
Shantung Chinese (Ed10), with special reference to the village of Taitou. L: 37N, 118E. T: 1930. B: VI, 105.

164: South China
Min Chinese (Ed6), with special reference to the hinterland of Swatow. L: 24N, 115E. T: 1920. B: I, 396.

165: Hainan
Li (Ed9). L: 19N, 109E. T: 1930. P: 220,000 in 1954. B: IV, 452.

166: Miao-Yao
Miao (Ed4), with special reference to the Yachio or Magpie Miao. L: 26N, 107E. T: 1940. P: 10,000 Yachio in 1940. B: I, 279.

167: Lolo-Nosu
Lolo (Ed2), with special reference to those of Liang Shan. L: 29N, 103E. T: 1940. B: I, 127.

168: Minchia
Minchia (Ed8). L: 26N, 100E. T: 1930. P: 400,000 in 1950. B: II, 127. Comment—Column 27: But sibling terms are used for FaBrCh; Column 64: Linguistic affiliation uncertain, possibly Si rather than Tb.

169: Upper Brahmaputra

Abor (Ee1). L: 28N, 95E. T: 1940. B: I, 127. Comment—Column 50: Rafts only.
170: Tibet
Tibetans (Ee4), with special reference to Central Tibet. L: 30N, 91E. T: 1920. P: 4,000,000 Central Tibetans in 1915. B: I, 396.
171: Sikkim
Lepcha (Ee3). L: 28N, 89E. T: 1930. B: I, 279.
172: Nepal
Sherpa (Ee6), with special reference to those of Khumbu. L: 28N, 87E. T: 1950 B: III, 442. Comment—Column 42: But smiths are Nepali, not Sherpa; Column 85: Tents of undescribed type are used during transhumance.
173: Kashmir
Kashmiri (Ef8), with special reference to the Muslim population of Kashmir province. L: 34N, 75E. T: 1890. P: 1,700,000 in Kashmir province in 1941. -B: V, 445.
174: North India
Pahari (Ef7), with special reference to the village of Sirkanda. L: 30N, 78E. T: 1950. P: 5,000,000. B: III, 331.
Gujarati (Ef9). L: 20N, 77E. T: 1920. P: 2,200,000 in 1921. B: New.
Others: Aryans (Ef3), Bengali (Ef2).
175: Bhil
Bhil (Ef5). L: 22N, 74E. T: 1900. P: 1,250,000. B: I, 542; II, 127.
176: Munda
Santal (Ef1). L: 24N, 87E. T: 1940. P: 2,730,000 in 1941. B: I, 128.
Hill Bhuiya (Eg7). L: 21N, 85E. T: 1930. B: I, 542. Comment—Column 36: Duration of the taboo coincides with the nursing period.
Kol (Eg8). L: 22N, 85E. T: 1940. P: 94,000 in 1941. B: II, 127. Comment: Column 24: The groups called "endogamous septs" are apparently not unilineal.
Baiga (Eg9). L: 22N, 81E. T: 1930. B: IV, 120.
Others: Ho (Ef4).
177: Northern Dravidians
Maria Gond (Eg3), with special reference to the Hill Maria. L: 19N, 81E. T: 1930. P: 12,000 Hill Maria in 1938. B: I, 280.
Muria Gond (Eg13). L: 20N, 81E. T: 1940. P: 220,000 in 1941. B: New.
Oraon (Ef6). L: 23N, 85E. T: 1940. P: 650,000 in 1951. B: II, 127.
Others: Bondo (Eg12), Koya (Eg11).
178: Indian Hunters and Gatherers
Chenchu (Eg1). L: 16N, 79E. T: 1940. P: 3,280 in 1941. B: I, 128. Comment—Column 50: Rafts only.
179: Southeast India
Telugu (Eg10), with special reference to the village of Shamirpet. L: 18N, 79E. T: 1950. B: IV, 250.
Coorg (Eg5). L: 12N, 76E. T: 1930. P: 40,000 in 1936. B: I, 397. Comment—Column 14: But formerly Eo.
Tamil (Eg2), with special reference to the agricultural castes in Tanjore, L: 11N, 79E. T: 1880. P: 3,000,000 in Tanjore in 1950. B: I, 128.
180: Nilgiri Hills
Toda (Eg4). L: 12N, 77E. T: 1900. B: I, 280.
181: Southwest India
Kerala (Eg6), with special reference to Northern Kerala and the Nayar caste. L: 11N, 76E. T: Prior to 1800. B: I, 397.
182: Sinhalese
Sinhalese (Eh6), with special reference to the Kandyan population. L: 7N, 80E. T: 1950. B: I, 397; II, 262. Comment—Column 14: But extended families are often found in well-to-do families; Column 24: Inferred from the preference for V residence and the existence of endogamous "kindreds" with a fiction of "common ancestry."

183: Vedda
Vedda (Eh4), with special reference to the Rock Vedda. L: 8N, 81E. T: 1900. B: I, 280; IV, 120. Comment—Column 80: Preferably caves and rock shelters.

184: Malagasy
Tanala (Eh3), with special reference to the Menabe. L: 22S, 47E. T: 1930. P: 170,000 in 1951. B: I, 280; III, 331. Comment—Column 27: But sibling terms are applied to cross-cousins of the same sex; Column 48: But formerly P.
Merina (Eh2). L: 19S, 46E. T: 1900. P: 1,000,000 in 1951. B: I, 128; III, 331. Comment—Column 27: Marriage is also allowed with FaBrDa but not MoSiDa; Column 73: But originally E.
Antandroy (Eh7). L: 25S, 46E. P: 255,000 in 1951. B: III, 331. Comment—Column 14: But McLeod reports Eq.
Sakalava (Eh8). L: 21S, 41E. T: 1900. P: 275,000 in 1951. B: III, 331. Comment—Column 30: But McLeod reports Jc.

185: Nicobar Islands
Nicobarese (Eh5), with special reference to the inhabitants of Car Nicobar. L: 9N, 92E. T: 1890. P: 9,000 in 1924. B: I, 397.

186: Andaman Islands
Andamanese (Eh1), with special reference to the Akar-Bale. L: 12N, 93E. T: 1870. P: 5,500 in 1858. B: I, 128. Comment—Column 27: Entry follows Man, but Radcliffe-Brown reports H.

187: Chittagong Hills
Chakma (Ei10). L: 23N, 92E. T: 1870. P: 125,000 in 1951. B: II, 262.
Mogh (Ei9). L: 20N, 92E. T: 1880. P: 66,000 in 1951. B: II, 262. Comment—Column 27: But S for male cross-cousins.

188: Kuki-Chin
Lakher (Ei4). L: 22N, 93E. T: 1930. P: 10,000. B: I, 280.
Purum (Ei6). L: 25N, 94E. T: 1930. P: 300 in 1936. B: I, 397.
Aimol (Ei11). L: 25N, 94E. T: 1910. P: 500 in 1931. B: II, 262.
Chin (Ei19). L: 22N, 94E. T: 1940. P: 350,00 in 1943. B: IV, 452.
Others: Thado (Ei12).

189: Garo
Garo (Ei1). L: 26N, 91E. T: 1900. P: 160,000 in 1901. B: I, 128; II, 404; IV, 452. Comment—Column 50: But M in one limited region; Column 76: The heir is a classificatory SiSo who is DaHu.

190: Khasi
Khasi (Ei8), with special reference to those of the Jaintia Hills. L: 26N, 92E. T: 1900. P: 175,000 in 1901. B: II, 127.

191: Naga
Ao (Ei14), with special reference to the Chongli. L: 27N, 94E. T: 1920. P: 30,000 in 1921. B: II, 262.
Lhota (Ei2). L: 27N, 94E. T: 1920. P: 20,000 in 1922. B: I, 128.
Angami (Ei13). L: 26N, 94E. T: 1910. B: II, 262.
Sema (Ei16). L: 26N, 95E. T: 1910. B: II, 262.
Others: Mikir (Ei17), Rengma (Ei15).

192: Kachin
Kachin (Ei5), with special reference to the Jinghpaw. L: 26N, 97E. T: 1940. P: 300,000. B: I, 397. Comment—Column 27: But O for FaSiDa(ms) and MoBrSo(ws).

193: Palaung-Wa
Palaung (Ei18), with special reference to the Katur. L: 23N, 97E. T: 1920. P: 100,000 in Burma, others in China. B: II, 262.

194: Burmese
Burmese (Ei3). L: 20N, 95E. T: 1950. P: 10,000,000 in 1931. B: I, 280; V, 446. Comment—Column 14: Or often Gm.

195: Karen

Karen (Ei7), with special reference to the Plains Karen. L: 17N, 97E. T: 1910. B: II, 127. Comment—Column 22: But there are agamous matrilineages which function in ancestor worship.

196: Thai

Siamese (Ej9). L: 15N, 100E. T: 1940. P: 18,000,000 in 1957. B: II, 128.

197: Akha

Akha (Ej7). L: 21N, 100E. T: 1950. P: 65,000 in Burma and Thailand; others in China and Laos. B: I, 542; IV, 453. Comment—Column 27: But S for male cross-cousins.

198: Lamet

Lamet (Ej1). L: 20N, 101E. T: 1940. P: 5,800. B: I, 128; II, 404.

199: Muong

Muong (Ej13). L: 21N, 105E. P: 250,000 in 1946. B: VI, 105.

200: Vietnamese

Annamese (Ej4). L: 17N, 107E. T: 1950. P: 22,000,000 Vietnamese. B: I, 280; IV, 453. Comment—Column 36: "... weaning begins at about 18 months."

201: Moi

Mnong Gar (Ej2), with special reference to the village of Sar Luk. L: 12N, 107E T: 1940. P: 146 in Sar Luk in 1948. B: I, 128. Comment—Column 25: MoYoBrDa only.

202: Cham-Jarai

Rhade (Ej10). L: 13N, 108E. T: 1950. P: 120,000 in 1960. B: II, 404. Comment —Column 74: Matrilineal.

Cham (Ej11), with special reference to the non-Muslim Cham of Vietnam. L: 11N, 108E. T: 1950. P: 100,000 in 1951. B: IV, 452. Comment—Column 69: But formerly C; Columns 74 and 76: Mainly from mother to youngest daughter.

203: Khmer

Cambodians (Ej5). L: 12N, 105E. T: 1950. P: 3,500,000 in 1950. B: I, 397.

204: Semang

Semang (Ej3), with special reference to the Jehai group. L: 6N, 101E. T: 1920. B: I, 280. Comment—Column 50: Bamboo rafts only.

205: Senoi

Senoi (Ej14), with special reference to the eastern Semai. L: 4N, 102E. T: 1960. P: 12,000 Semai in 1961. B: New. Comment—Column 50: Bamboo rafts only.

206: Malays

Malays (Ej8), with special reference to those of Trengganu. L: 5N, 103E. T: 1940. P: 1,250,000. B: II, 128.

207: Sea Gypsies

Selung (Ej6). L: 12N, 98E. T: 1920. B: I, 398. Comment—Column 20: Nomadic boat communities; Column 80: Houseboats.

Tawi-Tawi Badjaw (Ia13). L: 5N, 120E. T: 1960. P: 1,425 in 1963. B: V, 446. Comment—Column 30: Nomadic boat communities; Column 80: Houseboats.

208: Formosan Aborigines

Atayal (Ia1). L: 24N, 121E. T: 1930. P: 33,000 in 1931. B: I, 129; IV, 453.

Paiwan (Ia6). L: 22N, 121E. T: 1930. P: 35,000 in 1960. B: I, 542; V, 446.

Ami (Ia9), with special reference to the southern Ami. L: 22N, 121E. T: 1930. P: 55,000 in 1960. B: V, 446. Comment—Column 14: Entry follows Ma buchi, but Wei reports B.

Bunun (Ia10). L: 24N, 121E. T: 1930. P: 18,000 in 1931. B: V, 446. Comment— Column 27: But O in address.

Puyuma (Ia11). L: 23N, 121E. T: 1930. P: 5,300 in 1931. B: V, 446.

Yami (Ia14). L: 22N, 122E. T: 1930. P: 1,560 in 1960. B: V, 446. Comment— Column 20: But Wei and Liu, unlike other sources, report patrilineages.

209: Highland Luzon

Sagada Igorot (Ia2). L: 17N, 121E. T: 1950. P: 10,000. B: I, 129; II, 263.
Kalinga (Ia16). L: 18N, 121E. T: 1910. P: 24,500 in 1939. B: New.
Ifugao (Ia3). L: 17N, 121E. T: 1920. P: 130,000 in 1939. B: I, 280.
Others: Bontok Igorot (Ia8).

210: Central Filipinos

Sugbuhanon (Ia12). L: 10N, 124E. T: 1950. P: 2,225,000 in 1964. B: V, 446.

211: Southern Philippines

Hanunoo (Ia5). L: 13N, 121E. T: 1950. P: 6,000 in 1950. B: I, 398.
Subanun (Ia4), with special reference to the eastern Subanun. L: 8N, 123E
T: 1950. P: 55,000 eastern Subanun in 1950. B: I, 280.
Tagbanua (Ia7). L: 10N, 119E. T: 1950. P: 7,000. B: II, 128. Comment—Column 12: Formerly B.
Others: Manobo (Ia15).

212: Borneo

Iban (Ib1), with special reference to the Ulu Ai group. L: 2N, 112E. T: 1950.
P: 11,500 in Ulu Ai in 1947. B: I, 129; I, 280.
Dusun (Ib5), with special reference to the village of Sensuron. L: 6N, 117E. T:
1920. P: 145,000. B: I, 398; V, 447.

213: Batak

Batak (Ib4), with special reference to the Toba. L: 2N, 99E. T: 1930. P: 1,000,
000 in 1959. B: I, 281.

214: Sumatran Malays

Minangkabau (Ib6). L: 1S, 101E. T: 1920. P: 2,000,000 in 1930. B: I, 398.

215: Offshore Sumatran Islands

Mentaweians (Ib7), with special reference to North Pageh. L: 3S, 100E. T: 1920.
P: 10,000 in 1930. B: II, 128. Comment—Column 24: The *uma,* though
possibly a localized quasi-patrilineage, is more probably a ramage; Column
25: Marriage forbidden only with a FaBrDa; Column 27: As reported by
Kruyt, but Loeb states that sibling terms are applied to FaBrCh; Column
74: Taro land is inherited from Mo to Da.

216: Indonesian Hunters and Gatherers

Kubu (Ib8), with special reference to the Ridan group. L: 3S, 103E. T: 1900. P:
7,000 Ridan in 1925. B: VI, 105.

217: Java

Javanese (Ib2), with special reference to south central Java. L: 7S, 110E. T: 1950.
P: 35,000,000 in 1956. B: I, 129; IV, 347. Comment—Column 50: But Mc in
the coastal towns.

218: Bali

Balinese (Ib3). L: 8S, 115E. T: 1950. P: 1,000,000 in 1950. B: I, 281; VI, 105.
Comment—Column 24: Geertz speaks of clans with a "noticeable ambilineal
element."

219: Sumba-Sumbawa

Sumbanese (Ic9), with special reference to eastern Sumba. L: 10S, 120E. T: 1930.
P: 100,000 Lumbanese in 1940. B: VI, 106.

220: Buginese-Macassarese

Macassarese (Ic1). L: 5S, 119E. T: 1940. P: 4,000,000 in 1950. B: I, 129.

221: Celebes

Toradja (Ic5), with special reference to the Bare'e group. L: 2S, 121E. T: 1900.
P: 200,000. B: I, 398. Comment—Column 44: But weaving has been recently introduced.

222: Flores

Ili-Mandiri (Ic7), with special reference to the village of Leloba in east Flores.
L: 8S, 123E. T: 1920. B: VI, 106.

223: Alor-Solor

Alorese (Ic2), with special reference to those of Atimelang. L: 8S, 125E. T:
1940. P: 10,000 in Atimelang in 1940. B: I, 281. Comment—Column 34: But
Nicolspeyer denies a belief in a supreme being.

224: Timor-Roti

Belu (Ic3), with special reference to the Mountain Belu. L: 9S, 126E. T: 1950. P: 82,000 in 1952 exclusive of those in Portuguese territory. B: I, 281. Comment—Column 27: But I between male cross-cousins; Column 76: Inheritance by widows, then daughters.

Others: Rotinese (Ic4).

225: Tanimbar

Tanimbarese (Ic6). L: 8S, 131E. T: 1930. P: 25,000. B: I, 542.

226: Kei-Aru

Kei Islanders (Ic8). L: 6S, 133E. T: 1890. P: 30,000 in 1930. B: VI, 106.

227: Moluccas

Ambonese (Ic11). L: 4S, 128E. T: 1950. P: 60,000 in 1930. B: New.

228: Halmahera

Tobelorese (Ic10). L: 1N, 128E. T: 1910. B: VI, 106.

229: Northwest Australia

Murngin (Id2). L: 12S, 136E. T: 1930. P: Nearly 1,000 in 1950. B: I, 281. Comment—Column 22: The matrimoieties are implicit and unnamed.

Tiwi (Id3). L: 12S, 131E. T: 1920. P: 1,000. B: I, 281; IV, 347. Comment— Column 80: The dwelling is "nothing more than a few piled-up tree branches" or a crude bark shelter.

Others: Murinbata (Id7).

230: Central Australia

Aranda (Id1). L: 24S, 134E. T: 1900. P: 2,000 in 1900. B: I, 129. Comment— Column 37: Also subincision.

Dieri (Id4). L: 28S, 138E. T: 1900. B: I, 398. Comment—Column 37: And subsequently also subincision.

Kariera (Id5). L: 21S, 118E. T: 1910. P: 650 in 1865. B: I, 398. Comment—Column 22: Implicit matrimoieties intersecting the patrimoieties to form four sections.

231: Southeast Australia

Wongaibon (Id9). L: 32S, 146E. T: 1910. B: New.

232: Tasmania

Tasmanians (Id8). L: 42S, 146E. T: 1830. P: Extinct since 1876, originally about 2,000. B: New. Comment—Column 12: Marriage by capture was common; Column 36: Children were weaned after two years of age; Column 50: Rafts only.

233: Northeast Australia

Wikmunkan (Id6), with special reference to the Archer River group. L: 14S, 142E. T: 1920. P: 150 in 1929. B: I, 542. Comment—Column 25: MoYoBrDa only.

234: Southeast New Guinea

Motu (Ie10), with special reference to the western Motu. L: 9S, 147E. T: 1950. P: 7,000 in 1954. B: III, 422.

Koita (Ie20). L: 9S, 147E. T: 1900. P: 2,000 in 1909. B: New.

Koiari (Ie24). L: 9S, 148E. T: 1870. B: New.

Mekeo (Ie22). L: 9S, 147E. T: 1900. P: 3,100 in 1897. B: New.

Mailu (Ie21). L: 10S, 149E. T: 1900. B: New. Comment—Column 27: But D for FaSiCh.

235: Gulf of Papua

Purari (Ie8). L: 7S, 145E. T: 1910. P: 8,000. B: II, 128.

Miriam (Ie14). L: 10S, 144E. T: 1900. B: IV, 120.

Kiwai (Ie13). L: 9S, 143E. T: 1920. B: IV, 120. Comment—Column 14: A localized lineage occupies a communal dwelling.

236: Merauke

Keraki (Ie5). L: 9S, 142E. T: 1930. P: 700 in 1926. B: I, 398. Comment—Column 25: The preferred union is with a classificatory, not an actual, cross-cousin.

Kimam (Ie18), with special reference to the village of Bamol. L: 7S, 138E. T: 1940. P: 7,000 in 1960. Comment—Column 20: Though exogamous, lineages are only incompletely patrilineal and, within a village, tend to be grouped into local moieties; Column 36: "Sexual intercourse is strictly prohibited for the time being."

Marindanim (Ie19), with special reference to the coastal inhabitants. L: 8S, 139E. T: 1910. P: 13,000 in 1910. B: VI, 106. Comment—Column 14: But the sexes live segregated in men's and women's houses; Column 27: Sibling terms are applied to FaBrCh, but there is a single term for all other cousins.

237: West Papuans
Mimika (Ie30). L: 4S, 135E. T: 1950. P: 8,500. B: New.

238: West New Guinea Highlands
Kapauku (Ie1), with special reference to those of the Kamu valley. L: 4S, 136E. T: 1950. P: 60,000 in 1955. B: I, 129; III, 422; V, 447.

Muju (Ie23). L: 6S, 141E. T: 1950. B: New.

239: East New Guinea Highlands
Siane (Ie17). L: 6S, 145E. T: 1940. P: 15,000 in 1953. B: IV, 453. Comment—Columns 14 and 16: Each married woman has a separate house where she is visited at night by her husband, who lives in a men's house; Column 36: From a report that children are weaned between three and six years of age.

Kakoli (Ie11). L: 6S, 144E. T: 1950. B: III, 423.

Enga (Ie7), with special reference to the Mae group. L: 6S, 144E. T: 1950. P: 26,000 Mae Enga. B: I, 542.

Kutubu (Ie16). L: 6S, 143E. T: 1940. P: 400 in 1940. B: IV, 250.

240: East Papuans
Wantoat (Ie2). L: 7S, 147E. T: 1920. P: 5,150 in 1954. B: I, 129. Comment—Column 24: A "skewed kindred" consisting of parts of both Ego's and his mother's patrilineages.

Orokaiva (Ie9). L: 9S, 148E. T: 1920. P: 9,000. B: II, 404.

Mafulu (Ie25). L: 8S, 147E. T: 1920. P: 9,000. B: New.

Ngarawapum (Ie26). L: 6S, 146E. T: 1940. P: 600 in 1945. B: New.

241: North Papuans
Kwoma (Ie12). L: 4S, 142E. T: 1930. B: IV, 120. Comment—Column 37: But 5 if slashing of the boy's penis is equated with circumcision.

Arapesh (Ie3). L: 4S, 144E. T: 1930. B: I, 281.

Abelam (Ie15). L: 4S, 145E. T: 1930. B: IV, 250.

Banaro (Ie27). L: 4S, 145E. T: 1910. B: New.

242: Northwest New Guinea Melanesians
Waropen (Ie6). L: 2S, 137E. T: 1930. P: 6,000 in 1937. B: I, 398.

243: Northeast New Guinea Melanesians
Wogeo (Ie4). L: 3S, 144E. T: 1930. P: 1,000. B: I, 281. Comment—Column 25: Marriage is preferential between children of cross-cousins.

Busama (Ie28). L: 7S, 147E. T: 1940. P: 1,300 in 1946. B: New.

Manam (Ie29). L: 4S, 145E. T: 1930. P: 3,500 in 1933. B: New. Comment—Marriage is preferred with FaFaSiSoDa.

244: Palau
Palauans (If1). L: 7N, 135E. T: 1940. P: 6,000 in 1960. B: I, 129. Comment—Column 35: But games of chance, at least those using playing cards, are of relatively recent European origin; Column 38: Formerly T; Column 48: But extinct today.

245: Yap
Yapese (If6). L: 9N, 138E. T: 1910. P: 3,700 in 1935. B: I, 399; II, 128. Comment—Columns 67 and 69: Complex stratification into nine social classes and seven ranks, of which three form an endogamous upper caste and four an endogamous lower caste.

246: Marianas Islands
Chamorro (If8), with special reference to those of Saipan. L: 15N, 145E. T: 1950. B: II, 263.

247: Central Caroline Islands
Trukese (If2), with special reference to the island of Romonum. L: 7N, 152E. T: 1940. P: 10,000 Trukese in 1947. B: I, 129; IV, 453. Comment—Column 38: But the men's house is now obsolescent; Column 76: But provisional land rights revert to the matrilineage of the deceased.
Ifaluk (If4). L: 7N, 147E. T: 1940. P: 250 in 1948. B: I, 282. Comment—Column 35: But the one game of strategy "was unquestionably borrowed from the Japanese by the young men who had worked on Yap"; Columns 74 and 76: Matrilineal but without information on the preferred heirs.
Carolinians of Saipan (If15). L: 15N, 146E. T: 1930. P: 1,100 in 1950. B: IV, 250.
Ulithians (If9). L: 10N, 140E. T: 1900. P: 420 in 1949. B: II, 263. Comment—Column 74: Basically matrilineal.
Others: Nomoians (If10).
248: Eastern Caroline Islands
Ponapeans (If5). L: 7N, 158E. T: 1910. P: 8,000 in 1935. B: I, 399; V, 447. Comment—Column 34: But largely nominal Christians today.
Kusaians (If11). L: 5N, 163E. T: 1860. P: 500 in 1905. B: II, 263. Comment—Column 34: But C since the acceptance of Christianity.
249: Nauru
Nauruans (If13). L: 1S, 166E. T: 1900. P: 3,300. B: II, 263.
250: Marshall Islands
Majuro (If3). L: 7N, 171E. T: 1940. P: 900 in 1947. B: I, 282. Comment—Column 74: Mixed; Column 76: But originally matrilineal.
Bikinians (If12). L: 12N, 165E. T: 1940. P: 170 in 1935. B: II, 263.
251: Gilbert Islands
Makin (If14). L: 3N, 173E. T: 1890. P: 2,000 in 1890. B: III, 423. Comment—Column 39: The pig was introduced by Europeans; Column 73: Within the leading ramage of the village.
Onotoa (If7). L: 2S, 174E. T: 1940. B: II, 129; V, 447. Comment—Column 14: Formerly Er.
252: Western Islands (of Bismarck Archipelago)
Aua (Ig13). L: 2S, 143E. T: 1900. B: New. Comment—Columns 14 and 16: A married man lives at the house of his sister and visits that of his wife or wives only for the evening meal and to sleep.
253: Admiralty Islands
Manus (Ig9). L: 2S, 147E. T: 1920. P: 2,000 in 1929. B: II, 129. Comment—Column 27: I between cross-cousins of same sex, C between MoBrSo and FaSiDa, H between FaSiSo and MoBrDa.
Usiai (Ig10). L: 2S, 147E. T: 1950. B: III, 332.
254: New Ireland
Lesu (Ig4). L: 3S, 153E. T: 1930. B: I, 282. Comment—Column 25: The preferred marriage is with the daughter of a cross-cousin.
255: New Britain
Lakalai (Ig7). L: 5S, 151E. T: 1950. B: I, 543.
256: Massim
Trobrianders (Ig2). L: 8S, 151E. T: 1910. B: I, 130.
Dahuni (Ig14), with special reference to the village of Wagawaga. L: 10S, 150E. T: 1900. P: 250 in Wagawaga in 1951. B: New. Comment—Column 16: Or possibly B.
Dobuans (Ig5). L: 10S, 151E. T: 1920. B: I, 399. Comment—Column 16: Alternating M and A for periods of a year at a time; Columns 74 and 76: Matrilineal, but the exact distribution is unreported.
257: Louisade Archipelago
Rossel Islanders (Ig11). L: 9S, 154E. T: 1920. P: 1,500 in 1925. B: IV, 250.
258: Buka
Kurtatchi (Ig3). L: 5S, 154E. T: 1930. B: I, 282. Comment—Columns 74 and 76: A man may leave his property to his sons, his sisters's sons, or both.

259: Bougainville
Siuai (Ig1). L: 6S, 155E. T: 1940. P: 4,650 in 1938. B: I, 130. Comment—Column 74: Matrilineal within the lineage.

260: Choiseul-Eddystone
Choiseulese (Ig12: 1102), with special reference to the Varisi. L: 6S, 156E. T: 1900. P: 1,000 Varisi in 1956. Comment—Column 12: But O when residence is uxorilocal.
Others: Simboese (Ig8).

261: Malaita-Ulawa
Ulawans (Ig6). L: 10S, 161E. T: 1900. P: 1,200 in 1909. B: I, 399.

262: Santa Cruz Islands
Santa Cruz (Ih9), with special reference to the inhabitants of Graciosa Bay. L: 11S, 166E. T: 1930. P: 2,500 in 1958. B: New. Comment—Column 27: But optionally I.

263: Banks Islands
Mota (Ih1). L: 14S, 168E. T: 1890. B: I, 130.

264: Malekula
Seniang (Ih2). L: 17S, 167E. T: 1930. B: I, 130.

265: Ambrym-Pentecost
Bunlap (Ih3). L: 16S, 168E. T: 1950. P: 90 in Bunlap village in 1953. B: I, 282. Comment—Column 25: Marriage is preferred with MoBrDaDa or MoMoBrDa.

266: Southern New Hebrides
Tannese (Ih10), with special reference to the Whitesands group. L: 20S, 168E. T: 1920. B: New.

267: Loyalty Islands
Lifu (Ih7). L: 21S, 163E. T: 1910. B: II, 129.

268: New Caledonia
Ajie (Ih5). L: 22S, 165E. T: 1860. P: 1,700 in 1955. B: I, 399.

269: Fiji
Lau Fijians (Ih4). L: 18S, 179E. T: 1920. B: IV, 347.
Vanua Levu (Ih8), with special reference to the village of Nakaroka. L: 17S, 179E. T: 1940. B: IV, 347. Comment—Column 74: Mixed but mainly patrilineal.

270: Rotuma
Rotumans (Ih6). L: 13S, 177E. T: 1890. B: I, 534; IV, 453.

271: Polynesian Outliers in Micronesia
Kapingamarangi (Ii7). L: 1N, 155E. T: 1910. P: 482 in 1950. B: V, 447.

272: Polynesian Outliers in Central Melanesia
Ontong-Javanese (Ii5). L: 5S, 160E. T: 1920. P: 700 in 1928. B: I, 399. Comment—Column 74: Taro plots descend from Mo to Da, but other land is owned collectively by ramages.
Others: Rennell Islanders (Ii10).

273: Polynesian Outliers in Eastern Melanesia
Tikopia (Ii2). L: 12S, 168E. T: 1930. P: 1,300 in 1929. B: I, 130.

274: Western Polynesians
Samoans (Ii1: 65), with special reference to American Samoa. L: 14S, 170W. T: 1920. P: 8,000 in American Samoa in 1926. B: I, 130; V, 447.
Pukapukans (Ii3). L: 11S, 166W. T: 1930. P: 500. B: I, 282. Comment—Column 27: But I for cross-cousins of opposite sex; Column 38: But young men enter a men's house at the age of 18 or 20.
Tongans (Ii12). L: 20S, 174W. T: 1850. P: 24,000 in 1921. B: VI, 106. Comment—Column 24: Or localized "stem kindreds"; Column 76: Mixed, with substantial shares to sisters' sons.
Ellice Islanders (Ii4), with special reference to the inhabitants of Vaitupu. L: 8S, 178E. T: 1890. B: I, 399; V, 447.
Tokelau (Ii6), with special reference to the inhabitants of Atafu. L: 9S, 172W.

T: 1900. P: 380 on Atafu in 1930. B: II, 129; VI, 106. Comment—Column 74: Land is collectively owned by ramages.

Uveans (Ii13). L: 13S, 176W. T: 1830. P: 4,400 in 1919. B: VI, 106. Comment —Column 74: Land is collectively owned by ramages.

Futunans (Ii8). L: 14S, 178W. T: 1840. P: 1,500 in 1923. B: VI, 106. Comment— Column 74: Land is collectively owned by ramages.

Niueans (Ii9). L: 19S, 169W. T: 1840. P: 3,720 in 1921. B: VI, 106.

275: *Southern Polynesians*

Maori (Ij2), with special reference to those of the North Island of New Zealand. L: 35S, 175E. T: 1820. P: 90,000 in 1940. B: I, 282.

276: *Eastern Polynesians*

Marquesans (Ij3). L: 9S, 140W. T: 1900. P: 15,000 in 1840. B: I, 280; II, 263; V, 447. Comment—Column 25: But Miranda states that "marriage was prohibited within the third degree of relationship."

Mangaians (Ij1). L: 22S, 158W. T: 1820. P: 1,250 in 1926. B: I, 130.

Mangarevans (Ij7). L: 20S, 134W. T: 1900. B: IV, 120.

Hawaiians (Ij6). L: 20N, 156W. T: 1800. B: II, 129.

Manihikians (Ij4). L: 10S, 160W. T: 1850. P: 400 in 1926. B: I, 399. Comment —Column 24: Or very probably R.

Raroians (Ij5). L: 16S, 142W. T: 1900. P: 109 in 1950. B: I, 399.

Tahitians (Ij8). L: 18S, 150W. T: 1900. B: IV, 120. Comment—Column 14: But large communal dwellings originally; Column 34: But C since adoption of Christianity.

Easter Islanders (Ij9). L: 27S, 190W. T: 1860. P: 450 in 1936. B: VI, 106.

Others: Tongarevans (Ij10).

277: *Western Eskimo*

Aleut (Na9), with special reference to the Athin. L: 54N, 167W. T: 1930. P: 1,500 Aleut in 1834. B: II, 545. Comment—Column 35: But chess was introduced by Russian traders; Column 48: But pottery is found in archeological sites.

Nunivak Eskimo (Na6). L: 60N, 166W. T: 1930. B: I, 400. Comment—Column 34: Belief in an otiose supreme being who is not, however, a creator.

Chugach Eskimo (Na10). L: 60N, 147W. T: 1930. P: 200 in 1933. B: II, 545.

Sivokakmeit (Na11). L: 63N, 170W. T: 1920. P: 293 in 1955. B: II, 545. Comment—Column 39: Reindeer were introduced in 1900, but the herds died out in the 1940s; Column 48: But pottery was given up sometime after 1912.

278: *Interior Eskimo*

Caribou Eskimo (Na21). L: 63N, 96W. T: 1900. P: 500 in 1923. B: III, 111. Comment—Column 27: One term for paternal cousin, another for maternal cousin; Column 40: Men scrape and women chew skins, but the preparation is strictly mechanical.

Nunamiut (Na12). L: 68N, 152W. T: 1950. P: 200 in 1953. B: II, 545; IV, 348.

279: *Central and Eastern Eskimo*

Angmagsalik Eskimo (Na24). L: 66N, 37W. T: 1880. P: 371 in 1884. B: III, 111. Comment—Column 36: "children are suckled until they are at least two years old."

Iglulik (Na22). L: 70N, 82W. T: 1920. P: 500 in 1922. B: III, 111; IV, 453. Comment—Column 27: For cross-cousins of opposite sex, but I for those of same sex and special terms for parallel cousins of same sex.

Copper Eskimo (Na3). L: 69N, 110W. T: 1920. B: I, 282. Comment—Column 42: But some cold working of native copper.

Tareumiut (Na2). L: 71N, 157W. T: 1880. P: 1,000 in 1880. B: I, 130; II, 545; VI, 107.

Polar Eskimo (Na14). L: 78N, 70W. T: 1880. P: 271 in 1926. B: II, 546. Comment—Column 36: Inferred from report that children are commonly suckled for five years or more.

Labrador Eskimo (Na23), with special reference to the Koksoagmiut. L: 58N,

65W. T: 1890. P: 1,100 in 1890. B: III, 111.

Baffinland Eskimo (Na13). L: 65N, 65W. T: 1880. B: II, 545.

Others: Greenlanders (Na25), Netsilik Eskimo (Na43), Taqagmiut (Na44).

280: Cree-Montagnais

Montagnais (Na32), with special reference to those of Lake St. John. L: 48N, 72W. T: 1880. P: 670 at Lake St. John in 1929. B: III, 112. Comment—Column 24: Or possibly Q.

Attawapiskat (Na7). L: 53N, 83W. T: 1900. B: I, 543. Comment—Column 24: Patrilocal bands.

Naskapi (Na5), with special reference to the northern bands. L: 58N, 70W. T: 1890. B: I, 399. Comment—Column 24: Or possibly Q.

Eastern Cree (Na31), with special reference to those of Albany and Moose Creek. L: 51N, 85W. T: 1850. B: III, 112. Comment—Column 24: Or possibly Q; Column 25: "there were no marriage restrictions."

281: Maritime Algonkians

Micmac (Na41). L: 47N, 65W. T: 1700. P: More than 3,000 in 1609. B: III, 113. Comment—Column 36: But 1 today.

Others: Penobscot (Ng4).

282: Ojibwa

Chippewa (Na36), with special reference to the Red Lake and White Earth bands. L: 49N, 96W. T: 1860. B: III, 113. Comment—Column 48: But pottery was made prior to the mid-nineteenth century.

Katikitegon (Na38), with special reference to the Lac Vieux Desert band. L: 46N, 92W. T: 1800. P: 76 in 1940. B: III, 113.

Rainy River Ojibwa (Na37). L: 49N, 92W. T: 1880. P: 244 in 1917. B: III, 113.

Northern Saulteaux (Na33), with special reference to those of the Berens River. L: 52N, 98W. T: 1870. P: More than 900 in 1930. B: III, 113.

Eastern Ojibwa (Na39), with special reference to the Kitchibuan of Parry Island. L: 46N, 85W. T: 1870. P: 150 in 1929. B: III, 113.

Nipigon (Na35). L: 50N, 88W. T: 1800. P: 820 in 1880. B: III, 113.

Pekangekum (Na34). L: 52N, 94W. T: 1940. P: 342 in 1949. B: III, 113. Comment—Column 31: The "co-residential group," not the band.

Others: Ottawa (Na40).

283: Northeastern Athapaskans

Slave (Na17). L: 61N, 120W. T: 1860. P: 400 in 1881. B: II, 546. Comment—Column 36: From statement that "breast feeding continued to the age of two or three years."

Chippewyan (Na30). L: 60N, 105W. T: 1880. B: III, 112.

Dogrib (Na15). L: 63N, 117W. T: 1860. P: 900 in 1959. B: II, 546.

Beaver (Na29). L: 58N, 117W. T: 1850. P: 380 in 1914. B: III, 112.

Satudene (Na16). L: 65N, 119W. T: 1860. B: II, 546.

Sekani (Na28). L: 56N, 123W. T: 1880. P: 160 in 1923. B: III, 112.

284: Carrier-Nahani

Kaska (Na4). L: 59N, 128W. T: 1920. P: 300 aboriginally. B: I, 283. Comment —Column 74: Trap lines are inherited by DaHu.

Carrier (Na19), with special reference to the Hwitsowitenne. L: 54N, 124W. T: 1880. P: "more than 300" in 1925. B: II, 546.

Tahltan (Na27). L: 58N, 131W. T: 1870. P: 50 in 1885. B: III, 112. Comment— Column 36: From statement that children were suckled for two to three years.

285: Upper Yukon

Kutchin (Na20), with special reference to the Tatlit or Peel River Kutchin. L: 66N, 135W. T: 1880. P: 337 Tatlit in 1958. B: II, 546.

286: Lower Yukon

Ingalik (Na8). L: 62N, 160W. T: 1880. B: II, 129.

287: South Central Alaska

Nabesna (Na1). L: 63N, 141W. T: 1930. P: 152 in 1930. B: I, 130. Comment— Column 14: But polygyny was formerly common.

Tanaina (Na26), with special reference to the Iliamna. L: 62N, 144W. T: 1870. P: 650 in 1932. B: III, 112.

Eyak (Nb5). L: 60N, 145W. T: 1890. P: 38 in 1933. B: I, 400. Comment—Column 16: An inference from conflicting residence data confirmed by de Laguna as probably correct; Column 64: Probably belongs to a Nadene phylum with Athapaskan, Haida, and Tlingit.

288: *Tlingit-Haida*

Tlingit (Nb22), with special reference to the Chilkat. L: 58N, 134W. T: 1880. P: 6,750 in 1880. B: III, 114. Comment—Column 74: Matrilineal inheritance with collective ownership.

Haida (Nb1). L: 54N, 132W. T: 1890. P: 1,000 in 1890. B: I, 130. Comment— Column 42: But men made artifacts of beaten copper.

289: *Tsimshian-Haisla*

Tsimshian (Nb7). L: 55N, 130W. T: 1880. B: I, 129. Comment—Column 42: But artifacts were made of beaten copper; Column 64: Probably Macro-Penutian.

Haisla (Nb8). L: 54N, 129W. T: 1880. P: 400 in 1930. B: II, 547.

290: *Kwakiutl-Bellacoola*

Bellacoola (Nb9). L: 52N, 127W. T: 1880. P: 300 in 1922. B: II, 547.

Kwakiutl (Nb3). L: 51N, 128W. T: 1890. B: I, 283.

Bellabella (Nb23). L: 52N, 128W. T: 1880. P: 330 in 1901. B: III, 114.

Alkatcho Carrier (Nb10). L: 53N, 126W. T: 1865. P: 100 in 1936. B: II, 547 Comment—Column 76: Inheritance reported as bilateral with a patrilineal bias.

291: *Nootka-Quileute*

Nootka (Nb11), with special reference to the Central Nootka. L: 49N, 126W. T: 1880. P: 6,000 aboriginally. B: II, 547.

Makah (Nb24). L: 48N, 125W. T: 1860. P: 654 in 1861. B: III, 114.

Quileute (Nb18). L: 48N, 125W. T: 1880. P: 285 in 1945. B: II, 548.

292: *Coast Salish*

Twana (Nb2). L: 48N, 123W. T: 1850. P: 600 in 1850. B: I, 130.

Quinault (Nb25). L: 47N, 124W. T: 1860. P: 200 in 1925. B: III, 114. Comment —Column 27: Or alternatively H.

Stalo (Nb27), with special reference to the Tait. L: 49N, 122W. T: 1880. P: 1,700 in 1951. B: III, 114. Comment—Column 34: Aboriginally, but the concept of a high god was introduced "as a result of early white contact."

Klallam (Nb16). L: 48N, 123W. T: 1860. P: 485 in 1881. B: II, 547.

Puyallup (Nb17). L: 47N, 122W. T: 1870. B: II, 547.

Cowichan (Nb26). L: 49N, 123W. T: 1880. B: III, 114.

Squamish (Nb13). L: 50N, 123W. T: 1880. B: II, 547.

Lummi (Nb15). L: 49N, 123W. T: 1880. B: II, 547. Comment—Column 38: But boys of fourteen or fifteen leave the village in quest of guardian spirits and do not return for a year or more.

Others: Comox (Nb14), Klahuse (Nb12).

293: *Chinook*

Wishram (Nd18). L: 46N, 121W. T: 1860. P: 1,000 in 1800. B: III, 212.

Chinook (Nb19). L: 46N, 124W. T: 1850. P: 100 in 1853. B: II, 548. Comment —Column 36: "Nursing continued for two or three years, sometimes longer."

Others: Tillamook (Nb20).

294: *Oregon Seabord*

Tolowa (Nb6). L: 42N, 124W. T: 1870. B: I, 400.

Alsea (Nb28). L: 44N, 124W. T: 1860. B: III, 114.

Coos (Nb21). L: 43N, 124W. T: 1860. B: II, 548.

Tututni (Nb31). L: 42N, 124W. T: 1870. B: III, 115.

Others: Siuslaw (Nb29).

295: *Northwest California*

Yurok (Nb4). L: 41N, 124W. T: 1850. P: 2,500 in 1850. B: I, 283.

Sinkyone (Nb39). L: 40N, 124W. T: 1860. B: III, 116.

Shasta (Nb32), with special reference to the Shastika or eastern Shasta. L: 41N, 122W. T: 1860. P: 2,000 in 1850. B: III, 115.

Chimariko (Nb33). L: 41N, 123W. T: 1860. P: 250 in 1849. B: III, 115. Comment—Column 48: Log rafts only.

Hupa (Nb35). L: 41N, 123W. T: 1860. P: 640 in 1870. B: III, 115.

Karok (Nb34). L: 42N, 123W. T: 1860. P: 600 in 1905. B: III, 115.

Wiyot (Nb36). L: 40N, 124W. T: 1860. P: 800 in 1853. B: III, 115. Comment—Column 27: But H for second cousins.

Others: Lassik (Nb37), Mattole (Nb38), Takelma (Nb30).

296: Northeast California

Atsugewi (Nc4). L: 41N, 121W. T: 1860. B: I, 400.

Yana (Nc11), with special reference to the Northern Yana. L: 41N, 122W. T: 1860. P: 35 in 1884. B: III, 207.

Achomawi (Nc10), with special reference to the Western Achomawi. L: 41N, 121W. T: 1860. P: 1,000 in 1900. B: III, 207.

297: Maidu-Wintun

Wintu (Nc14), with special reference to the Northeastern Wintu. L: 41N, 122W. T: 1860. B: III, 207.

Maidu (Nc12), with special reference to the Northeastern or Mountain Maidu. L: 40N, 121W. T: 1850. P: 250 Northern Maidu in 1905. B: III, 207. Comment—Column 31: For the hamlet, but 3 for the hamlet cluster.

Nisenan (Nc13), with special reference to the Hill and Mountain Nisenan. L: 39N, 121W. T: 1850. B: III, 207. Comment—Column 36: But Faye states that children were nursed "till they were four or five years old."

Nomlaki (Nc1). L: 39N, 122W. T: 1850. P: 300 in 1954. B: I, 131.

Patwin (Nc22), with special reference to the Hill Patwin. L: 39N, 122W. T: 1850. P: 150 in 1924. B: III, 208.

298: Pomo-Yuki

Yuki (Nc7). L: 40N, 123W. T: 1850. P: 2,000 aboriginally. B: II, 130; III, 207.

Eastern Pomo (Nc18). L: 39N, 123W. T: 1860. B: III, 208.

Coast Yuki (Nc15). L: 39N, 124W. T: 1860. P: 500 in 1850. B: III, 208.

Wappo (Nc20). L: 38N, 123W. T: 1860. B: III, 208. Comment—Column 46: Skins were scraped but not actually tanned.

Northern Pomo (Nc17), with special reference to those of Kalekau. L: 39N, 123W. T: 1860. B: III, 208.

Southern Pomo (Nc19), with special reference to those near Santa Rosa. L: 38N, 123W. T: 1860. B: III, 208.

Others: Huchnom (Nc16).

299: Miwok-Yokut·

Monachi (Nc23). L: 37N, 119W. T: 1870. P: More than 500 in 1920. B: III, 209. Comment—Column 20: Mo in some subgroups.

Yokuts (Nc3), with special reference to those of the Northern Foothills. L: 36N, 120W. T: 1850. P: 550 in 1910. B: I, 283; III, 206.

Miwok (Nc5), with special reference to the Central Sierra group. L: 38N, 120W. T: 1850. B: I, 400; III, 206.

Wukchumni (Nc25). L: 36N, 119W. T: 1860. B: III, 209.

Lake Yokuts (Nc24), with special reference to the Chunut and Tachi. L: 36N, 120W. T: 1860. B: III, 209. Comment—Column 27: After Gifford, but Gayton reports H for all Yokuts.

Others: Lake Miwok (Nc21), Salinan (Nc26).

300: Kern River

Tubatulabal (Nc2). L: 36N, 118W. T: 1850. P: 145 in 1932. B: I, 283.

Kawaiisu (Nc27). L: 35N, 118W. T: 1860. B: III, 209.

301: Southwest California

Luiseno (Nc33). L: 33N, 117W. T: 1860. P: 1,300 in 1870. B: III, 210; IV, 453.

Comment—Column 34: But the deity Chingishnish had certain attributes of a high god.

Cahuilla (Nc31), with special reference to the Desert Cahuilla. L: 33N, 116W. T: 1870. P: 750 Cahuilla in 1920. B: III, 210. Comment—Column 12: But Strong reports B.

Serrano (Nc30). L: 34N, 117W. T: 1870. P: Some 100 in 1910. B: III, 209.

Gabrielino (Nc29). L: 34N, 118W. T: 1770. P: 5,000 in 1770. B: III, 209.

Cupeno (Nc32). L: 33N, 117W. T: 1870. P: 200 in 1910. B: III, 210.

Others: Chumash (Nc28).

302: Diegueno

Diegueno (Nc6), with special reference to the Southern Diegueno. L: 32N, 116W. T: 1850. P: 700. B: I, 543; III, 206.

Kiliwa (Nc34). L: 31N, 115W. T: 1880. P: 36 in 1929. B: III, 210. Comment— Column 38: But boys were secluded for two months at puberty; Column 76: But the widow took precedence over the eldest son.

303: Washo

Washo (Nd6). L: 39N, 120W. T: 1850. P: 850 in 1960. B: I, 543; IV, 447. Comment—Column 20: There are weak agamous patrimoieties whose sole function is to oppose each other in games; Column 64: Probably Macro-Hokan.

304: Central Great Basin

Wadadokado or Harney Valley Paiute (Nd22). L: 43N, 119W. T: 1870. P: 200 in 1870. B: III, 212.

Kidutokado or Surprise Valley Paiute (Nd24). L: 42N, 120W. T: 1870. P: 150 in 1873. B: III, 212.

White Knife Shoshoni (Nd43). L: 41N, 117W. T: 1860. P: 800 aboriginally. B: III, 214. Comment—Column 24: But Steward reports only marriage with a pseudo-cross-cousin; Column 27: But cross-cousins of opposite sex are called "breast siblings."

Kuyuidokado or Pyramid Lake Paiute (Nd27). L: 40N, 119W. T: 1860. P: 700 in 1866. B: III, 213.

Agaiduka or Lemhi River Shoshoni (Nd46). L: 44N, 112W. T: 1860. P: 600 in 1860. B: III, 214. Comment—Column 39: But a few people had horses; Column 44: But rare.

Panamint (Nd32), with special reference to those of Saline Valley. L: 36N, 117W. T: 1850. P: 65 in 1870. B: III, 213.

Gosiute (Nd48), with special reference to those of Deep Creek. L: 40N, 114W. T: 1860. B: III, 215. Comment—Column 12: But Malouf reports B; Column 80: Caves or circular windbreaks of brush, but no houses.

Eastern Mono or Owens Valley Paiute (Nd30). L: 37N, 118W. P: 1,000 in 1870. B: III, 213. Comment—Column 28: But plots of wild seeds were irrigated.

Hukundika Shoshoni (Nd5). L: 42N, 112W. T: 1870. B: I, 400. Comment— Column 48: But pottery was made at an earlier period.

Others: Atsakudokwa Paiute (Nd23), Beatty Shoshoni (Nd33), Elko Shoshoni (Nd42), Ely Shoshoni (Nd38), Hamilton Shoshoni (Nd37), Koso (Nd31), Lida Shoshoni (Nd34), Mahaguaduka Shoshoni (Nd35), Moanunts Ute (Nd59), Panguitch Paiute (Nd50), Sawakudokwa Paiute (Nd25), Spring Valley Shoshoni (Nd39), Tagotoka Paiute (Nd21), Toedokado Paiute (Nd28), Tubaduka Shoshoni (Nd40), Tukudika Shoshoni (Nd47), Tunava Paiute (Nd29), Wadaduka Shoshoni (Nd41), Wadakuht Paiute (Nd26), Wiyambituka Shoshoni (Nd36), Yahanduka Shoshoni (Nd44).

305: Southern Paiute

Kaibab (Nd53). L: 36N, 113W. T: 1860. P: 600 in 1850. B: III, 215. Comment —Column 28: But only a few families practiced agriculture.

Shivwits (Nd52). L: 36N, 117W. T: 1860. P: 300 in 1873. B: III, 215. Comment —Column 12: But Lowie reports S.

San Juan Paiute (Nd56). L: 36N, 111W. T: 1860. B: III, 216.

Antarianunts (Nd49). L: 37N, 110W. T: 1860. B: III, 215.

Chemehuevi (Nd54). L: 35N, 115W. T: 1860. P: 350 in 1920. B: III, 215. Comment—Column 34: Coyote a creator but not a supreme being.
Others: Las Vegas Paiute (Nd55), Moapa (Nd51), Panguitch (Nd50).

306: Plateau Yumans

Walapai (Nd65). L: 36N, 114W. T: 1870. P: 1,000 in 1870. B: III, 217.

Havasupai (Nd3). L: 36N, 112W. T: 1880. B: I, 283; III, 211.

Yavapai (Nd66), with exclusive reference to the Northeastern Yavapai. L: 35N, 112W. T: 1870. P: 500 in 1870. B: III, 217.

Tolkepaya or Western Yavapai (Nd67). L: 34N, 114W. T: 1870. P: 500 in 1870. B: III, 217.

Keweyipaya or Southeastern Yavapai (Nh23). L: 34N, 111W. T: 1870. B: III, 333.

307: Eastern Great Basin

Southern Ute (Nd2), with special reference to the Wimonantci. L: 38N, 109W. T: 1860. B: III, 210. Comment—Column 28: Practiced only by a few families; Column 48: But women made clay pipes.

Wind River Shoshoni (Nd64), with special reference to the Kucundika. L: 43N, 109W. T: 1860. P: 1,600 in 1869. B: III, 216.

Bohogue Shoshoni (Nd45). L: 43N, 112W. T: 1860. P: 1,500 in 1867. B: III, 214.

Bannock (Nd63), with special reference to the Eastern Bannock. L: 43N, 112W. T: 1860. P: 600 in 1869. B: III, 216. Comment—Column 48: But pottery was made in the prehistoric period.

Uncompahgre Ute (Nd62). L: 39N, 107W. T: 1860. B: III, 216.

Uintah Ute (Nd58). L: 40N, 112W. T: 1860. B: III, 216.

Others: Moache Ute (Nd60), Pahvant Ute (Nd57), Taviwatsiu Ute (Nd61).

308: Lutuami

Klamath (Nc8). L: 43N, 122W. T: 1860. P: 1,200 in 1854. B: III, 207; IV, 447.

Modoc (Nc9). L: 42N, 122W. T: 1860. P: 300 in 1910. B: III, 207. Comment—Column 34: The creator was a culture hero rather than a high god.

309: Sahaptin

Tenino (Nd1). L: 45N, 121W. T: 1850. P: 1,200 in 1850. B: I, 131. Comment—Column 39: But some horses were obtained by trade from tribes to the east.

Nez Perce (Nd20). L: 45N, 115W. T: 1850. P: 6,000 in 1800. B: III, 212.

Umatilla (Nd19). L: 46N, 119W. T: 1860. B: III, 212.

Others: Klikitat (Nd17).

310: Interior Salish

Sinkaietk (Nd15). L: 49N, 120W. T: 1880. P: 300 in 1930. B: III, 212. Comment—Column 14: But large communal dwellings in the winter; Column 74: Given away to close relatives, especially siblings.

Sanpoil (Nd4). L: 48N, 119W. T: 1870. P: 660 in 1860. B: I, 283; III, 211. Comment—Column 35: But poker has become popular in recent times; Column 76: Distributed among close male relatives.

Flathead (Nd12). L: 46N, 113W. T: 1860. B: III, 211. Comment—Column 14: In summer, but Er in winter; Column 36: "children were not weaned until they were three years old."

Coeur d'Alene (Nd14). L: 48N, 117W. T: 1860. P: 500 in 1905. B: III, 212. Comment—Column 76: Distributed among relatives; Column 85: Also CGRCG, EGRGB, and CGRCH.

Others: Kalispel (Nd13), Wenatchi (Nd16).

311: Northern Plateau

Chilcotin (Nd8), with special reference to the Alexis Creek and Redstone bands. L: 52N, 122W. T: 1880. P: 600 in the 1840s. B: III, 211. Comment—Column 44: But bands influenced by the Coast Salish did some weaving.

Shuswap (Nd11), with special reference to the Southeastern Shuswap. L: 51N, 120W. T: 1850. B: III, 211. Comment—Column 78: Division among close relatives, including cousins; Column 85: Also RSRGM.

Lillooet (Nd9). L: 50N, 125W. T: 1860. P: 4,000 in 1850. B: III, 211.

Thompson (Nd10). L: 50N, 122W. T: 1860. B: III, 211.

312: Kutenai

Kutenai (Nd7), with special reference to the Lower Kutenai. L: 50N, 117W. T: 1880. P: 1,200 in 1891. B: II, 130; III, 211. Comment—Column 14: But communal dwellings in winter; Column 39: But horses were few; Column 48: But the pots were sun-dried, not fired; Column 76: But formerly seized by relatives.

313: Northwest Plains

Gros Ventre (Ne1). L: 49N, 109W. T: 1870. B: I, 131.

Blackfoot (Ne12). L: 51N, 112W. T: 1850. P: 1,600 in 1809. B: III, 332.

Blood (Ne13). L: 51N, 115W. T: 1850. P: 800 in 1809. B: III, 332.

Piegan (Ne18). L: 49N, 115W. T: 1850. P: 2,800 in 1809. B: III, 333.

Sarsi (Ne7). L: 54N, 110W. T: 1880. B: II, 130.

314: Northeast Plains

Assiniboin (Ne11). L: 48N, 106W. T: 1870. P: 3,000 in 1890. B: III, 332. Comment—Column 34: But the Great Spirit is not specifically reported as a creator; Column 36: From statement that children "were weaned when they were about three years old."

Plains Cree (Ne19). L: 45N, 94W. T: 1850. B: III, 333.

Teton (Ne8). L: 43N, 103W. T: 1870. B: II, 130; V, 447.

Bungi (Ne14), with special reference to the Turtle Mountain band. L: 51N, 103W. T: 1850. P: 7,000 in 1958. B: III, 332; New.

Santee (Ne20). L: 45N, 94W. T: 1850. B: III, 333.

315: Upper Missouri

Hidatsa (Ne15). L: 47N, 101W. T: 1860. P: 471 in 1905. B: III, 333; V, 447. Comment—Column 50: Skin bullboats; Column 74: Probably from Mo to Da.

Crow (Ne4). L: 45N, 108W. T: 1870. P: 1,800 in 1935. B: I, 283.

Mandan (Ne6). L: 47N, 101W. T: 1830. B: I, 543. Comment—Column 74: Land was owned by women and inherited from Mo to Da.

316: Southern Plains

Arapaho (Ne9). L: 40N, 103W. T: 1860. P: 2,300 in 1904. B: III, 332. Comment—Column 48: But pottery was made at an earlier date.

Cheyenne (Ne5). L: 39N, 104W. T: 1860. P: 4,700 in 1870. B: I, 400. Comment—Column 48: But pottery disappeared after European contact.

Kiowa-Apache (Ne2). L: 36N, 99W. T: 1870. P: 200 in 1934. B: I, 131. Comment—Column 32: The Kiowa-Apache formed one band of the Kiowa tribe.

Comanche (Ne3). L: 33N, 100W. T: 1870. B: I, 283.

Kiowa (Ne17). L: 36N, 99W. T: 1860. P: 1,165 in 1905. B: III, 333. Comment—Column 14: "The basic economic and social group . . . was a group of brothers and their wives and children"; Column 64: Probably belongs to a Tanoan-Kiowa phylum.

317: Caddo

Wichita (Nf5). L: 34N, 98W. T: 1860. P: 500 in 1950. B: I, 400.

Hasinai (Nf8). L: 31N, 95W. T: 1770. B: II, 130.

318: Pawnee-Arikara

Pawnee (Nf6), with special reference to the Skidi. L: 42N, 100W. T: 1860. P: 10,000 in 1780. B: I, 544; IV, 453. Comment—Column 22: Though not specifically attested, matrilineages are suggested by analysis of the kinship terminology; Column 24: Or perhaps B.

Arikara (Ne10). L: 46N, 101W. T: 1860. P: 1,650 in 1871. B: III, 332. Comment—Column 50: Skin bullboats: Column 74: Probably from Mo to Da.

319: Prairie Siouans

Omaha (Nf3). L: 41N, 96W. T: 1850. P: 1,200. B: I, 284. Comment—Column 16: In hunting camps, but possibly U in the villages.

Ponca (Nf12). L: 43N, 99W. T: 1850. P: 825 in 1880. B: V, 447.

Oto (Nf11). L: 40N, 95W. T: 1870. B: IV, 250.

Iowa (Nc10). L: 41N, 95W. T: 1870. B: IV, 250.

Winnebago (Nf2). L: 44N, 88W. T: 1850. B: I, 131.

320: Central Algonkians

Fox (Nf7). L: 45N, 95W. T: 1830. B: II, 130. Comment—Column 34: Possibly reflecting Christian influence.

Shawnee (Nf13), with special reference to the Kispokotha band. L: 37N, 85W. T: 1820. P: 1,160 in 1930. B: New.

Potawatomi (Na42). L: 44N, 85W. T: 1760. P: 2,000 in 1760. B: IV, 120.

Menomini (Nf9). L: 46N, 88W. T: 1870. P: 1,600 in 1900.

Miami (Nf4). L: 40N, 86W. T: 1720. P: 6,000 in 1718. B: I, 400.

321: Iroquois

Iroquois (Ng10), with special reference to the Seneca. L: 43N, 77W. T: 1750. B: IV, 121. Comment—Column 36: "A mother nurses her child for two to three years"; Column 38: Boys were segregated for one year at puberty.

Huron (Ng1). L: 44N, 78W. T: 1640. P: 24,000 in 1640. B: I, 131; II, 130; IV, 453.

322: Middle Atlantic Algonkians

Delaware (Ng6), with special reference to the Munsee. L: 41N, 75W. T: 1700. P: 8,000 in 1600. B: II, 401.

323: Cherokee-Yuchi

Cherokee (Ng5). L: 36N, 83W. T: 1750. P: 20,000 in 1729. B: I, 401.

Yuchi (Ng11). L: 35N, 86W. T: 1750. P: 1,140 in 1832. B: IV, 121. Comment— Column 16: At a late period, but probably originally M: Column 27: But O terminology was borrowed from the Shawnee in the eighteenth century.

324: Muskogee

Creek (Ng3). L: 33N, 84W. T: 1750. P: Under 20,000 aboriginally. B: I, 284. Comment—Column 42: But aboriginally men did some work in copper, and probably also in silver and gold, though without the use of fire.

Choctaw (Ng12). L: 33N, 88W. T: 1760. P: 15,000. B: New.

Timucua (Ng8). L: 27N, 82W. T: 1560. B: II, 131.

Others: Seminole (Ng2).

325: Lower Mississippi

Natchez (Ng7). L: 32N, 91E. T: 1700. P: 3,000 in 1700. B: II, 130; III, 423. Comment—Column 22: Matrilineages were subsequently borrowed from the Creek, but descent was always matrilineal with respect to social classes; Column 27: Mixed C and E terms, at least at a later date; Columns 67 and 69: Four social classes with caste-like features.

326: Texas Coast

Karankawa (Ne16). L: 29N, 96W. T: 1800. P: Fewer than 200 in 1814. B: III, 333. Comment—Column 14: But a shelter often accommodated two families; Column 35: "No gambling or guessing games were noted"; Column 64: Probably Macro-Hokan.

327: Apache

Chiricahua (Nh1). L: 31N, 108W. T: 1880. P: 1,000 in 1880. B: I, 131.

Jicarilla (Nh16). L: 36N, 104W. T: 1870. B: II, 265.

Mescalero (Nh15). L: 33N, 103W. T: 1870. B: II, 264.

Lipan (Nh24). L: 30N, 100W. T: 1880. B: IV, 250.

328: Eastern Pueblos

Tewa (Nh11), with special reference to San Ildefonso. L: 36N, 106W. T: 1900. P: 126 in San Ildefonso in 1937. B: II, 264. Comment—Column 3: For the Tewa as a whole, but 3 for San Ildefonso; Column 39: But O aboriginally.

Taos (Nh6). L: 37N, 106W. T: 1890. P: 700 in 1930. B: I, 401. Comment—Column 39: But O aboriginally.

Isleta (Nh10). L: 35N, 107W. T: 1920. P: 1,036 in 1930. B: II, 264.

Picuris (Nh9). L: 36N, 106W. T: 1920. P: 100. B: II, 264. Comment—Column 20: But there were agamous ceremonial patrimoieties.

329: Central Pueblos
Santa Ana (Nh12). L: 35N, 107W. T: 1920. P: 242 in 1934. Comment—Column 39: But O aboriginally; Column 48: But pottery is no longer made today.
Sia (Nh25). L: 36N, 107W. T: 1920. P: 327 in 1957. B: IV, 453. Comment—Column 39: But aboriginally O; Column 44: But formerly P.
Jemez (Nh8). L: 36N, 107W. T: 1920. P: 650 in 1937. B: II, 131; V, 448.
Cochiti (Nh7). L: 36N, 106W. T: 1890. P: 600. B: I, 544. Comment—Column 39: But O aboriginally.

330: Western Pueblos
Hopi (Nh18). L: 36N, 111W. T: 1920. P: 3,500 in 1950. B: II, 265. Comment—Column 42: But men work in silver today; Column 74: Matrilineal inheritance within the lineage.
Zuni (Nh4). L: 35N, 109W. T: 1910. P: 2,250 in 1941. B: I, 284. Comment—Column 74: A man's land is inherited by his daughters.
Hano (Nh2). L: 36N, 111W. T: 1950. P: 400 in 1950. B: I, 132. Comment—Column 39: But O aboriginally.
Acoma (Nh13). L: 35N, 108W. T: 1920. P: 1,250 in 1941. B: II, 264.
Others: Laguna (Nh14).

331: Navaho
Navaho (Nh3). L: 37N, 110W. T: 1930. P: 50,000 in 1950. B: I, 284. Comment —Column 39: But O aboriginally; Column 42: But O aboriginally; Column 76: But usually Pe today.
Western Apache (Nh17). L: 34N, 110W. T: 1870. P: 4,700 in 1940. B: II, 265. Comment—Column 46: But M in some bands; Column 73: But alternatively C.

332: River Yumans
Maricopa (Nh5). L: 33N, 113W. T: 1850. P: 700 in 1850. B: I, 401. Comment—Column 27: But sibling terms are applied to cross-cousins of opposite sex.
Cocopa (Nh19). L: 32N, 115W. T: 1850. B: II, 265.
Yuma (Nh22). L: 33N, 114W. T: 1860. B: II, 265.
Mohave (Nh21). L: 35N, 114W. T: 1850. B: II, 265.
Kamia (Nh20). L: 33N, 115W. T: 1860. P: 250 in 1849. B: II, 265.

333: Pima-Papago
Papago (Ni2). L: 31N, 112W. T: 1930. P: 5,000. B: I, 284. Comment—Column 20: But there are five agamous and nearly functionless patronymic name groups.
Pima (Ni6). L: 31N, 111W. T: 1840. P: 20,000. B: New. Comment—Column 20: But there were five agamous patronymic name groups and agamous patrimoieties; Column 39: Aboriginally, but subsequently qB.

334: Seri
Seri (Ni4). L: 29N, 112W. T: 1900. P: 200 in 1960. B: I, 401; II, 131.

335: Cahita
Yaqui (Ni7). L: 28N, 110W. T: 1870. B: New. Comment—Column 39: Aboriginally, but Bm today.

336: Tarahumara
Tarahumara (Ni1). L: 28N, 107W. T: 1930. B: I, 132. Comment—Column 39: But O aboriginally; Column 42: Iron working is done by itinerant Mexican smiths.

337: Huichol
Huichol (Ni3). L: 23N, 104W. T: 1920. P: 4,000. B: I, 401. Comment—Column 35: Zingg specifically reports "an absence of games."

338: Chichimec
Chichimec (Ni5). L: 22N, 100W. T: 1570. B: IV, 454. Comment—Items marked by asterisks are not specifically attested for the sixteenth century but are inferred as probable from subsequent ethnographic reports.

339: Tarascans

Tarasco (Nj8). L: 19N, 101W. T: Sixteenth century. B: New. Comment—Column 42: Work was done in gold, silver, and copper.

340: Totonac

Totonac (Nj4). L: 20N, 97W. T: 1940. P: 100,000 B: I, 401. Comment—Column 28: Aboriginally Jc; Column 42: But gold was worked aboriginally; Column 37: But Palerm reports that boys were circumcised aboriginally.

341: Aztec

Aztec (Nj2). L: 19N, 99W. T: 1520. B: I, 284; II, 131. Comment—Column 24: The "calpulli," since they were definitely agamous and nonunilineal, are classed as ramages.

342: Puebla Nahuatl

Tlaxcalans (Nj9), with special reference to the municipio of San Bernardino Contla. L: 19N, 98W. T: 1960. P: 300,000 in 1960. B: New. Comment—Column 32: Integrated into the Mexican state.

343: Chinantec-Mazatec

Chinantec (Nj1). L: 18N, 96W. T: 1940. P: 40,000. B: I, 132.
Others: Mazatec (Nj5).

344: Mixe-Zoque

Mixe (Nj7), with special reference to those of Ayutla. L: 17N, 95W. T: 1930. B: New.

Popoluca (Nj3), with special reference to the Sierra branch. L: 18N, 95W. T: 1940. P: 10,000. B: I, 401. Comment—Column 39: Also a few horses, mules, and cattle.

Others: Huave (Nj6).

345: Mixtec-Zapotec

Zapotec (Nj10). L: 17N, 96W. T: 1940. P: 215,000 in 1950. B: New. Comment—Column 32: Integrated into the Mexican state.

346: Lowland Maya

Yucatec Maya (Sa6). L: 18N, 90W. T: 1520. B: I, 544.

Chorti (Sa3). L: 14N, 89W. T: 1930. B: I, 284. Comment—Column 39: Also a few cattle, which "are of little importance"; Column 67: Though the Chorti themselves are egalitarian, the co-resident Ladinos are stratified into classes.

Lacandon (Sa10). L: 17N, 92W. T: 1900. P: More than 200,000 in 1900. B: IV, 121. Comment—Column 32: Integrated into the Mexican state.

347: Highland Maya

Quiche (Sa13), with special reference to the village of Chichicastenango. L: 15N, 91W. T: 1930. P: 25,000 in the Chichicastenango jurisdiction. B: New. Comment—Column 67: But aboriginally D; Column 69: The Indians form an ethnic caste with respect to the dominant Ladinos.

Mam (Sa8), with special reference to the village of Santiago Chimaltenango. L: 15N, 92W. T: 1930. B: II, 132. Comment—Column 32: Integrated into the Guatemalan state; Column 48: Traded from a neighboring village.

Others: Cakchiquel (Sa11), Tzeltal (Sa2).

348: Lenca-Jicaque

Lenca (Sa12). L: 14N, 88W. B: VI, 107. Comment—Column 44: Formerly P.

349: Miskito-Ulva

Miskito (Sa9). L: 13N, 85W. T: 1920. P: 6,000 in 1944. B: II, 132. Comment—Column 24: Or possibly Q.

350: Talamanca

Bribri (Sa5). L: 9N, 83W. T: 1950. P: 4,000 in 1960, including the kindred Cabecar tribe. B: II, 131. Comment—Column 22: Formerly M; Column 35: Absence of games is specifically reported by Gabb.

351: Cuna

Cuna (Sa1), with special reference to those of the San Blas archipelago. L: 9N, 78W. T: 1940. P: 21,000 San Blas Cuna in 1940. B: I, 132; II, 265. Comment

—Column 35: Ball games and checkers have recently been introduced; Column 44: But only hammocks today.

352: Choco
    Choco (Sa4), with special reference to those of Panama. L: 8N, 78W. T: 1960. P: 5,000. B: I, 401. Comment—Column 64: Probably Macro-Cariban.

353: Antillean Arawak
    Taino (Sb8). L: 19N, 75W. T: 1520. P: Extinct. B: VI, 107. Comment—Column 22: Descent may well have been matrilineal, like inheritance.

354: Antillean Carib
    Callinago (Sb1). L: 15N, 61W. T: 1650, P: Extinct. B: I, 132. Comment—Columns 74 and 76: Probably matrilineal.
    Black Carib (Sa7). L: 16N, 89W. T: 1940. P: 30,000. B: II, 131. Comment—Column 24: Solien reports "nonunilineal descent groups"; Chapter 69: Though egalitarian themselves, the Black Carib form an ethnic caste in Honduran society.

355: Sierra Nevada de Santa Marta
    Cagaba (Sb2). L: 11N, 74W. T: 1940. P: 2,000 in 1941. B: I, 284. Comment—Column 39: Also a few cattle.

356: Goajiro
    Goajiro (Sb6). L: 12N, 72W. T: 1940. P: 18,000. B: II, 132.

357: Paraujano
    Paraujano (Sb5). L: 11N, 72W. T: 1950. P: 1,350 in 1958. B: I, 402.

358: Motilon
    Yupa (Sb7), with special reference to the Pariri. L: 9N, 72W. T: 1950. P: 156 in 1954. B: IV, 454. Comment—Column 24: Or possibly Q.
    Others: Iroka (Sb3).

359: Guahibo
    Guahibo (Sc4), with special reference to the seminomadic groups. L: 5N, 69W. T: 1960. P: 12,000 in 1966. B: New.

360: Middle Orinoco
    Yaruro (Sc2). L: 7N, 68W. T: 1950. B: I, 133; II, 405.

361: Saliva
    Piaroa (Sc8). L: 5N, 67W. T: 1950. B: II, 266; IV, 454. Comment—Column 14: but the inhabitants of the communal dwelling may constitute a matrilocal extended family; Column 24: Or perhaps Q; Column 34: A high god who is apparently not a creator.

362: South Venezuelan Arawak
    Wapishana (Sc5). L: 3N, 60W. T: 1900. B: I, 402. Comment—Column 14: Each polygynous family has its own section in a communal house; Column 24: Or quite possibly Q.
    Piapoco (Sc17). L: 6N, 68W. T: 1950. P: A few hundred. B: IV, 454.
    Curipaco (Sc9). L: 5N, 67W. T: 1950. B: II, 266; IV, 454.

363: Orinoco-Ventuari Carib
    Yabarana (Sc7). L: 5N, 66W. T: 1950. B: II, 132; IV, 454. Comment—Column 24: Or possibly Q.
    Makitare (Sc16). L: 3N, 65W. T: 1920. B: II, 267; III, 423; IV, 454. Comment—Column 14: Each nuclear family occupies a separate apartment in a communal dwelling, but a married man is subject to the authority of his father-in-law; Column 24: Or possibly Q.
    Panare (Sc13). L: 6N, 66W. T: 1950. P: 750 in 1954. B: II, 266; IV, 454. Comment—Column 14: But the inhabitants of a communal dwelling approximate an extended family: Column 24: Or quite possibly Q.
    Others: Waica (Sd4).

364: Yanoama
    Sanema (Sd8). L: 4N, 66W. T: 1950. P: 2,500. B: IV, 455.

365: Shiriana
Shiriana (Sd6). L: 4N, 63W. T: 1960. P: 5,000 in 1960. B: IV, 454. Comment—Column 28: But a few groups grow a little manioc.

366: Guiana Carib
Barama River Carib (Sc3). L: 5N, 59W. T: 1930. B: I, 285. Comment—Column 24: From statement that brothers tend to live together in a settlement.
Waiwai (Sd7). L: 1N, 59W. T: 1950. P: 180 in 1954. B: IV, 454. Comment—Column 14: But an entire village occupies a communal dwelling; Column 34: A creator who is not a high god.
Macusi (Sc12). L: 4N, 59W. T: 1910. B: II, 266; V, 448.
Taulipang (Sc15). L: 4N, 62W. T: 1910. B: II, 267.
Camaracoto (Sc11). L: 6N, 63W. T: 1930. B: II, 266. Comment—Column 12: Or alternatively B.
Others: Carinya (Sb4), Rucuyen (Sc14).

367: Orinoco Delta
Warrau (Sc1), with special reference to the Winikina. L: 9N, 62W. T: 1950. P: 8,000 in 1950. B: I, 132.

368: Coastal Arawak
Locono (Sc10). L: 6N, 57W. T: 1900. B: II, 266.

369: Bush Negroes
Saramacca (Sc6). L: 4N, 56W. T: 1920. B: II, 132. Comment—Column 64: A pidgin language based on Portuguese with strong influences from other Indo-European languages and Niger-Congo.

370: Palikur
Palikur (Sd3). L: 3N, 52W. T: 1920. P: 240. B: I, 402.

371: Lower Amazon Tupi
Tapirape (Sd2). L: 11S, 52W. T: 1930. P: 149 in 1939 (since extinct). B: I, 285; II, 132.
Tenetehara (Sj6). L: 3S, 46W. T: 1930. P: 2,000. B: I, 403. Comment—Column 39: Animal husbandry is recent; Column 48: But pottery was formerly made.

372: Maue-Mundurucu
Mundurucu (Sd1). L: 6S, 58W. T: 1950. P: 1,250 in 1952. B: I, 133; I, 285; II, 287. Comment—Column 16: But men sleep apart from their wives in a men's house; Column 27: MoBrCh equated with SiCh, FaSiSo equated with MoBr, and a special term for FaSiDa.
Maue (Sd5). L: 4S, 57W. T: 1950. P: 1,400 in 1958. B: IV, 454. Comment—Column 39: But a few pigs are kept today; Column 48: But formerly P.

373: Siriono-Guarayu
Siriono (Se1). L: 16S, 64W. T: 1940. P: 2,000 in 1940. B: I, 133. Comment—Columns 22 and 24: Possibly L and O, respectively, though descent is specifically reported to be bilateral.

374: Pano
Amahuaca (Se8). L: 10S, 72W. T: 1950. B: III, 423.
Chacobo (Se11). L: 12S, 67W. T: 1960. P: 145 in 1960. B: New.
Conibo (Se9). L: 9S, 74W. T: 1920. P: 1,200 in 1940. B: IV, 121. Comment—Column 22: But some authors infer matrilineal descent.

375: Upper Amazon
Cocama (Se10). L: 1N, 79W. B: VI, 107. Comment—Column 20: A probable inference; Column 25: Preferential marriage with SiDa.

376: Tucuna
Tucuna (Se2). L: 3S, 70W. P: 3,000 in 1940. B: I, 133. Comment—Column 64: Perhaps Macro-Arawakan.

377: Peba
Yagua (Se4). L: 3S, 72W. T: 1940. P: 1,000 in 1940. B: I, 285. Comment—Column 14: But an entire settlement occupies a communal dwelling.

378: Tucano

Cubeo (Se5). L: 1N, 71W. T: 1940. P: 2,000. B: I, 402; IV, 455. Comment—
Column 14: But each family has a separate apartment in a communal
dwelling; Column 73: Alternatively Q.

379: Witoto
Witoto (Se6). L: 1S, 74W. T: 1900. P: 15,000. B: I, 544. Comment—Column
14: Each family has a separate apartment in a communal dwelling.

380: Jivaro
Jivaro (Se3). L: 3S, 78W. T: 1930. P: 5,000 in 1956. B: I, 285; III, 334; IV, 455

381: Tunebo
Tunebo (Sf4). L: 7N, 72W. T: 1950. P: 2,000. B: I, 402; II, 405.

382: Chibcha
Chibcha (Sf6). L: 5N, 72W. T: 1540. P: 1,000,000 aboriginally. B: II, 132.
Comment—Columns 22 and 24: Possibly L and O, respectively, in view of
reported matrilineal succession; Column 34: The Sun was the chief deity,
but another god was the creator.

383: Paez
Paez (Sf5). L: 3N, 76W. T: 1900. B: I, 545. Comment—Column 39: But O
aboriginally.

384: Cayapa
Cayapa (Sf3). L: 1N, 79W. T: 1910. P: 2,000. B: I, 285; II, 267; V, 448.

385: Campa
Campa (Sf7). L: 8S, 75W. T: 1900. P: 5,000 in 1930. B: IV, 121.

386: Highland Peru
Inca (Sf1). L: 13S, 72W. T: 1520. P: Several million. B: I, 133.

387: Aymara
Aymara (Sf2). L: 16S, 69W. T: 1940. P: 600,000 in 1936. B: I, 285. Comment—
Column 32: Formerly integrated into the Inca state, today into the Bolivian
and Peruvian states; Column 39: Aboriginally Co; Column 69: But the
Aymara form a lower caste in Bolivian society.

388: Araucanians
Mapuche (Sg2), with special reference to those of Cholchol. L: 39S, 68W. T:
1880. P: 200,000. B: I, 285; II, 267; IV, 455. Comment—Column 27: But
usually H outside of Cholchol; Column 39: Aboriginally Co; Column 42:
Aboriginally O.

389: Alacaluf
Alacaluf (Sg5). L: 52S, 74W. T: 1900. P: 200 in 1900. B: II, 132.

390: Yahgan
Yahgan (Sg1). L: 55S, 69W. T: 1870. P: 2,500 in 1866. B: I, 133; II, 267.

391: Patagonians
Tehuelche (Sg4), with special reference to the northern bands. L: 46S, 70W. T:
1870. P: 1,400 in 1870. B: I, 545. Comment—Column 35: But games of
chance (dice) were borrowed from the Spaniards; Column 39: But O prior
to 1725; Columns 42 and 44: But silversmithing and loom weaving are
relatively recent introductions.
Ona (Sg3), with special reference to the Shelknam. L: 54S, 69W. T: 1880. P:
2,000 in 1880 (300 in 1910). B: I, 402; IV, 348. Comment—Column 20: But
some scholars have inferred patrilineal descent.

392: Guaycuru
Toba (Sh8), with special reference to those of the Argentinian Chaco. L: 25S,
60W. T: 1960. P: Nearly 10,000 in 1964. B: IV, 455; V, 448. Comment—
Column 34: But aboriginally O; Column 50: Formerly M.
Abipon (Sh3). L: 29S, 61W. T: 1800. P: 2,000 in 1767. B: I, 286.
Caduveo (Sh4). L: 22S, 57W. T: 1940. P: 150 in 1937. B: I, 403.

393: Mascoi
Lengua (Sh9). L: 23S, 59W. T: 1890. P: 2,300 in 1940. B: New. Comment—
Column 35: An inference from scanty data; Column 39: But a few live-

stock have recently been acquired; Column 80: Windbreaks of mats supported by sticks.

394: Mataco

Mataco (Sh1). L: 24S, 63W. T: 1860. P: 20,000 in 1900. B: I, 133. Comment—Column 14: But N today.

Choroti (Sh5). L: 22S, 62W. T: 1910. P: 2,500 in 1915. B: I, 403. Comment—Column 35: But games of chance are not indigenous; Column 39: But both small and large livestock have recently been introduced.

395: Chiriguano

Chiriguano (Sh7). L: 20S, 63W. T: 1900. B: II, 133. Comment—Column 35: But games of chance are not indigenous; Column 39: But some sheep and cattle are kept today; Column 48: But tanning is not aboriginal.

396: Zamuco

Chamacoco (Sh6). L: 20S, 59W. T: 1890. B: II, 133.

397: Terena

Terena (Sh2). L: 21S, 58W. T: Before 1850. P: 3,000 in 1946. B: I, 133.

398: Guato

Guato (Si6). L: 19S, 58W. T: 1900. P: 100 in 1901. B: I, 545.

399: Nambicuara

Nambicuara (Si4). L: 12S, 59W. T: 1940. P: Fewer than 1,500. B: I, 286. Comment—Column 48: But some groups make crude pottery.

400: Paressi

Paressi (Si7), with special reference to the Cozarimi. L: 15S, 58W. T: 1910. P: 340 Paressi in 1908. B: VI, 107. Comment—Column 39: But pigs are kept today.

401: Bororo

Bororo (Si1). L: 16S, 55W. T: 1920. P: Nearly 1,000 in 1936. B: I, 133.

Umotina (Si8). L: 15S, 57W. T: 1940. P: 65 in 1949. B: New.

402: Bacairi

Bacairi (Si3). L: 14S, 55W. T: 1940. P: 250 in 1947. B: I, 286. Comment—Column 24: Patrifamilies strongly suggest quasi-lineages; Column 38: Boys at puberty go into seclusion for from two months to a year.

403: Camayura

Camayura (Si5). L: 12S, 54W. T: 1940. B: 110 in 1948. B: I, 403. Comment—Column 24: Or possibly Q.

404: Trumai

Trumai (Si2). L: 12S, 53W. T: 1930. P: 43 in 1938. B: I, 133. Comment—Column 24: An inference from the "tendency for patrilineally related males to live together" and from the statement that "the establishment of a patrilineal lineage" was prevented by the high death rate.

405: Caraja

Caraja (Sj1). L: 12S, 50W. T: 1950. P: 8,000 in 1939. B: I, 134; II, 133. Comment—Column 20: But there are three agamous patrilineal groups which function only in the ceremonial and political life of the men; Column 44: But not aboriginal.

406: Southern Ge

Sherente (Sj2). L: 9S, 48W. T: 1850. P: 2,140 in 1951. B: I, 134.

407: Apinaye-Coroa

Apinaye (Sj7). L: 6S, 49W. T: 1920. P: 160 in 1937. Comment—Columns 20 and 22: Parallel descent, i.e., patrilineal for males and matrilineal for females.

Coroa (Sj9). L: 8S, 52W. T: 1950. B: IV, 455. Comment—Column 20: Contrary to earlier reports of matrilineal descent, Dreyfus insists that moiety affiliation does not depend upon kinship, that there are no unilineal kin groups, and that the exogamous name groups are based on "cross descent," matrilineal for males and patrilineal for females; Column 52: Formerly F.

408: Timbira

Ramcocamecra (Sj4). L: 7S, 45W. T: 1930. P: 300 in 1930. B: I, 286; V, 448.

409: Guarani
>   Cayua (Sj10). L: 26S, 54W. T: 1950. B: New. Comment—Column 14: But formerly En; Column 39: But a few horses are kept today.

410: Caingang
>   Aweikoma (Sj3). L: 28S, 50W. T: 1910. P: 106 in 1934. B: I, 286.

411: Botocudo
>   Botocudo (Sj5). L: 18S, 42W. T: 1880. P: 5,100 in 1880 (90 in 1939). B: I, 403. Comment—Column 48: But pottery has been made in recent times; Column 64: Possibly Macro-Ge.

412: Coastal Tupi
>   Tupinamba (Sj8). L: 8S, 35W. T: 1600. P: 10,000. B: II, 133. Comment—Column 35: Probable on the basis of incomplete data.

Codes

Various items of ethnographic information on the 862 societies covered in this summary are presented in four tables in codified or symbolic form. Separate columns are devoted to particular subjects, and they are numbered in such a way as to facilitate the entry of the codified data on punch cards for machine calculations. Absence of information on any item is indicated in the tables by a period (.), whether it is due to deficiencies in the sources or to failure to assess them fully. An asterisk (*) in any column refers to a clarifying comment under the name of the society in "Classification by Clusters." The symbols used in the various columns, consisting in every case of numbers and/or letters, are defined below.

Column 1: Regional Identification. Each entry consists of a capital letter followed by a lower-case letter and then a number. The capitals refer to the six major ethnographic regions, as follows:

A Africa, exclusive of Madagascar and the northern and northeastern portions of the continent.
C Circum-Mediterranean, including Europe, Turkey and the Caucasus, the Semitic Near East, and northern and northeastern Africa.
E East Eurasia, excluding Formosa, the Philippines, Indonesia, and the area assigned to the Circum-Mediterranean but including Madagascar and other islands in the Indian Ocean.
I Insular Pacific, embracing all of Oceania as well as areas like Australia, Indonesia, Formosa, and the Philippines that are not always included therewith.
N North America, including the indigenous societies of this continent as far south as the Isthmus of Tehuantepec.
S South America, including the Antilles, Yucatan, and Central America as well as the continent itself.

The lower-case letters indicate the ten lesser areas into which each major region is arbitrarily divided. The numbers denote individual societies within each area, in the order of their original inclusion in the Atlas. They need not be entered on punch cards, since the code numbers in Column 3 will suffice.

Column 3: Code Number and Name of Society. For punch-card purposes, societies have been assigned code numbers in the order of their original listing. No punch-card position is required for the name, but four positions should be reserved for the code numbers, which run into the thousands.

Column 7: Subsistence Economy. A set of five digits indicates the estimated relative dependence of the society on each of the five major types of subsistence activity. The first digit refers to the gathering of wild plants and small land fauna; the second, to hunting, including trapping and fowling; the third, to fishing, including shellfishing and the pursuit of large aquatic animals; the fourth, to animal husbandry; the fifth, to agriculture. The symbols are defined as follows:

46

0) Zero to 5 per cent dependence.
1) 6 to 15 per cent dependence.
2) 16 to 25 per cent dependence.
3) 26 to 35 per cent dependence.
4) 36 to 45 per cent dependence.
5) 46 to 55 per cent dependence.
6) 56 to 65 per cent dependence.
7) 66 to 75 per cent dependence.
8) 76 to 85 per cent dependence.
9) 86 to 100 per cent dependence.

Column 12: Mode of Marriage. The prevailing mode of obtaining a wife is indicated by the following symbols:

B Bride-price or bride-wealth, i.e., transfer of a substantial consideration in the form of livestock, goods, or money from the groom or his relatives to the kinsmen of the bride.
D Dowry, i.e., transfer of a substantial amount of property from the bride's relatives to the bride, the groom, or the kinsmen of the latter.
G Gift exchange, i.e., reciprocal exchange of gifts of substantial value between the relatives of the bride and groom, or a continuing exchange of goods and services in approximately equal amounts between the groom or his kinsmen and the bride's relatives.
O Absence of any significant consideration, or bridal gifts only.
S Bride-service, i.e., a substantial material consideration in which the principal element consists of labor or other services rendered by the groom to the bride's kinsmen.
T Token bride-price, i.e., a small or symbolic payment only.
X Exchange, i.e., transfer of a sister or other female relative of the groom in exchange for the bride.

Lower-case letters following a capital indicate alternative modes of marriage or supplementary practices.

Column 14: Family Organization. The prevailing form of domestic or familial organization is indicated by the following symbols:

E Large extended families, i.e., corporate aggregations of smaller family units occupying a single dwelling or a number of adjacent dwellings and normally embracing the families of procreation of at least two siblings or cousins in each of at least two adjacent generations.
F Small extended families, i.e., those normally embracing the families of procreation of only one individual in the senior generation but of at least two in the next generation. Such families usually dissolve on the death of the head.
G Minimal extended or "stem" families, i.e., those consisting of only two related families of procreation (disregarding polygamous unions), particularly of adjacent generations.
M Independent nuclear families with monogamy.
N Independent nuclear families with occasional or limited polygyny.
O Independent polyandrous families.
P Independent polygynous families, where polygyny is general and not reported to be preferentially sororal, and where co-wives are not reported to occupy separate dwellings or apartments.
Q The same as P except that co-wives typically occupy separate quarters.
R Independent polygynous families, where polygyny is common and preferentially sororal, and where co-wives are not reported to occupy separate quarters.
S The same as R except that co-wives typically occupy separate quarters.

Lower-case letters from m to s, following E, F, or G, indicate the marital composition of the component familial units in extended families, e.g., Gm for stem families with monogamy.

Column 16: Marital Residence. The prevailing profile of marital residence in the society is expressed by the following symbols:

A Avunculocal, i.e., normal residence with or near the maternal uncle or other male matrilineal kinsmen of the husband.

B Ambilocal, i.e., residence established optionally with or near the parents of either the husband or the wife, depending upon circumstances or personal choice, where neither alternative exceeds the other in actual frequency by a ratio greater than two to one. If the differential frequency is greater than this, the symbols Uv or Vu are used to denote, respectively, a marked preponderance of uxorilocal or virilocal practice.

C Optionally uxorilocal or avunculocal. This may be the case in a uxorilocal society where many men marry a MoBrDa and thus, in fact, live avunculocally.

D Optionally patrilocal (or virilocal) or avunculocal.

M Matrilocal, i.e., normal residence with or near the female matrilineal kinsmen of the wife. Cf. U Uxorilocal.

N Neolocal, i.e., normal residence apart from the relatives of both spouses or at a place not determined by the kin ties of either.

O Nonestablishment of a common household, i.e., where both spouses remain in their natal households, sometimes called "duolocal" or "natolocal" residence.

P Patrilocal, i.e., normal residence with or near the male patrilineal kinsmen of the husband. Cf. V Virilocal.

U Uxorilocal. Equivalent to "matrilocal" but confined to instances where the wife's matrikin are not aggregated in matrilocal and matrilineal kin groups.

V Virilocal. Equivalent to "patrilocal" but confined to instances where the husband's patrikin are not aggregated in patrilocal and patrilineal kin groups.

Lower-case letters following a capital indicate either culturally patterned alternatives to, or numerically significant deviations from, the prevailing profile. Lower-case letters preceding a capital indicate the existence of a different rule or profile for the first years or so of marriage, e.g., uP for initial uxorilocal residence followed by permanent patrilocal residence.

Column 19: Community Organization. The prevalence of local endogamy, agamy, and exogamy, together with the presence or absence of localized kin groups, is indicated by the following symbols:

A Agamous communities without localized clans or any marked tendency toward either local exogamy or local endogamy.

C Clan-communities, each consisting essentially of a single localized exogamous kin group or clan. Cs if also segmented into clan-barrios.

D Demes, i.e., communities revealing a marked tendency toward local endogamy but not segmented into clan-barrios.

E Exogamous communities, i.e., those revealing a marked tendency toward local exogamy without having the specific structure of clans.

S Segmented communities, i.e., those divided into barrios, wards, or hamlets, each of which is essentially a localized kin group, a clan or ramage, in the absence of any indication of local exogamy. Large extended families, indicated by E in Column 14, are treated as clan-barrios if they are integrated by a rule of ambilineal, matrilineal, or patrilineal descent.

T Segmented communities where a marked tendency toward local exogamy is also specifically reported.

The specific structure of the clans indicated by C, S, or T, i.e., whether ambilocal, matrilocal, or patrilocal, is revealed by the rule of residence in Column 16.

Column 20: Patrilineal Kin Groups and Exogamy. A capital letter indicates the largest type of kin group reported for the society. A lower-case letter following a capital indicates the largest kin group characterized by exogamy, if it is different. The symbols are defined as follows:

E Patrilineal exogamy, i.e., extension of incest taboos to known patrilineal kinsmen in the absence of true patrilineal kin groups, provided such extension does not apply generally to bilateral kinsmen of equal remoteness.
L Lineages of modest size, i.e., patrilineal kin groups whose core membership is normally confined to a single community or a part thereof.
M Moieties, i.e., maximal lineages when there are only two such in the society.
O Absence of any patrilineal kin groups and also of patrilineal exogamy.
P Phratries, i.e., maximal lineages when there are more than two and when sibs are also present. Segmentary lineage systems in which segments of a lower order of magnitude are equivalent to sibs are also designated by P.
S Sibs ("clans" in British usage), i.e., lineages whose core membership normally comprises residents of more than one community.

Column 22: Matrilineal Kin Groups and Exogamy. The symbols are the same as those for Column 20 except that they refer to matrilineal rather than patrilineal groups and practices. Societies with double descent are readily identified by the appearance of L, M, P, or S symbols in both Column 20 and Column 22.

Column 24: Cognatic Kin Groups. The presence or probable absence, and the typology, of ambilineal and bilateral kin groups are indicated by the following symbols.

A Ambilineal descent inferred from the presence of ambilocal extended families, true ramages being absent or unreported.
B Bilateral descent as inferred from the absence of reported ambilineal, matrilineal, or patrilineal kin groups, kindreds being absent or unreported.
K Bilateral descent with specifically reported kindreds, i.e., Ego-oriented bilateral kin groups or categories.
O Absence of cognatic kin groups as inferred from the presence of unilineal descent.
Q Bilateral descent with reported or probable quasi-lineages, i.e., cognatic groups approximating the structure of lineages but based on filiation rather than on unilineal or ambilineal descent.
R Ramages, i.e., ancestor-oriented ambilineal kin groups, if they are agamous, endogamous, or not specifically stated to be exogamous.
S Exogamous ramages specifically reported.

When both kindreds and ramages are reported for the same society, they are indicated by a capital followed by a lower-case letter. When entered on punch cards, Rk and Kr must be treated separately, since this column lacks space for a second symbol.

Column 25: Cousin Marriage. The rules or practices governing the marriageability or nonmarriageability of first cousins, and in some instances also of second cousins, are indicated by the following symbols:

C Duolateral cross-cousin marriage, i.e., marriage allowed with either MoBrDa or FaSiDa but forbidden with a parallel cousin. A lower-case letter is appended to indicate preferential, as opposed to merely permitted unions, i.e., Cc, Cm, or Cp, respectively, for a symmetrical, matrilateral, or patrilateral preference.

D Duolateral marriage with paternal cousins only. Da or Dp for a preference for FaBrDa or FaSiDa respectively.

E Duolateral marriage with maternal cousins only. Em for a preference for MoBrDa.

F Duolateral marriage with an uncle's daughter only. Fa or Fm for a preference for FaBrDa or MoBrDa respectively.

G Duolateral marriage with an aunt's daughter only. Gp for a preference for FaSiDa

M Matrilateral cross-cousin marriage, i.e., unilateral marriage with a MoBrDa only. Mm if preferred rather than merely permitted.

N Nonlateral marriage, i.e., unions forbidden with any first or second cousin.

O Nonlateral marriage when evidence is available only for first cousins.

P Patrilateral cross-cousin marriage, i.e., unilateral marriage with a FaSiDa only. Pp if preferred rather than merely permitted.

Q Quadrilateral marriage, i.e., marriage allowed with any first cousin. Qa for the Arabic or Islamic variant in which the FaBrDa is the preferred mate. Qc, Qm, and Qp for other preferences.

R Nonlateral marriage in which all first cousins and some but not all second cousins are forbidden as spouses. Rr for the type of preferential marriage with particular second cross-cousins only, notably MoMoBrDaDa or FaMoBrSoDa, often reported of societies with subsection systems.

S Nonlateral marriage in which unions are forbidden with any first cousin but are permitted with any second cousin (or at least any who is not a lineage mate). Ss if second-cousin marriage is preferred rather than merely permitted.

T Trilateral marriage, i.e., marriage allowed with any first cousin except an ortho-cousin or lineage mate. Tc, Tm, and Tp, respectively for preferences for a bilateral, matrilateral, or patrilateral cross-cousin.

Two positions will be required for punch-card entries. In the one registering capital letters, the unusual forms of duolateral marriage—D, E, F, and G—may be grouped together. In the second, registering preferential or "prescriptive" unions, the lower-case letters (a, c, m, p, r, and s) should be distinguished and all other instances grouped under a separate category to indicate the absence of preferential rules.

Column 27: Kinship Terminology for Cousins. The prevailing pattern of kinship terminology employed for first cousins is indicated by the following symbols:

C Crow, i.e., FaSiCh equated with Fa or FaSi and/or MoBrCh with Ch or BrCh(ws).

D Descriptive or derivative, rather than elementary, terms employed for all cousins.

E Eskimo, i.e., FaBrCh, FaSiCh, MoBrCh, and MoSiCh equated with each other but differentiated from siblings.

H Hawaiian, i.e., all cousins equated with siblings or called by terms clearly derivative from those for siblings.

I Iroquois, i.e., FaSiCh equated with MoBrCh but differentiated from both siblings and parallel cousins.

O Omaha, i.e., MoBrCh equated with MoBr or Mo and/or FaSiCh with SiCh(ms) or Ch.

S Sudanese, i.e., FaSiCh and MoBrCh distinguished alike from siblings, parallel cousins, and each other but without conforming to either the Crow, the descriptive, or the Omaha patterns.

Z Mixed or variant patterns not adequately represented by any of the foregoing symbols. The details are given under "Classification by Clusters."

Column 28: Type and Intensity of Agriculture. Capital letters symbolize the intensity of cultivation, as follows:

C Casual agriculture, i.e., the slight or sporadic cultivation of food or other plants incidental to a primary dependence upon other subsistence practices.
E Extensive or shifting cultivation, as where new fields are cleared annually, cultivated for a year or two, and then allowed to revert to forest or brush for a long fallow period.
H Horticulture, i.e., semi-intensive agriculture limited mainly to vegetable gardens or groves of fruit trees rather than the cultivation of field crops.
I Intensive agriculture on permanent fields, utilizing fertilization by compost or animal manure, crop rotation, or other techniques so that fallowing is either unnecessary or is confined to relatively short periods.
J Intensive cultivation where it is largely dependent upon irrigation.
O Complete absence of agriculture.

A second symbol, a lower-case letter, indicates the principal type of crop under the following categories:

c Cereal grains, e.g., maize, millet, rice, or wheat, when at least as important as any other type of crop.
n Non-food crops only, e.g., cotton or tobacco.
r Roots or tubers, e.g., manioc, potatoes, taro, or yams, when more important than cereal grains and at least as important as tree crops or vegetables.
t Tree fruits, e.g., bananas, breadfruit, coconuts, or dates, when more important than cereal grains and root crops. Sago, unless specifically reported to be cultivated, is treated as a gathered product rather than a cultivated one.
v Vegetables, e.g., cucurbits, greens, or legumes, when more important than other crops.

Column 30: Settlement Pattern. The prevailing type of settlement pattern is indicated by the following symbols:

B Fully migratory or nomadic bands.
H Separated hamlets where several such form a more or less permanent single community.
N Neighborhoods of dispersed family homesteads.
S Seminomadic communities whose members wander in bands for at least half of the year but occupy a fixed settlement at some season or seasons, e.g., recurrently occupied winter quarters.
T Semisedentary communities whose members shift from one to another fixed settlement at different seasons or who occupy more or less permanently a single settlement from which a substantial proportion of the population departs seasonally to occupy shifting camps, e.g., during transhumance.
V Compact and relatively permanent settlements, i.e., nucleated villages or towns.
W Compact but impermanent settlements, i.e., villages whose location is shifted every few years.
X Complex settlements consisting of a nucleated village or town with outlying homesteads or satellite hamlets. Urban aggregations of population are not separately indicated since Column 31 deals with community size.

Column 31: Mean Size of Local Communities. The average population of local communities, whatever the pattern of settlement, is computed from census data or other evidence and is ranked in one of the following categories:

1 Fewer than 50 persons.
2 From 50 to 99 persons.

3 From 100 to 199 persons.
4 From 200 to 399 persons.
5 From 400 to 1,000 persons.
6 More than 1,000 persons in the absence of indigenous urban aggregations.
7 One or more indigenous towns of more than 5,000 inhabitants but none of more than 50,000.
8 One or more indigenous cities with more than 50,000 inhabitants.

Column 32: Jurisdictional Hierarchy. The number of jurisdictional levels in each society is shown by a pair of digits, of which the first indicates the number of levels up to and including the local community and the second those transcending the local community. Thus 20 represents the theoretical minimum, e.g., independent nuclear or polygynous families and autonomous bands or villages, whereas 44 represents the theoretical maximum, e.g., nuclear families, extended families, clan-barrios, villages, parishes, districts, provinces, and a complex state. The second digit incidentally provides a measure of political complexity, ranging from 0 for stateless societies, through 1 or 2 for petty and larger paramount chiefdoms or their equivalent, to 3 or 4 for large states. Different types of organization on the same level, e.g., a consanguineal lineage and its localized equivalent, are counted as one, and organizations not held to be legitimate, e.g., imposed colonial regimes, are excluded.

Column 34: High Gods. A high god is defined, following Swanson, as a spiritual being who is believed to have created all reality and/or to be its ultimate governor, even though his sole act was to create other spirits who, in turn, created or control the natural world. The range of beliefs is indicated by the following symbols:

A A high god present but otiose or not concerned with human affairs.
B A high god present and active in human affairs but not offering positive support to human morality.
C A high god present, active, and specifically supportive of human morality.
O A high god absent or not reported in substantial descriptions of religious beliefs.

Column 35: Types of Games. Following Roberts, only games with an outcome, i.e., a winner and a loser, are treated, and their classification and incidence are indicated by the following symbols:

A Games of physical skill only, whether or not they may also involve incidental elements of chance or strategy, e.g., foot racing, wrestling, the hoop-and-pole game.
B Games of chance only, with no significant element of either physical skill or strategy involved, e.g., dice games.
C Games of physical skill and of chance both present.
O No games of any of the three types.
P Games of strategy only, involving no significant element of physical skill, e.g., chess, go, poker. Whether or not an element of chance is also involved is considered irrelevant.
Q Games of physical skill and of strategy present, but not games of chance.
R Games of chance and of strategy present, but not games of physical skill.
S Games of all three types present.

Column 36: Post-Partum Sex Taboos. The normal duration of post-partum sex taboos, i.e., those requiring a lactating mother to refrain from sexual intercourse, is rated according to the following scale:

0 No taboo, especially where the husband is expected to have intercourse with his wife as soon as possible after childbirth for the alleged benefit of the child.
1 Short post-partum taboo, lasting not more than one month.
2 Duration of from more than a month to six months.
3 Duration of from more than six months to one year.
4 Duration of from more than one year to two years.
5 Duration of more than two years.

Column 37: Male Genital Mutilations. The practice of circumcision or any of its variants, e.g., Polynesian "supercision," when culturally normative and not sporadic or merely optional, and the age at which it typically occurs are indicated by the following symbols:

0 Absent or not generally practiced.
1 Performed shortly after birth, i.e., within the first two months.
2 Performed during infancy, i.e., from two months to two years of age.
3 Performed during early childhood, i.e., from two to five years of age.
4 Performed during late childhood, i.e., from six to ten years of age.
5 Performed during adolescence, i.e., from eleven to fifteen years of age.
6 Performed during early adulthood, i.e., from sixteen to 25 years of age.
7 Performed during maturity, i.e., from 25 to 50 years of age.
8 Performed in old age, i.e., after 50 years of age.
9 Circumcision customary, but the normal age is unspecified or unclear.

Column 38: Segregation of Adolescent Boys. Several degrees and modes of segregating boys at or approaching puberty are indicated by the following symbols:

A Absence of segregation, adolescent boys residing and sleeping in the same dwelling as their mothers and sisters.
P Partial segregation, adolescent boys residing or eating with their natal families but sleeping apart from them, e.g., in a special hut or in a cattle shed.
R Complete segregation, in which adolescent boys go to live as individuals with relatives outside the nuclear family, e.g., with grandparents or with a maternal or paternal uncle.
S Complete segregation, in which adolescent boys go to live as individuals with non-relatives, e.g., as retainers to a chief or as apprentices to specialists.
T Complete segregation, in which boys reside with a group of their own peers, e.g., in bachelor dormitories, military regiments, or age-villages.

Column 39: Type of Animal Husbandry. The predominant type of domestic animals kept in the particular society is indicated by the following symbols:

B Bovine animals, e.g., cattle, mithun, water buffaloes, yaks.
C Camels or other animals of related genera, e.g., alpacas, llamas.
D Deer, e.g., reindeer.
E Equine animals, e.g., horses, donkeys.
O Absence or near absence of domestic animals other than bees, cats, dogs, fowl, guinea pigs, or the like.
P Pigs the only domestic animals of consequence.

S Sheep and/or goats when larger domestic animals are absent or much less important.

A preposited lower-case p indicates that animals were employed in plow cultivation prior to the contact period; a lower-case q indicates that plow cultivation, though not aboriginal, was well established at the period of observation. A postposited lower-case m indicates that domestic animals are milked other than sporadically; a lower-case o indicates the absence or near absence of milking.

Columns 42 to 62, in Table C, are devoted to a series of technological and economic activities and to types of specialization in their performance, but they employ an identical set of symbols, consisting of a capital and, in some cases, also a lower-case letter. The capital letters indicate specialization by sex, as follows:

D Differentiation of specific tasks by sex but approximately equal participation by both sexes in the total activity.
E Equal participation by both sexes without marked or reported differentiation in specific tasks.
F Females alone perform the activity, male participation being negligible.
G Both sexes participate, but females do appreciably more than males.
I Sex participation irrelevant, especially where production is industrialized.
M Males alone perform the activity, female participation being negligible.
N Both sexes participate, but males do appreciably more than females.
O The activity is absent or unimportant in the particular society.
P The activity is present, but sex participation is unspecified in the sources consulted.

When not followed by a lower-case letter, the foregoing symbols imply that the activity, if present, is normally performed by many or most adult men, women, or both. Specialization by age or occupational status, where reported to be present, is indicated by one of the following symbols in lower case:

a Senior age specialization, i.e., the activity is largely performed by men and/or women beyond the prime of life.
b Junior age specialization, i.e., the activity is largely performed by boys and/or girls before the age of puberty.
c Craft specialization, i.e., the activity is largely performed by a small minority of adult males or females who possess specialized skills. Occupational castes are treated as instances of craft specialization.
i Industrial specialization, i.e., the activity is largely removed from the domain of a division of labor by sex, age, or craft specialization and is performed mainly by industrialized techniques of production.

It remains to define the several columns to which the above sets of symbols are applied.

Column 42: Metal Working. Only such arts as smelting, casting, and forging, which involve the application of fire, are indicated.

Column 44: Weaving. Only the manufacture of true cloth on a loom or frame is indicated—not the manufacture of nets, baskets, mats, or nonwoven fabrics like barkcloth or felt.

Column 46: Leather Working. Only the dressing of skins, e.g., by tanning, is indicated, not the manufacture of artifacts from raw hides or undressed skins.

Column 48: Pottery. Only the manufacture of earthenware utensils is indicated.

Column 50: Boat Building. Only the construction of true water craft is indicated, not the making of simple floats, rafts, or the like.

Column 52: House Construction. Only the actual building of a permanent dwelling or the erection of a transportable shelter is indicated, not the acquisition or preliminary preparation of the materials used.

Column 54: Gathering. For the definition of this and subsequent subsistence activities see the code for Column 7.

Column 56: Hunting.

Column 58: Fishing.

Column 60: Animal Husbandry.

Column 62: Agriculture.

The remaining columns are those incorporated in Table D.

Column 64: Linguistic Affiliation. Presented herewith is a classification of the linguistic stocks or families of the world and, for some of the better analyzed ones, the subfamilies into which they are divided. In some cases an indication is given of the possible grouping of families into phyla characterized by more remote relationships. Only for the New Guinea area is a reasonably satisfactory and generally acceptable grouping of languages into families still unavailable, and we have followed a suggestion by Greenberg that the non-Malayo-Polynesian languages of this area form a single phylum, which we designate as "Papuan." The following symbols indicate the 78 presumably distinct linguistic families for which it is likely that more than a single representative will appear in the tables.

Aa Afro-Asiatic or Hamito-Semitic. Subfamilies: AaB Berber; AaC Cushitic; AaD Chadic; AaE Egyptian; AaS Semitic.
Ac Araucanian.
Ag Algonkian. Probably forms a Macro-Algonkian phylum with Ritwan (Ri).
Ak Abasgo-Kerketian or Circassian. Possibly forms a Caucasic phylum with Checheno-Lesghian (Cl) and Georgian (Gr).
Al Altaic. Possibly forms a Ural-Atlantic phylum with Uralic (Ur). Subfamilies: AlG Tungusic; AlM Mongolic; AlT Turkic.
Am Annam-Muong. Possibly related to Mon-Khmer (Mk) or Thai-Kadai (Tk).
Ar Arawakan. Possibly forms a Macro-Arawakan phylum with Tacana and Tucuna.
At Athapaskan. Probably forms a Nadene phylum with Eyak, Haida, and Tlingit. Subfamilies: AtN Northern; AtP Pacific; AtS Southern.
Au Australian. Possibly forms an Indo-Pacific phylum with Andamanese, Papuan (Pa), and Tasmanian.
Be Betoyan or Tucanoan.

Bo Bororan. Possibly forms a Macro-Ge phylum with Botocudo, Caingang (Cg) and Ge (Ge).
Ca Cariban. Possibly forms a Macro-Cariban phylum with Choco and Peban (Pb).
Cd Caddoan.
Cg Caingang. Possibly belongs to a Macro-Ge phylum.
Ch Chibchan. Possibly forms a Macro-Chibchan phylum with Misumalpan (Ms).
Cl Checheno-Lesghian. Possibly belongs to a Caucasic phylum.
Cm Chemakuan. Probably forms a Mosan phylum with Salishan (Sa) and Wakashan (Wa).
Cn Chari-Nile or Macro-Sudanic. Subfamilies: CnC Central Sudanic; CnE Eastern Sudanic or Nilotic; CnK Kunaman; CnN Nubian.
Cp -Cahuapanan.
Cq Chiquitoan. Possibly forms a Macro-Guaycuran phylum with Guaycuran (Gu) and Mataco-Mateguayo (Mm).
Dr Dravidian.
Es Eskimauan or Eskimo-Aleut.
Ge Ge. Possibly belongs to a Macro-Ge phylum.
Gr Georgian, Grusian, or Kartvelian. Possibly belongs to a Caucasic phylum.
Gu Guaycuran. Probably belongs to a Macro-Guaycuran phylum with Mataco-Mateguayo (Mm) and possibly also with Chiquitoan (Cq).
Ho Hokan. Probably forms a Macro-Hokan phylum with Chumash, Coahuilteco, Jicaque, Karankawa, Salina, Seri, Supanec, Tequistlatec, Tonkawa, and Washo. Subfamilies: HoC Chimarikan; HoE Esselenian; HoK Karok or Quoratean; HoP Pomo or Kulanapan; HoS Shastan or Shasta-Achomawi; HoY Yuman; HoZ Yanan.
Ie Indo-European. Subfamilies: IeA Albanian; IeB Baltic or Balto-Slavic; IeC Celtic; IeG Germanic; IeH Hellenic or Greek; IeI Indic; IeM Armenian; IeP: Persian or Iranian; IeR Romance or Italic; IeS Slavic.
Ir Iroquoian.
Jr Japano-Ryukuan.
Ka Kanuric or Central Saharan.
Ke Kechumaran or Quechua-Aymara.
Kh Khoisan or Click.
Kk Katukinan or Catukina.
Km Koman.
Ko Kordofanian.
Kr Keresan.
Lu Luorawetlan or Paleo-Siberian.
Ma Mayan.
Mi Mixtecan. Probably forms a Mixteco-Zapotecan phylum with Zapotec (Za).
Mk Mon-Khmer or Austroasiatic. Subfamilies: MkC Cambodian or Mon-Khmer proper; MkK Khasi-Nicobarese; MkM Munda or Kolarian; MkS Semang-Sakai.
Mm Mataco-Mateguayo. Probably belongs to a Macro-Guaycuran phylum.
Mn Mascoian.
Mp Malayo-Polynesian or Austronesian. Possibly forms a Macro-Austronesian phylum with Thai-Kadai (Tk).
Ms Misumalpan. Possibly belongs to a Macro-Chibchan phylum.
My Miao-Yao.
Mz Mizocuavean.
Na Nahuatlan or Mexicano. Forms a Uto-Aztecan phylum with Piman (Pi), Shoshonean (Ss), and Taracahitian (Tc).
Nc Niger-Congo or Nigritic. Subfamilies: NcA Atlantic or West Atlantic; NcB Bantoid or Central; NcE Eastern or Adamawa-Eastern; NcG Gur or Voltaic; NcI Ijo or Ijaw; NcK Kwa; NcM Mande.
Nm Natchez-Muskogean.
Om Oto-Manguean.

Op Oregon Penutian. Probably forms a Macro-Penutian phylum with Kusan, Penutian (Pe), Sahaptin (Sh), Tsimshian, and Yakonan (Ya). Subfamilies: OpC Chinookan; OpK Kalapooian; OpT Takilman or Takelma.

Pa Papuan or Indo-Pacific. A probable phylum (not a family) of non-Malayo-Polynesian languages in New Guinea and adjacent islands in Indonesia and Melanesia. Greenberg also tentatively classes Andamanese, Australian (Au), and Tasmanian with this phylum.

Pb Peban. Possibly belongs to a Macro-Cariban phylum.

Pe Penutian. Probably forms a Macro-Penutian phylum with Kusan, Oregon Penutian (Op), Sahaptin (Sh), Tsimshian, and Yakonan (Ya). Subfamilies: PeC Costanoan; PeM Maidu or Pujunan; PeN Miwok or Moquelumnan; PeW Wintun or Copehan; PeY Yokuts or Mariposan.

Pi Piman, Pima-Tepehuan, or Sonoran. Forms a Uto-Aztecan phylum with Nahuatlan (Na), Shoshonean (Ss), and Taracahitian (Tc).

Pn Panoan.

Pu Puinavean.

Ri Ritwan. Probably belongs to a Macro-Algonkian phylum.

Sa Salishan. Probably belongs to a Mosan phylum.

Sh Sahaptin. Probably belongs to a Macro-Penutian phylum. Subfamilies: ShL Lutuamian; ShS Shahaptian; ShW Waiilatpuan.

Si Sinitic. Probably forms a Sino-Tibetan phylum with Tibeto-Burman (Tb).

Ss Shoshonean. Forms a Uto-Aztecan phylum with Nahuatlan (Na), Piman (Pi), and Taracahitian (Tc).

Sx Siouan.

Ta Tanoan. Probably forms a Tanoan-Kiowa phylum with Kiowan. Subfamilies: TaE Tewa; TaI Tiwa; TaO Towa.

Tb Tibeto-Burman. Probably forms a Sino-Tibetan phylum with Sinitic (Si).

Tc Taracahitian. Forms a Uto-Aztecan phylum with Nahuatlan (Na), Piman (Pi), and Shoshonean (Ss).

Tg Tupi-Guarani. Possibly forms a Macro-Tupian phylum with Witotan (Wi) and Zaparoan (Zp).

Th Tehuelchean or Chonan.

Tk Thai-Kadai. Possibly belongs to a Macro-Austronesian phylum.

Tu Tunican.

Ur Uralic. Possibly forms a Ural-Altaic phylum with Altaic (Al). Subfamilies: UrF Finnic; UrS Samoyedic; UrU Ugric.

Wa Wakashan. Probably belongs to a Mosan phylum.

Wi Witotan. Possibly belongs to a Macro-Tupian phylum.

Xx An isolated linguistic family not known to be related to any other and confined to the society in question or to a very small cluster of neighboring and culturally similar groups.

Xy A linguistic family confined to the society in question or its immediate neighbors but presumed to be related to other languages within a larger phylum.

Ya Yakonan. Probably belongs to a Macro-Penutian phylum.

Yp Yunga-Puruhan.

Yu Yukian.

Za Zapotecan. Probably belongs to a Mixteco-Zapotecan phylum.

Zm Zamucoan.

Zp Zaparoan. Possibly belongs to a Macro-Tupian phylum.

Column 67: Class Stratification. The degree and type of class differentiation, excluding purely political and religious statuses, is indicated by the following symbols:

C Complex stratification into social classes correlated in large measure with extensive differentiation of occupational statuses.

D Dual stratification into a hereditary aristocracy and a lower class of ordinary commoners or freemen, where traditionally ascribed noble status is at least as decisive as control over scarce resources.

E Elite stratification, in which an elite class derives its superior status from, and perpetuates it through, control over scarce resources, particularly land, and is thereby differentiated from a propertyless proletariat or serf class.

O Absence of significant class distinctions among freemen (slavery is treated in Column 71), ignoring variations in individual repute achieved through skill, valor, piety, or wisdom.

W Wealth distinctions, based on the possession or distribution of property, present and socially important but not crystallized into distinct and hereditary social classes.

Combinations of a capital and a lower-case letter, e.g., Cd, indicate that the prevailing system exhibits important features of two of the types defined above.

Column 69: Caste Stratification. The degree and type of caste differentiation is indicated by the following symbols:

C Complex caste stratification in which occupational differentiation emphasizes hereditary ascription and endogamy to the near exclusion of achievable class statuses.

D One or more despised occupational groups, e.g., smiths or leather workers, distinguished from the general population, regarded as outcastes by the latter, and characterized by strict endogamy.

E Ethnic stratification, in which a superordinate caste withholds privileges from and refuses to intermarry with a subordinate caste (or castes) which it stigmatizes as ethnically alien, e.g., as descended from a conquered and culturally inferior indigenous population, from former slaves, or from foreign immigrants of different race and/or culture.

O Caste distinctions absent or insignificant.

Combinations of a capital and a lower-case letter indicate a combination or mixture of two of the types defined above.

Column 71: Slavery. The forms and prevalence of slave status, treated quite independently of both class and caste status, are indicated by the following symbols:

H Hereditary slavery present and of at least modest social significance.

I Incipient or nonhereditary slavery, i.e., where slave status is temporary and not transmitted to the children of slaves.

O Absence or near absence of slavery.

S Slavery reported but not identified as hereditary or nonhereditary.

A postposited f indicates that slavery, though no longer practiced at the time level specified in "Classification into Clusters," had existed at an earlier period.

Column 73: Succession to the Office of Local Headman. Without reference to rules of succession prevailing on higher levels of political integration, those applying to the office of local headman (or a close equivalent) are indicated by the following symbols:

A Nonhereditary succession through appointment by some higher authority.
C Nonhereditary succession through informal consensus.
E Nonhereditary succession through election or some other mode of formal consensus.
I Nonhereditary succession through influence, e.g., of wealth or social status.
M Hereditary succession by a sister's son.
N Hereditary succession by a matrilineal heir who takes precedence over a sister's son, e.g., a younger brother.
O Absence of any office resembling that of a local headman.
P Hereditary succession by a son.
Q Hereditary succession by a patrilineal heir who takes precedence over a son.
S Nonhereditary succession on the basis primarily of seniority or age.

Column 74: Inheritance of Real Property. The rule or practice governing the disposition or transmission of a man's property in land (exclusive of any dower right of his widow) is indicated by the following symbols:

C Inheritance by children of either sex or both.
D Inheritance by children, but with daughters receiving less than sons.
M Matrilineal inheritance by a sister's son or sons.
N Inheritance by matrilineal heirs who take precedence over sisters' sons.
O Absence of individual property rights in land or of any rule of inheritance governing the transmission of such rights.
P Patrilineal inheritance by a son or sons.
Q Inheritance by patrilineal heirs who take precedence over sons.

Lower-case letters following capitals indicate the distribution of the inheritance among several individuals of the same category, as follows:

e Equal or relatively equal distribution among all members of the category.
p Primogeniture, i.e., predominant inheritance by the senior member of the category.
q Exclusive or predominant inheritance by the member of the category adjudged best qualified, either by the deceased or by his surviving relatives.
u Ultimogeniture, i.e., predominant inheritance by the junior member of the category.

Column 76: Inheritance of Movable Property. The symbols are the same as for Column 74, with the qualification that O also includes the destruction, burial, or giving away of movable property.

In actual application the codes for Columns 74 and 76 have proved inadequate, and the coded data in these columns should consequently be used only with great circumspection.

Column 78: Norms of Premarital Sex Behavior. The following symbols define the standards of sex behavior prevailing for unmarried females:

A Premarital sex relations allowed and not sanctioned unless pregnancy results.
E Premarital sex relations precluded by a very early age of marriage for females.
F Premarital sex relations freely permitted and subject to no sanctions.
T Trial marriage; monogamous premarital sex relations permitted with the expectation of marriage if pregnancy results, promiscuous relations being prohibited and sanctioned.
P Premarital sex relations prohibited but weakly sanctioned and not infrequent in fact.
V Insistence on virginity; premarital sex relations prohibited, strongly sanctioned, and in fact rare.

The prevailing type of dwelling is indicated by five adjacent symbols representing five outstanding features of shape, construction, and materials.

Column 80: Ground Plan of Dwelling. The symbols used are the following:

C Circular.
E Elliptical or elongated with rounded ends.
P Polygonal.
Q Quadrangular around (or partially around) an interior court.
R Rectangular or square.
S Semicircular.

Column 81: Floor Level. The symbols used are the following:

E Elevated slightly above the ground on a raised platform of earth, stone, or wood.
G Floor formed by or level with the ground itself.
P Raised substantially above the ground on piles, posts, or piers.
S Subterranean or semi-subterranean, ignoring cellars beneath the living quarters.

Column 82: Wall Material. The symbols used are the following:

A Adobe, clay, or dried brick.
B Bark.
F Felt, cloth, or other fabric.
G Grass, leaves, or other thatch.
H Hides or skins.
M Mats, latticework, or wattle.
O Open walls, including cases where they can be temporarily closed by screens.
P Plaster, mud and dung, or wattle and daub.
R Walls indistinguishable from roof or merging into the latter. Cf. Column 84.
S Stone, stucco, concrete, or fired brick.
W Wood, including logs, planks, poles, bamboo, or shingles.

Column 83: Shape of Roof (or of walls and roof where not distinct). The symbols used are the following:

B Beehive shaped with pointed peak.
C Conical.
D Dome shaped or hemispherical.
E Semi-hemispherical.
F Flat or horizontal.
G Gabled, i.e., with two slopes.
H Hipped or pyramidal, i.e., with four slopes.
R Rounded or semi-cylindrical.
S Shed, i.e., with one slope.

Column 84: Roofing Material. The symbols used are the following:

B Bark.
E Earth or turf.
F Felt, cloth, or other fabric.
G Grass, leaves, brush, or other thatch.
H Hides or skins.
I Ice or snow.
M Mats.
P Plaster, clay, mud and dung, or wattle and daub.

S Stone or slate.
T Tile or fired brick.
W Wood, including logs, planks, poles, bamboo, or shingles.

Columns 85 to 89: Secondary or Alternative House Type. The same symbols as in Columns 80 to 84 are employed to characterize any different house type of significance in the culture, e.g., a more recent or introduced type or one occupied during seasonal migrations as opposed to that used in more permanent settlements.

Tables

TABLE A

1	3	7	12	14	16	19	20	22	24	25	27
Aa1	1: Kung	82000	S	Fn	uB	E	O	O	K	N	E
Aa2	101: Dorobo	46000	B	M	P	C	S	O	O	O	O
Aa3	102: Nama	13150	Gb	N	uP	C	S	O	O	C	I
Aa5	202: Mbuti	63100	Xb	N	B	A	O	O	B	N	H
Aa6	301: Sandawe	11125	B	N	bP	C	L	O	O	Mm	Z*
Aa7	636: Naron	73000	T	N	bVu	E	O	O	B	O	.
Aa9	726: Hatsa	55000	B	N	Vn	.	O	O	B	.	.
Ab1	2: Herero	13060	B	Fq	Va	E	Ps	S	O	Cp	I
Ab2	3: Swazi	11026	B	Es	Pn	Cs	S	O	O	C	I
Ab3	103: Lozi	12124	Ts	Q	uVa	A	O	O	Rk	N	H
Ab4	104: Thonga	01135	B	Es	P	C	Sl	O	O	S	O
Ab5	203: Mbundu	11125	B	Q	Pa	Cs	Lo	Lo	O	Cm	I
Ab6	204: Venda	11026	B	Es	P	S	Sl	Lo	O	Cm	I
Ab7	302: Nyaneka	01144	B	Fq	vA	C	O	S	O	C	I
Ab8	303: Sotho	11035	B	Q	uP	A	So	O	O	Qc	I
Ab9	401: Ndebele	01045	B	Q	P	A	S	O	O	N	I
Ab10	402: Pondo	00055	B	Fq	P	E	S	O	O	O	I
Ab12	404: Zulu	01045	B	Fq	P	C	S	O	O	N	I
Ab13	405: Tswana	01045	B	S	uP	S	O*	O	Q*	Qc	I
Ab14	406: Lovedu	10036	B	Q	P	C	Sl	O	O	Cm	I
Ab16	408: Lenge	11125	B	Fq	P	C	S	O	O	S	O
Ab18	410: Shona	11125	B*	S	Pu	C	Sl	O	K	O	O
Ab19	411: Ambo	01135	B	Q	bVn	.	O	S	O	S*	H
Ac1	4: Ila	10036	B	Fq	Va	A	L	S	O	Pp	I
Ac2	5: Pende	10126	T	Q	vAv	Cs	O	Sl	O	Pp	C*
Ac3	105: Bemba	11107	St	S	uCv	A	O	S	K	Cc	I
Ac4	106: Kuba	01216	B*	Fn	vA	S	O	S	O	N	H
Ac5	205: Lamba	02206	St	N	uCu	A	O	S	O	Cm	I
Ac6	206: Ndembu	02116	T	Q	uAv	C	O	Sl	O	Cc	I
Ac7	304: Yao	01216	O	En	Ma	S	O	Sl	O	Cp	I
Ac8	305: Yombe	02215	B	Q	A	C	O	Sl	O	O	.
Ac9	351: Ngoni	01216	T	Q	Vu	A	O	O	Q*	C	I
Ac10	637: Chewa	12115	St	Q	uAu	S	O	S	O	Cc	I
Ac11	668: Luvale	01306	T	Fq	Av	C	O	S	O	Cc	I
Ac12	698: Chokwe	03115	T	N	A	C	O	S	O	Cm	I
Ac13	703: Lake Tonga	10414	B	N	Av	S	O	Sl	O	Cm	I
Ac14	728: Kongo	11116	B	N	A	C	O	S	O	C	.
Ac17	731: Suku	12106	B	Q	Va	A	O	So	O	Cp	I
Ac18	732: Sundi	11116	B	Fq	A	C	O	Sl	O	.	.
Ac21	735: Bunda	01117	B	Q	A	C	O	S	O	Cc*	I
Ac22	736: Dzing	12115	B	Q	Av	E	O	S	O	O	I
Ac23	737: Lele	01117	B	Q	vAn	A	O	S	O	O*	I
Ac25	739: Songo	12115	B	Q	Av	E	O	L	O	Tc	I
Ac28	742: Luimbe	02412	B	Q	D	E	O	S	O	Cc	I
Ac30	744: Pl. Tonga	01126	B	Fq	uDn	A	O	S	O	C*	I
Ac33	747: Lala	01216	S	N	uAn	C	O	S	O	M	I
Ac34	748: Luapula	01315	St	N	uAn	A	O	Sl	O	Cc	I
Ac36	750: Tumbuka	02017	B*	S	P*	E	S*	O*	O	Cc	I
Ac38	752: Nyanja	01216	S	Q	Ma	A	O	S	O	Cc	I
Ad1	6: Bajun	01414	B	M	uNu	A	Lo	O	O	Qa	D
Ad2	7: Nyoro	01126	B	Q	P	S	S	O	O	O	D
Ad3	107: Chagga	01036	B	Q	Pn	C	S	O	O	N	O
Ad4	108: Kikuyu	00037	B	Q	P	C	S	O	O	N	O
Ad6	208: Nyakyusa	01126	B	Q	N	A	Lo	O	K	N	I
Ad7	306: Ganda	01117	B	Q	Nv	E	S	O	O	O	I

TABLE B

1	3	28	30	31	32	34	35	36	37	38	39
Aa1	1: Kung	O	B	1	30	B	A	2	0	P	O
Aa2	101: Dorobo	O	B	1	20	O	.	2	6	.	O
Aa3	102: Nama	O	B	3	21	O	S	2	0*	P	Bm
Aa5	202: Mbuti	O	B	1	20	O	.	5	5	T	O
Aa6	301: Sandawe	Ec	N	.	21	A	.	.	4	.	Bm
Aa7	636: Naron	O	B	1	20	A	.	5	0	.	O
Aa9	726: Hatsa	O	B	1	20	.	.	.	0	.	O
Ab1	2: Herero	O	B	.	30	.	.	.	9	P	Bm
Ab2	3: Swazi	Ec	H	.	33	O	.	.	5	P	qBm
Ab3	103: Lozi	Ic	T	2	23	A	.	.	0	.	Bm
Ab4	104: Thonga	Ec	V	.	22	.	S	4	5	R	Bm
Ab5	203: Mbundu	Ec	V	4	32	A	Q	.	0	P	Bo
Ab6	204: Venda	Ic	V	4	32	B	S	5	6*	T	Bm
Ab7	302: Nyaneka	Ec	H	.	32	.	.	.	5	.	Bm
Ab8	303: Sotho	Ic	H	4	33	O	.	.	0	.	qBm
Ab9	401: Ndebele	Ec	X	7	33	A	.	.	0	T	Bm
Ab10	402: Pondo	Ic	N	.	32	.	.	.	.	.	qBm
Ab12	404: Zulu	Ec	N	.	33	.	.	.	0	T	Bm
Ab13	405: Tswana	Ec	X	7	32	C	.	1	6	T	Bm
Ab14	406: Lovedu	Ic	H	5	32	A	.	2	5	A	qBm
Ab16	408: Lenge	Ec	H	.	31	.	.	.	.	.	So
Ab18	410: Shona	Ec	H	3	22	C	.	.	5	.	Bm
Ab19	411: Ambo	Ec	N	.	32	.	Q	3	5	P	Bm
Ac1	4: Ila	Ec	T	4	31	A	Q	5	0	P	Bm
Ac2	5: Pende	Er	V	.	31	.	.	.	.	.	So
Ac3	105: Bemba	Ec	W	3	32	B	.	2	0	R	So
Ac4	106: Kuba	Ec	W	3	32	A	S	2	1	P	So
Ac5	205: Lamba	Ec	V	.	22	A	Q	1	0	.	O
Ac6	206: Ndembu	Ec	W	1	22	.	.	.	.	R	So
Ac7	304: Yao	Ec	H	3	31	O	Q	4	4	.	O
Ac8	305: Yombe	Ec	V	4	31	.	.	.	9	R	So
Ac9	351: Ngoni	Ec	V	3	23	O	.	.	0*	T	Bm
Ac10	637: Chewa	Ec	V	3	32	O	.	2	0	P	Bm
Ac11	668: Luvale	Ec	V	.	31	A	.	.	5	R	So
Ac12	698: Chokwe	Er	V	.	22	.	.	.	.	R	So
Ac13	703: Lake Tonga	Er	H	2	30	A	.	.	.	.	So
Ac14	728: Kongo	Er	V	.	31*	.	.	.	5	R	So
Ac17	731: Suku	Er	V	2	33	A	.	5	5	P	So
Ac18	732: Sundi	Et	V	2	31	.	.	.	9	R	So
Ac21	735: Bunda	Ec	N	.	22	.	.	.	.	T	So
Ac22	736: Dzing	Er	W	3	31	.	.	.	.	R	So
Ac23	737: Lele	Ec	V	3	31	O	.	.	.	T	So
Ac25	739: Songo	Er	V	.	31	.	.	.	.	T	So
Ac28	742: Luimbe	Ec	V	.	31	.	.	.	.	.	Bo
Ac30	744: Pl. Tonga	Ec	H	4	30	B	.	4	0	P	Bm
Ac33	747: Lala	Ec	V	2	21	A	.	.	0	.	So
Ac34	748: Luapula	Er	V	5	32	B	.	.	5	.	So
Ac36	750: Tumbuka	Ec	V	.	32*	B	.	4	0	.	So*
Ac38	752: Nyanja	Ec	N	.	31	.	.	.	0	.	So
Ad1	6: Bajun	Ec	V	.	20	.	.	.	5	A	Bm
Ad2	7: Nyoro	Ic	N	5	23	A	Q	.	0	A	Bm
Ad3	107: Chagga	Jc	N	5	21	O	S	2	5	A	Bm
Ad4	108: Kikuyu	Ic	V	4	30	B	Q	2	6	T	Bm
Ad6	208: Nyakyusa	It	V	3	22	A	O	*	0	T	Bm
Ad7	306: Ganda	It	V	7	23	A	Q	4	0	P	Bm

TABLE C

1	3	42	44	46	48	50	52	54	56	58	60	62
Aa1	1: Kung	O	O	M	O	O	F	G	M	O	O	O
Aa2	101: Dorobo	O	O	F	O	O	F	G	M	O	O	O
Aa3	102: Nama	M	O	G	F	O	D	F	M	M	D	O
Aa5	202: Mbuti	O	O	O	O	O	G	G	N	E	O	O
Aa6	301: Sandawe	.	.	.	.	.	.	F	M	F	M	G
Aa7	636: Naron	O	O	M	O	O	F	F	M	O	O	O
Aa9	726: Hatsa	O	O	M	.	O	.	F	M	O	O	O
Ab1	2: Herero	Mc	O	M	.	O	.	F	M	O	E	O
Ab2	3: Swazi	Mc	O	M	.	.	E	F	M	O	M	G
Ab3	103: Lozi	Mc	O	M	F	M	D	G	M	N	M	G
Ab4	104: Thonga	Mc	O*	O	F	M	M	F	M	M	M	G
Ab5	203: Mbundu	Mc	O	P	F	M	M	F	M	N	M	G
Ab6	204: Venda	Mc*	P*	P	Fc	O	D	G	M	O	M	G
Ab7	302: Nyaneka	.	.	.	.	.	.	O	M	E	M	E
Ab8	303: Sotho	Mc	O	.	F	.	M	F	M	O	M	G
Ab9	401: Ndebele	Mc	O	Mc	F	.	N	F	M	O	M	G
Ab10	402: Pondo	.	.	.	.	.	.	F	M	N	N	G
Ab12	404: Zulu	Mc	O	M	F	M	M	O	M	O	M	G
Ab13	405: Tswana	Mc	O	M	Fc	O	.	O	M	O	N	G
Ab14	406: Lovedu	Mc*	O	M	F	O	N	F	M	O	.	G
Ab16	408: Lenge	.	.	.	.	.	.	F	M	.	Mb	G
Ab18	410: Shona	.	.	.	.	.	.	F	M	N	M	E
Ab19	411: Ambo	Mc	O	M	F	O	M	G	M	N	Nb	F
Ac1	4: Ila	Mc	O	G	F	M	D	F	M	M	M	G
Ac2	5: Pende	.	.	.	.	.	.	O	F	.	.	G
Ac3	105: Bemba	Mc	O	P	F	P	D	G	M	N	.	G
Ac4	106: Kuba	Mc	M	P	O	.	.	O	M	N	O	G
Ac5	205: Lamba	Mc	.	.	F	M	.	O	M	N	O	E
Ac6	206: Ndembu	Mc	O	.	.	P	.	O	M	N	.	G
Ac7	304: Yao	Mc	O	O	F	P	M	O	M	M	.	G
Ac8	305: Yombe	Mc	F	.	F	P	.	.	M	N	.	G
Ac9	351: Ngoni	Mc	.	.	F	.	.	O	M	O	M	G
Ac10	637: Chewa	Mc	O	P	F	P	.	F	M	M	N	N
Ac11	668: Luvale	Mc	P	.	P	.	.	.	Mc	D	.	N
Ac12	698: Chokwe	Mc	.	.	P	.	.	.	M	N	.	G
Ac13	703: Lake Tonga	Mc	.	.	P	P	.	.	.	M	.	F
Ac14	728: Kongo	Mc	.	.	.	.	.	D	M	N	.	G
Ac17	731: Suku	Mc	.	.	F	.	M	.	M	E	.	G
Ac18	732: Sundi	Mc	.	M	G	P	M	E	M	M	N	G
Ac21	735: Bunda	.	.	.	.	.	.	.	M	D	.	G
Ac22	736: Dzing	.	.	.	.	.	.	.	M	G	M	G
Ac23	737: Lele	Mc	M	.	F	.	M	F	M	F	.	G
Ac25	739: Songo	.	.	.	.	.	.	D	M	.	.	G
Ac28	742: Luimbe	Mc	P	.	P	.	.	.	M	M	.	G
Ac30	744: Pl. Tonga	Mc	.	.	F	.	M	F	M	N	M	G
Ac33	747: Lala	O*	.	.	F	.	.	.	M	N	N	G
Ac34	748: Luapula	Mc	O*	M	F	M	.	.	M	M	.	G
Ac36	750: Tumbuka	Mc	.	.	.	.	.	.	M	.	.	G
Ac38	752: Nyanja	Mc	M	.	F	P	.	.	M	M	.	G
Ad1	6: Bajun	O*	.	O*	O*	.	.	O	M	M	N	E
Ad2	7: Nyoro	Mc	O	Mc	Mc	Mc	D	O	M	Mc	N	G
Ad3	107: Chagga	Mc	O	P	O	O	N	O	M	O	D	D
Ad4	108: Kikuyu	Mc	O	M	Fc	O	D	O	M	O	M	G
Ad6	208: Nyakyusa	Mc	P	O	P	M	M	O	M	N	M	N
Ad7	306: Ganda	Mc	O	Mc	Mc	Mc	M	O	M	M	M	G

TABLE D

1	3	64	67	69	71	73	74	76	78	80–84	85–89
Aa1	1: Kung	Kh	O	O	O	P	O	O	E	CGRDG	SGREG
Aa2	101: Dorobo	CnE	O	O	O	C	Pp	Ce	.	CGRDG	————
Aa3	102: Nama	Kh	W	O	O	P	O	Pp	A	CGRDM	————
Aa5	202: Mbuti	CnC*	O	O	O	O	O	O	A	CGRDG	————
Aa6	301: Sandawe	Kh	O	O	O	.	.	Pe	.	CGRDG	RGPFE
Aa7	636: Naron	Kh	O	O	O	P	O	O	.	SGREG	————
Aa9	726: Hatsa	Kh	O	O	O	S	O	Q.	.	CGRDG	————
Ab1	2: Herero	NcB	W	O	Hf	Q	O	Np	.	CGRBP	————
Ab2	3: Swazi	NcB	D	O	O	P	Pp	Pp	.	CGRBG	CGPCG
Ab3	103: Lozi	NcB	D	O	H	P	Pq	Pq	.	CGPCG	RG.GG
Ab4	104: Thonga	NcB	D	O	O	Q	O	Pe	F	CGPCG	————
Ab5	203: Mbundu	NcB	D	O	H	P	P.	M.	.	CGPCG	————
Ab6	204: Venda	NcB	D	O	If	P	O	Pp	A*	CGPCG	————
Ab7	302: Nyaneka	NcB	D	O	Sf	M	Mp	Mp	.	CGMCG	————
Ab8	303: Sotho	NcB	D	O	O	P	O	Pp	.	CGPCG	————
Ab9	401: Ndebele	NcB	E	E	O	A	Pp	Pp	.	CGRBG	CGPCG
Ab10	402: Pondo	NcB	W	O	O	P	Pp	Pp	.	CGRBG	CGPCG
Ab12	404: Zulu	NcB	D	O	O	P	Pp	Pp	.	CGRBG	————
Ab13	405: Tswana	NcB	Ed	E	O	P	Pp	Pp	P	CGACG	————
Ab14	406: Lovedu	NcB	D	O	O	.	.	Q.	A	CG.CG	————
Ab16	408: Lenge	NcB	.	O	O	Q	.	.	.	CGPCG	————
Ab18	410: Shona	NcB	.	.	S	Q	Pp	Pp	.	CG.CG	————
Ab19	411: Ambo	NcB	Dw	O	Hf	A	O	Ne	.	CGWCG	————
Ac1	4: Ila	NcB	W	O	Hf	M	O	Nq	F	CGPCG	————
Ac2	5: Pende	NcB	D	O	Sf	M	.	Mp	.	RG.HG	————
Ac3	105: Bemba	NcB	D	O	If	N	Np	Nq	E	CGPCG	————
Ac4	106: Kuba	NcB	D	E	H	S	O	Np	.	RGGGG	————
Ac5	205: Lamba	NcB	O	O	S	M	.	Np	.	CGPCG	————
Ac6	206: Ndembu	NcB	.	O	Sf	N	.	N.	.	RGP.G	————
Ac7	304: Yao	NcB	O	O	Hf	M	.	Np	A	CG.CG	RG..G
Ac8	305: Yombe	NcB	D	O	I	N	Np	Np	.	RGWGG	————
Ac9	351: Ngoni	NcB	D	O	If	.	P	Pp	.	CG.CG	————
Ac10	637: Chewa	NcB	O	O	Sf	N	N.	N.	E	CGGCG	————
Ac11	668: Luvale	NcB	O	O	H	M	.	M.	F	RGPGG	CGPCG
Ac12	698: Chokwe	NcB	D	O	S	M	Mp	Mp	.	CGRBG	————
Ac13	703: Lake Tonga	NcB	O	O	Hf	M	M.	M.	.	CG.CG	————
Ac14	728: Kongo	NcB	D	O	Hf	N	Np	Np	F	RGMGG	RPGGG
Ac17	731: Suku	NcB	D	O	I	N	Np	Np	.	RGWGG	————
Ac18	732: Sundi	NcB	.	.	If	N	.	Ne	.	RGWGG	————
Ac21	735: Bunda	NcB	D	O	If	N	Me	Me	.	RGGHG	————
Ac22	736: Dzing	NcB	.	.	Sf	M	N.	N.	.	RGMGG	————
Ac23	737: Lele	NcB	D	D*	Sf	N	.	Ne	.	RGWGG	————
Ac25	739: Songo	NcB	O	O	Hf	N	Np	Np	.	RGPHG	————
Ac28	742: Luimbe	NcB	.	O	.	N	Np*	Np*	.	RGGHG	————
Ac30	744: Pl. Tonga	NcB	O	O	If	N	Nq	Nq	F	CGPCG	————
Ac33	747: Lala	NcB	D	O	Hf	N	Np	Np	F	CGPCG	————
Ac34	748: Luapula	NcB	D	O	Sf	N	Nq	Nq	.	CGMCG	————
Ac36	750: Tumbuka	NcB	D	O	If	P*	Pp	Pp	.	CG.CG	————
Ac38	752: Nyanja	NcB	O	O	H	N	Np	Np	.	CGPCG	————
Ad1	6: Bajun	NcB	O	D	Hf	P	Ce	Ce	.	RGWGG	CG.CG
Ad2	7: Nyoro	NcB	D	O	Hf	P	Pp	Pp	.	CGRBG	————
Ad3	107: Chagga	NcB	D	O	O	P	Pp	Pp	P	CGMCG	————
Ad4	108: Kikuyu	NcB	W	O	O	N	Pp	Pp	.	RG.FE	CGPCG
Ad6	208: Nyakyusa	NcB	O	O	If	E	Qp	Qp	E	CGACG	RGAGG
Ad7	306: Ganda	NcB	D	O	Hf	A	Pq	Pq	P	CGRBG	————

TABLE A. *Continued*

1	3	7	12	14	16	19	20	22	24	25	27
Ad8	307: Hehe	01036	B	Fp	Pn	C	S	O	O	Cm	I
Ad9	352: Gisu	01126	B	Q	Pn	C	Sl	O	O	N	H
Ad10	629: Shambala	01036	B	Q	P	C	S	O	O	O	H
Ad11	638: Bena	01036	Bs	Q	uNu	A	S	O	K	C	I
Ad13	669: Chiga	02026	B	Ẽq	P	C	S	O	O	Mm	I
Ad14	704: Luguru	01018	Bs	N	M	S	O	S	O	Cm	C
Ad15	757: Iwa	01018	Bs	Q	P	C	S	O	O	Cc	.
Ad16	758: Ngonde	01126	B	S	N	E	Lo	O	O	O	H
Ad17	759: Safwa	01126	Bs	Q	Pn	E	S	O	O	.	.
Ad19	761: Fipa	00316	Bs	Q	P	.	Sl	O	O	O	I
Ad20	762: Nyamwezi	11017	B*	N	uVu	E	O	O	R	O	I
Ad21	763: Pimbwe	01216	B	Q	P	.	S*	O*	O	N	S
Ad22	764: Sukuma	00037	B*	Q	uVa	A	O	O	R	N	C
Ad24	766: Gogo	01045	B	Fq	Pn	C	Sl	O	O	Cm	I
Ad26	768: Turu	00055	B	Fq	P	C	S	O	O	O	H
Ad29	771: Hadimu	00226	B	Q	P	.	O	O	R*	Q	H
Ad30	772: Digo	01216	B	Q	Pu	S	S	L	O	O	.
Ad32	774: Giriama	01027	B	Ẽq	P	E	P	O	O	O	S
Ad33	775: Pokomo	01306	B	N	P	A	S	O	O	O	H
Ad35	777: Meru	01036	B	Q	P	C	S	O	O	O	.
Ad39	781: Sonjo	00028	B	N	P	S	S	O	O	O	.
Ad41	783: Vugusu	00046	B	N	P	C	S	O	O	N	D
Ad42	784: Haya	00235	B	Q	P	E	S	O	O	O	O
Ad44	786: Konjo	01315	B	Q	P	C	Sl	O	O	.	I
Ad45	787: Nyankole	01045	B	Q	Pn	.	Sl	O	K	O	H
Ad46	788: Soga	00026	B	Q	P	A	S	O	O	N	O
Ae1	8: Amba	11116	Xb	Q	Pa	C	S	O	O	N	O
Ae2	9: Kpe	01135	B	Q	Pa	S	Sl	L	O	N	.
Ae3	109: Fang	11215	B	Fq	P	Cs	S	O	O	N	O
Ae4	110: Nkundo	11206	B	Eq	Pa	Cs	S	E	O	N	C
Ae5	209: Bamileke	01018	B	Q	P	S	L	O	O	N	.
Ae6	210: Luba	12214	B	Q	P	A	L	O	O	O	.
Ae7	308: Babwa	02107	B	Fq	P	Cs	L	O	O	.	H
Ae8	309: Rundi	00136	T	Q	Pn	S	S	O	O	Cc	I
Ae9	640: Fut	01018	B	Fq	P	S	L	O	O	O	.
Ae10	641: Ruanda	01045	B	Q	P	C	Sl	O	O	C	I
Ae11	670: Songola	12502	B	S	P	C	S	O	O	N	H
Ae12	699: Duala	00316	B	Q	P	Cs	Sl	O*	O	.	I
Ae14	793: Ha	00145	B	Fq	P	C	S	O	O	C	I
Ae15	794: Hunde	01135	B	Q	P	C	S	O	O	.	I
Ae17	796: Rega	02215	B	Q	P	A	S	O	O	O	I
Ae22	801: Kutshu	02215	B	Fq	P	A	S	O	O	O	I
Ae28	807: Ngala	01414	B	Eq	P	A	S	O	O	.	.
Ae29	808: Poto	00712	B	Eq	P	Cs	S	O	O	O	H
Ae38	817: Ndoko	01108	B	Eq	D	E	O	S	O	.	.
Ae39	818: Ngombe	02206	B	Eq	P	S	Sl	O	O	N	Z*
Ae41	820: Kota	12016	B	N	P	S	S	O	O	O	.
Ae48	827: Bafia	00226	B*	Q	Pa	C	Pl	O	O	.	.
Ae50	829: Bamum	01117	B	Fq	P	S	L	O	O	.	.
Ae51	830: Banen	11017	Xb	Q	P	C	L	O	O	.	.
Ae55	834: Ndob	01117	B	Fq	P	S	L	O	O	.	H
Ae56	835: Nsaw	01018	S	Fq	Pn	S	Sl	O	O	O	.
Af1	10: Fon	02125	Bs	Q	Pu	S	P	O	O	T	D
Af2	11: Kissi	00019	Bs	Ẽq	P	T	Sl	O	O	Mm	H
Af3	111: Ashanti	01207	B	Fq	oAv	A	Sl	S	O	Cm	D

TABLE B. *Continued*

1	3	28	30	31	32	34	35	36	37	38	39
Ad8	307: Hehe	Ic	N	.	32	.	.	5	0	P	Bm
Ad9	352: Gisu	Et	N	.	31	A	.	.	6	P	Bm
Ad10	629: Shambala	It	V	3	32	.	.	.	3	T	Bm
Ad11	638: Bena	Jc	V	.	22	C	.	4	0	T	Bm
Ad13	669: Chiga	Ec	N	.	30	.	.	.	0	A	Bm
Ad14	704: Luguru	Ec	H	.	30	.	.	4	.	.	So
Ad15	757: Iwa	Ec	V	3	22	A	.	.	0	.	So
Ad16	758: Ngonde	It	V	.	22	O	.	.	0	T	Bm
Ad17	759: Safwa	Ec	V	.	21	.	.	.	.	T	Bm
Ad19	761: Fipa	Ec	V	3	22	A	.	.	0	T	Bm*
Ad20	762: Nyamwezi	Ec	V	2	22	.	.	.	0	T	So
Ad21	763: Pimbwe	Ec	V	.	22	A	.	.	0	.	So
Ad22	764: Sukuma	Ic	N	.	32	.	.	.	0	T	Bm
Ad24	766: Gogo	Ec	N	5	31	.	.	.	5	.	Bm
Ad26	768: Turu	Ic	N	.	30	.	.	.	9	P	Bm
Ad29	771: Hadimu	Er	V	.	23	C	.	.	5	.	Bm
Ad30	772: Digo	Er	V	.	21	C	.	.	9	.	So
Ad32	774: Giriama	Ec	V	.	33	O	.	.	5	.	Bm
Ad33	775: Pokomo	Jc	V	.	21	.	.	.	5	T	O
Ad35	777: Meru	Ec	N	.	30	.	.	.	5	T	Bm
Ad39	781: Sonjo	Jc	V	5	20	.	.	.	5	.	Sm
Ad41	783: Vugusu	Ec	N	4	30	.	.	.	5	.	Bm
Ad42	784: Haya	It	N	4	22	A	.	.	0	.	Bm
Ad44	786: Konjo	Er	N	.	20	A	.	.	0	.	So
Ad45	787: Nyankole	Ec	N	3	23	A	.	.	0	.	Bm
Ad46	788: Soga	It	N	.	22	.	.	.	0	R	Bm
Ae1	8: Amba	Et	H	3	30	O	.	.	0*	A	So
Ae2	9: Kpe	Er	V	2	30	A	.	4	4*	.	Bo
Ae3	109: Fang	Er	V	2	30	A	A*	4	5	A	So
Ae4	110: Nkundo	Er	H	.	42	A	.	1	4	P	So
Ae5	209: Bamileke	Ec	H	.	42	.	.	.	0	P	O
Ae6	210: Luba	Er	V	.	33	.	.	.	.	.	So
Ae7	308: Babwa	Et	H	.	42	.	.	.	0	P	O
Ae8	309: Rundi	It	N	.	33	A	Q	2	0	A	Bm
Ae9	640: Fut	Ec	V	.	31	B	.	.	.	.	So
Ae10	641: Ruanda	Ic	N	.	33	A	Q	.	0	A	Bm
Ae11	670: Songola	Et	V	.	21	.	.	.	9	T	So
Ae12	699: Duala	Er	V	.	32	A	A	.	4	A*	So
Ae14	793: Ha	Ic	N	.	32	A	.	.	0	P	Bm
Ae15	794: Hunde	It	V	.	22	.	.	.	0	.	Bm
Ae17	796: Rega	Et	X	.	21	.	.	.	9	.	So
Ae22	801: Kutshu	Er	V	.	31	.	.	.	9	.	So
Ae28	807: Ngala	Er	V	4	31	A	C	.	3	.	So
Ae29	808: Poto	Et	V	.	31	.	.	.	9	.	So
Ae38	817: Ndoko	Er	V	.	30	.	.	.	.	.	O
Ae39	818: Ngombe	Er	V	3	41	O	O	3	3	A	O
Ae41	820: Kota	Et	V	.	30	.	.	.	5	P	So
Ae48	827: Bafia	Ec	N	.	30	.	.	.	5	T	So
Ae50	829: Bamum	Ec	V	.	43	B	.	.	9	.	So
Ae51	830: Banen	Er	N	.	20	A	.	.	5	.	So
Ae55	834: Ndob	Ec	V	.	41	.	.	.	.	.	So
Ae56	835: Nsaw	Ec	V	5	42	B	.	.	.	.	So
Af1	10: Fon	Er	V	7	33	O	S	3	6	P	So
Af2	11: Kissi	Ec	V	3	41	.	.	.	5	P	Bo
Af3	111: Ashanti	Er	V	7	42	A	Q	1	0	R*	So

TABLE C. *Continued*

1	3	42	44	46	48	50	52	54	56	58	60	62
Ad8	307: Hehe	Mc	.	.	.	.	M	O	M	O	M	G
Ad9	352: Gisu	Mc	O	P	G	O	.	O	M	.	N	G
Ad10	629: Shambala	Mc	.	.	.	.	.	.	M	F	M	G
Ad11	638: Bena	Mc	O	.	F	M	M	G	M	M	M	G
Ad13	669: Chiga	.	.	.	.	.	.	O	M	M	M	G
Ad14	704: Luguru	.	.	.	.	.	.	.	M	M	.	N
Ad15	757: Iwa	Mc	P	.	.	.	.	.	M	.	M	E
Ad16	758: Ngonde	Mc	P	.	P	P	.	.	M	N	M	N
Ad17	759: Safwa	.	.	.	.	.	.	F	M	.	M	E
Ad19	761: Fipa	Mc	M	.	F	.	M	.	M	N	N	G
Ad20	762: Nyamwezi	.	.	.	.	.	.	G	M	.	M	G
Ad21	763: Pimbwe	.	.	.	.	.	.	.	M	M	M	G
Ad22	764: Sukuma	Mc	.	.	P	.	.	.	M	O	N	G
Ad24	766: Gogo	Mc	.	.	.	O	.	.	M	O	M	G
Ad26	768: Turu	Mc	.	.	.	.	.	.	.	O	N	G
Ad29	771: Hadimu	Mc	O*	O	M*	Mc	Mc	.	M	D	N	E
Ad30	772: Digo	Mc	.	.	P	M	.	F	M	.	N	G
Ad32	774: Giriama	Mc	.	.	P	.	.	.	M	.	N	G
Ad33	775: Pokomo	Mc	.	.	.	P	.	.	M	M	O	G
Ad35	777: Meru	Mc	O	M	F	.	D	.	M	O	M	G
Ad39	781: Sonjo	Mc	.	.	Fc	O	.	O	M	O	D	D
Ad41	783: Vugusu	Mc	.	.	.	.	O	.	M	M	N	G
Ad42	784: Haya	Mc	.	.	.	.	.	.	M	M	M	G
Ad44	786: Konjo	Mc	O	.	P	.	.	.	.	M	M	N
Ad45	787: Nyankole	Mc	.	.	M	.	M	.	M	.	M	G
Ad46	788: Soga	Mc	D	O	Mc	Mc	.	.	Mc	M	M	G
Ae1	8: Amba	Mc	O	.	F	O	M	.	M	M	M	G
Ae2	9: Kpe	Mc*	.	.	P	M	.	N	M	F	M	G
Ae3	109: Fang	Mc	O	.	F	P	.	G	M	N	M	G
Ae4	110: Nkundo	Mc	M	O	F	M	M	F	M	N	O	G
Ae5	209: Bamileke	M	Mc	.	F	.	M	O	M	O	.	G
Ae6	210: Luba	Mc	.	.	.	.	.	.	F	M	N	.	G
Ae7	308: Babwa	.	.	.	.	.	.	.	M	G	.	G
Ae8	309: Rundi	Mc	O	P	Dc	M	N	O	Mc	M	M	E
Ae9	640: Fut	M	O	.	F	O	M	.	M	O	.	G
Ae10	641: Ruanda	Mc	O	M	Fc	M	.	D	Mc	.	M	E
Ae11	670: Songola	.	.	.	.	.	.	.	M	N	.	G
Ae12	699: Duala	Mc*	.	.	P	P	.	.	M	N	.	G
Ae14	793: Ha	Mc	.	F	Mc	P	M	.	M	.	M	G
Ae15	794: Hunde	Mc	.	.	.	.	.	.	M	M	M	D
Ae17	796: Rega	.	.	.	.	.	.	G	M	N	.	G
Ae22	801: Kutshu	.	.	.	.	.	.	.	M	.	.	G
Ae28	807: Ngala	.	O	P	F	P	.	.	M	E	.	G
Ae29	808: Poto	Mc	.	.	F	.	.	M	M	N	.	G
Ae38	817: Ndoko	.	.	.	.	.	.	.	M	F	.	G
Ae39	818: Ngombe	Mc	O	O	O	O	N	F	M	E	G	G
Ae41	820: Kota	Mc	.	.	.	.	.	.	M	F	.	G
Ae48	827: Bafia	Mc	E	.	G	.	.	.	.	N	.	G
Ae50	829: Bamum	Mc	P	P	F	P	D	.	M	.	D	G
Ae51	830: Banen	Mc	O	.	F	.	D	.	M	E	D	G
Ae55	834: Ndob	Mc	.	.	F	.	M	.	M	F	.	G
Ae56	835: Nsaw	.	.	.	F	.	M	.	M	.	.	G
Af1	10: Fon	Mc	Mc	P	Fc	P	.	O	M	M	E	G
Af2	11: Kissi	.	.	.	.	.	.	O	M	N	N	E
Af3	111: Ashanti	Mc	Mc	.	F	.	.	O	M	M	.	D

TABLE D. *Continued*

1	3	64	67	69	71	73	74	76	78	80–84	85–89
Ad8	307: Hehe	NcB	D	O	Hf	.	.	De	.	RG.FE	———
Ad9	352: Gisu	NcB	W	O	If	Q	Pe	Pe	A*	CGPCG	———
Ad10	629: Shambala	NcB	D	.	H	P	Pe	Pe	.	CGRCG	RGPHG
Ad11	638: Bena	NcB	D	O	Hf	A	Pe	Pe	.	RGMGG	RG.FE
Ad13	669: Chiga	NcB	O	O	If	.	.	Pe	.	CGRBG	———
Ad14	704: Luguru	NcB	O	D	Hf	P	Ce	Ce	.	RGWGG	CG.CG
Ad15	757: Iwa	NcB	D	O	If	Q	Qp	Qp	.	CGPCG	RGA..
Ad16	758: Ngonde	NcB	D	O	If	A	Qp	Qp	.	CG.CG	———
Ad17	759: Safwa	NcB	.	O	I	P	Qe	Qe	.	CGACG	———
Ad19	761: Fipa	NcB	D	O	Sf	E	.	.	.	RGAGG	CGPCG
Ad20	762: Nyamwezi	NcB	D	O	I	*	*	*	.	CGPCG	RGPFE
Ad21	763: Pimbwe	NcB	D	O	Sf	E	*	*	.	CGPCG	———
Ad22	764: Sukuma	NcB	D	O	Sf	A	Pp	*	F	CGACG	———
Ad24	766: Gogo	NcB	D	O	I	P	O	Pp	.	QGAFE	———
Ad26	768: Turu	NcB	O	D	O	O	Pe	Pe	.	QS.FE	———
Ad29	771: Hadimu	NcB	D	.	Hf	E	De	De	.	RGGHG	———
Ad30	772: Digo	NcB	.	.	S	Q	Np	Np	.	RG.RG	———
Ad32	774: Giriama	NcB	O	.	I	O	Pp	Pp	.	RG.GG	———
Ad33	775: Pokomo	NcB	O	O	I	O	Pp	Pp	.	CGPDG	———
Ad35	777: Meru	NcB	O	O	Sf	O	Pe	Pe	.	CGPCG	———
Ad39	781: Sonjo	NcB	E	D	O	E	Pe	Pe	V	CGWCG	———
Ad41	783: Vugusu	NcB	W	O	.	.	Pe	Pe	F	CGPCG	———
Ad42	784: Haya	NcB	D	O	I	P	Pp	Pp	.	CGRBG	———
Ad44	786: Konjo	NcB	O	O	.	P	.	.	.	CGRBG	———
Ad45	787: Nyankole	NcB	E	E	If	.	Pp	Pp	.	CGRBG	———
Ad46	788: Soga	NcB	D	O	Hf	A	Pe	Pe	.	CGACG	CGRBG
Ae1	8: Amba	NcB	O	E	O	O	Pp	Pe	F	CGRBG	RGP.G
Ae2	9: Kpe	NcB	W	O	If	O	Pp	.	.	RGMGG	———
Ae3	109: Fang	NcB	W	E	O	P	O	Pp	F	RGBGG	———
Ae4	110: Nkundo	NcB	O	E	If	Q	Qp	Qp	F	RGWGG	———
Ae5	209: Bamileke	NcB	D	O	Hf	P	Pq	Pq	.	RGACG	———
Ae6	210: Luba	NcB	D	O	Hf	Q	Qp	Qp	E	RG..G	———
Ae7	308: Babwa	NcB	O	O	I	.	Pp	Pp	.	CG.CG	RG.GG
Ae8	309: Rundi	NcB	C*	E	If	P	Pp	Pp	V	CGRBG	———
Ae9	640: Fut	NcB	D	O	Hf	P	.	.	.	RGPHG	———
Ae10	641: Ruanda	NcB	C*	E	If	P	Pe	Pe	V	CGRBG	———
Ae11	670: Songola	NcB	O	O	H	Q	.	.	.	RG.GG	———
Ae12	699: Duala	NcB	W	O	Hf	P	.	Pp	.	REMGM	———
Ae14	793: Ha	NcB	D	O	Sf	P	Pp	Pp	.	CGRBG	———
Ae15	794: Hunde	NcB	C*	E	S	.	Pp	Pp	.	CGWCG	———
Ae17	796: Rega	NcB	O	O	O	Q	Qe	Qe	V	RGBRG	———
Ae22	801: Kutshu	NcB	O	O	S	P	Pp	Pp	.	RG.GG	———
Ae28	807: Ngala	NcB	W	O	H	.	Pp	Pp	.	RGMGG	RPMGG
Ae29	808: Poto	NcB	O	O	H	Q	Pe	Qe	F	RGGHG	———
Ae38	817: Ndoko	NcB	O	O	S	N	Np	Np	.	RG...	———
Ae39	818: Ngombe	NcB	O	O	If	C	Qq	O	F	RGPGG	———
Ae41	820: Kota	NcB	O	E*	Sf	P	Qe	Qe	E	RGBGG	———
Ae48	827: Bafia	NcB	O	O	S	P	.	.	A	RGPGG	RGBGG
Ae50	829: Bamum	NcB	D	O	H	P	Pq	Pq	E	RGPDG	CGPCG
Ae51	830: Banen	NcB	O	O	H	P	Pe	Pe	.	QGPGM	———
Ae55	834: Ndob	NcB	.	O	Sf	.	P.	P.	.	RGPHG	———
Ae56	835: Nsaw	NcB	D	O	Sf	.	.	.	.	QGPHG	———
Af1	10: Fon	NcK	Dc	O	H	P	Pp	Pp	V	RGAHG	———
Af2	11: Kissi	NcA	O	O	Hf	.	Pe	Pe	.	CEACG	———
Af3	111: Ashanti	NcK	D	O	If	E	Np	Np	V	QGAGG	———

TABLE A. *Continued*

1	3	7	12	14	16	19	20	22	24	25	27
Af4	112: Yako	11017	B	Fq	uPa	S	L	L	O	Cp	I
Af5	211: Mende	01007	Bt	Fq	Pc	S	L	O	O	Mm	H
Af6	212: Oyo Yoruba	00118	Bs	Eq	P	S	S	O	K	O	H
Af7	310: Bete	01117	B	Fq	P	Cs	L	O	O	O	.
Af8	311: Nupe	10117	B	Eq	P	S	Lo	O	O	C	H
Af9	642: Baule	01216	T	Eq	Av	S	O	Sl	O	C	.
Af10	643: Ibo	01018	B	Eq	P	S	Sl	O	O	N	O
Af11	644: Toma	01216	B	Q	P	Cs	Sl	O	O	T	.
Af13	672: Igbira	11215	S	Ep	P	S	L	O	O	N	O
Af14	700: Sherbro	10216	B	Fp	Va	.	O	L*	O*	N	H
Af15	705: Kpelle	11116	Bs	P	Pu	S	Sl	O	O	M	.
Af19	919: Efik	01315	B	Eq	P	S	S	O	O	O	D
Af20	920: Ibibio	01216	Bs	Fq	P	S	L	O	O	O	D
Af22	922: Itsekiri	11512	T	P	Pn	S	Lo	O	Rk	N	.
Af23	923: Afikpo	10216	Bs	Fq	P	S	Lo	S	O	Tp	.
Af24	924: Edo	11017	St	Gp	P	S	S	O	O	O	H
Af25	925: Isoko	10315	Bs	Ep	P	S	L	O	O	O	H
Af28	928: Gbari	11026	St	Eq	P	S	L	O	O	S	O
Af32	932: Egba	01018	Bs	Ep	P	S	S	O	O	O	H
Af33	933: Ekiti	00217	B	Ep	P	S	S	O	O	N	H
Af36	936: Ewe	01216	Bs	Ep	oP	S	Sl	O	O	C	H
Af42	942: Fanti	01117	B	Fp	oDn	A	L	Sl	O	Cm	D
Af43	943: Ga	01414	B	Ep	Op	S	Lo	O*	O	Qm	H
Af49	949: Sapo	01216	B	Q	P	Cs	Sl	O	O	O	.
Af51	951: Gagu	13015	B	Fp	P	S	L	O	O	.	.
Af52	952: Guro	12025	B	Ep	P	S	L	O	O	.	.
Af54	954: Gbande	01117	B	Q	P	S	Sl	O	O	O	.
Af56	956: Ngere	00226	B	Q	Pa	S	Sl	O	O	O	.
Af57	957: Temne	00226	Bs	Fp	Pa	C	Sl	O	O	O	E
Ag1	12: Bambara	20125	Bs	Eq	P	S	Sl	O	O	Cm*	I
Ag2	13: Yatenga	10027	B	Eq	P	S	S	O	O	N	H
Ag3	113: Dogon	20026	St	En	P	T	L	O	O	O*	I
Ag4	114: Tallensi	10027	Bs	Fq	Pn	C	S	E	O	N	H
Ag5	213: Birifor	11116	Bs	Eq	Pa	C	S	Ml	O	Cp	C
Ag6	214: Futajalonke	00055	Bs	Q	P	S	Lo	O	O	Qc	I
Ag7	312: Bozo	10603	Bs	Ep	P	.	Lo	O	O	Q	.
Ag8	313: Coniagui	21016	St	N	vAv	A	O	Sl	O	T	.
Ag9	645: Malinke	11116	Bs	Eq	P	A	Sl	O	O	C	I
Ag10	673: Konkomba	11116	St	Q	P	Cs	Sl	O	O	T	I*
Ag11	674: Lobi	21016	S	Q	Va	A	O	Sl	O	Cp	C
Ag12	675: Nankanse	01126	B	Fq	Pa	Cs	S	E	O	O	H
Ag13	706: Kasena	11026	B	Fq	P	Cs	S	O	O	O	H
Ag16	961: Banyun	00217	St	Fp	P	.	L	O	O	T	.
Ag18	963: Bijogo	10225	O	N	M	.	O	S	O	O	.
Ag19	964: Diola	10324	Bs	Ep	P	.	L	O	O	O	.
Ag21	966: Bassari	11026	B	N	Pa	A	O	Sl	O	.	.
Ag22	967: Serer	10225	Bs	Eq	Pa	A	E	S	O	C	.
Ag25	970: Soninke	10027	B	Fq	P	A	So	O	O	Q	.
Ag26	971: Susu	01126	B	Ep	P	S	Sl	O	O	Cc	I
Ag27	972: Diula	11017*	B	Ep	Pn	S	So	O	O	Q	.
Ag30	975: Bobo	01027	St	Eq	P	S	L	O	O	.	.
Ag31	976: Minianka	11026	Bs	Ep	P	S	L	O	O	.	.
Ag32	977: Senufo	20017	Bs	Eq	P	S	Sl	O	O	C	.
Ag41	986: Kusasi	00037	Bs	Ep	P	C	S	E	O	O	H

TABLE B. *Continued*

1	3	28	30	31	32	34	35	36	37	38	39
Af4	112: Yako	Er	V	7	40	O	.	4	0	.	Bo
Af5	211: Mende	Ec	X	5	41	A	S	5	5	T*	So
Af6	212: Oyo Yoruba	Er	V	8	43	A	.	5	2	A	So
Af7	310: Bete	Er	V	5	40	.	.	.	.	.	So
Af8	311: Nupe	Ec	H	5	32	C	.	5	4	P	So
Af9	642: Baule	Er	V	.	31	.	.	.	0	.	So
Af10	643: Ibo	Er	H	4	41	A	.	*	1	A	Bo
Af11	644: Toma	Ec	V	4	31	A	S	.	5	T	Bo
Af13	672: Igbira	Er	V	.	31	A	.	.	2	A	Bo
Af14	700: Sherbro	Er	V	.	32	A	.	.	9	.	Bo
Af15	705: Kpelle	Ec	V	4	31	A	S	.	5	T	Bo
Af19	919: Efik	Er	V	.	41	A	.	3	1	.	Bo
Af20	920: Ibibio	Er	H	5	41	A	.	.	2	A	Bo
Af22	922: Itsekiri	Ec	V	.	31	A	.	.	2	.	So
Af23	923: Afikpo	Ir	V	6	41	O	.	3	1	P	Bo
Af24	924: Edo	Er	V	8	43	A	.	.	2	.	So
Af25	925: Isoko	Er	X	.	41	A	.	5	3	A	So
Af28	928: Gbari	Ic	V	.	31	B	.	3	0*	.	So
Af32	932: Egba	Er	V	7	42	A	.	.	9	.	So
Af33	933: Ekiti	Er	V	7	42	A	.	5	9	A	Bo
Af36	936: Ewe	Er	X	.	42	A	.	.	3	.	So
Af42	942: Fanti	Er	V	.	41	A	.	.	0	.	So
Af43	943: Ga	Ec	X	.	30	O	.	.	1	.	So
Af49	949: Sapo	Ec	V	2	31	.	A	4	9	.	Bo
Af51	951: Gagu	Ec	V	5	40	.	.	.	0	.	So
Af52	952: Guro	Ec	V	4	41	.	.	.	0	.	Bo
Af54	954: Gbande	Ec	V	5	31	A	S	.	5	.	Bo
Af56	956: Ngere	Ec	V	4	31	A	S	4	5	.	Bo
Af57	957: Temne	Ec	X	.	32	A	.	5	5	.	Bo
Ag1	12: Bambara	Ic	V	7	41*	O	.	5	5	.	Bm
Ag2	13: Yatenga	Ic	N	7	42	A	P	3	4	T	Bo
Ag3	113: Dogon	Ic	V	3	41	.	.	.	5	.	Bo
Ag4	114: Tallensi	Ic	N	5	40	O	C	5	0	A	Bm
Ag5	213: Birifor	Ec	N	3	40	A	.	5	0	A	Bo
Ag6	214: Futajalonke	Ec	X	.	42	C	.	.	5	P	Bm
Ag7	312: Bozo	Jc	T	.	41	C	.	.	5	T	O
Ag8	313: Coniagui	Ec	V	2	31	A	.	4	4	T	Bo
Ag9	645: Malinke	Ec	V	.	31	.	.	.	5	P	Bo
Ag10	673: Konkomba	Ec	H	.	30	A	.	5	0	A	Bo
Ag11	674: Lobi	Ec	N	3	30	.	.	.	0	.	Bo
Ag12	675: Nankanse	Ec	N	.	40	A	.	5	0	A	Bm
Ag13	706: Kasena	Ec	V	.	41	.	.	5	0	A	Bo
Ag16	961: Banyun	Ec	N	.	30	.	.	.	5	P	P
Ag18	963: Bijogo	Ec	V	.	31	.	.	.	0	.	Bo
Ag19	964: Diola	Ec	V	.	31	.	.	.	5	.	Bm
Ag21	966: Bassari	Ec	V	.	21	A	.	5	4	P	Bo
Ag22	967: Serer	Ec	N	.	32	.	.	.	.	P	Bm
Ag25	970: Soninke	Ec	V	.	32	C	.	.	5	.	Bm
Ag26	971: Susu	Ec	V	.	31	.	.	.	9	.	Bm
Ag27	972: Diula	Er	V	.	41	C	.	.	2	P	So
Ag30	975: Bobo	Ec	N	4	40	.	.	.	5	.	So
Ag31	976: Minianka	Ec	V	.	42	.	.	.	5	.	So
Ag32	977: Senufo	Jc	V	.	41	.	.	.	2	.	So
Ag41	986: Kusasi	Ic	N	.	30	A	.	5	0	.	Bm

TABLE C. *Continued*

1	3	42	44	46	48	50	52	54	56	58	60	62
Af4	112: Yako	.	.	.	.	O	M	E	M	O	M	D
Af5	211: Mende	Mc	M	P	F	P	M	N	M	G	.	D
Af6	212: Oyo Yoruba	Mc	D	P	F	.	M	F	O	.	F	N
Af7	310: Bete	.	.	.	.	.	.	O	M	B	.	G
Af8	311: Nupe	Mc	D	.	F	P	.	G	M	.	M	N
Af9	642: Baule	Mc	.	.	.	.	.	.	M	E	.	N
Af10	643: Ibo	Mc	O	O	F	.	.	.	M	N	.	G
Af11	644: Toma	Mc	M	M	F	.	.	.	M	N	.	G
Af13	672: Igbira	Mc	P	.	P	.	.	.	M	N	.	G
Af14	700: Sherbro	Mc	M	.	.	M	M	.	M	N	.	G
Af15	705: Kpelle	Mc	M	.	F	O	N	M	M	G	.	G
Af19	919: Efik	.	.	.	.	P	.	.	M	M	M	D
Af20	920: Ibibio	.	M	.	P	.	.	.	M	N	M	G
Af22	922: Itsekiri	Mc	O	.	F	M	.	.	M	N	.	*
Af23	923: Afikpo	Mc	O	O	F	.	N	.	.	N	.	G
Af24	924: Edo	Mc	Mc	Mc	P	.	M	F	M	.	.	D
Af25	925: Isoko	Mc*	O	.	P	M	.	M	M	M	.	G
Af28	928: Gbari	Mc	M	Mc	F	P	.	.	M	.	.	N
Af32	932: Egba	Mc	D	.	F	.	.	.	M	.	F	N
Af33	933: Ekiti	Mc	D	.	F	.	.	.	.	.	.	N
Af36	936: Ewe	Mc	M	.	F	P	.	.	M	M	.	E
Af42	942: Fanti	Mc	M	.	F	.	.	.	M	M	.	E
Af43	943: Ga	.	.	.	.	.	.	.	M	M	.	N
Af49	949: Sapo	Mc	.	.	F	.	.	.	M	N	.	G
Af51	951: Gagu	.	.	.	.	.	.	M	M	F	.	G
Af52	952: Guro	.	.	.	.	.	.	.	M	F	.	N
Af54	954: Gbande	Mc	M	P	F	O	.	.	M	D	.	G
Af56	956: Ngere	Mc	.	O	F	.	O*	.	M	E	.	G
Af57	957: Temne	Mc*	M	Mc*	F	.	.	.	Mc	G	.	D
Ag1	12: Bambara	Mc	M	Mc	Fc	M	N	G	M	N	D	N
Ag2	13: Yatenga	Mc	M	Mc	Fc	O	N	F	M	O	Mb	E
Ag3	113: Dogon	Mc	.	Mc	.	.	.	E	M	O	M	N
Ag4	114: Tallensi	Mc	O	M	F	O	N	F	M	N	N	N
Ag5	213: Birifor	M	M	P	F	.	D	F	M	E	M	N
Ag6	214: Futajalonke	Mc	.	.	.	.	.	O	O	O	D	N
Ag7	312: Bozo	.	.	.	.	.	.	O	O	M	O	N
Ag8	313: Coniagui	Mc	D	.	F	O	.	F	M	O	Eb	D
Ag9	645: Malinke	Mc	.	Mc	.	Mc	.	F	M	M	M	N
Ag10	673: Konkomba	Mc	.	P	F	.	N	F	M	N	Mb	D
Ag11	674: Lobi	.	.	.	.	.	.	F	M	E	Mb	N
Ag12	675: Nankanse	M	.	M	F	.	N	.	M	N	M	N
Ag13	704: Kasena	Mc	P	.	F	.	.	.	.	.	.	N
Ag16	961: Banyun	.	.	.	.	.	.	M	M	F	F	N
Ag18	963: Bijogo	.	.	.	.	.	.	M	M	D	.	N
Ag19	964: Diola	.	.	.	.	.	.	.	M	D	N	G
Ag21	966: Bassari	Mc	.	.	F	.	M	F	M	M	M	D
Ag22	967: Serer	Mc	Mc	Mc	.	P	.	.	M	D	D	N
Ag25	970: Soninke	Mc	.	Mc	.	.	.	.	.	.	*	N
Ag26	971: Susu	Mc	.	Mc	P	.	.	.	.	.	M	N
Ag27	972: Diula	Mc	.	.	.	.	.	M	O	.	N
Ag30	975: Bobo	Mc	.	.	.	.	.	F	M	F	.	N
Ag31	976: Minianka	Mc	M	.	Fc	.	.	.	M	.	.	N
Ag32	977: Senufo	Mc	.	Mc	F	.	.	F	M	M	.	N
Ag41	986: Kusasi	Mc	.	M	F	.	N	.	.	.	.	N

TABLE D. *Continued*

1	3	64	67	69	71	73	74	76	78	80–84	85–89
Af4	112: Yako	NcB	O	O	If	N	P.	Ne	.	RGWGG	————
Af5	211: Mende	NcM	D	O	Hf	Q	Qe	Qe	.	CGPCG	RGPGG
Af6	212: Oyo Yoruba	NcK	Cd	O	If	Q	Qe*	Qe*	P	QGAGG	————
Af7	310: Bete	NcK	O	O	O	S	O	Qe	.	RGP.G	————
Af8	311: Nupe	NcK	Cd	O	Hf	S	Qp	De	V	CGACG	————
Af9	642: Baule	NcK	O	O	H	N	Np	Np	F	RGPGG	————
Af10	643: Ibo	NcK	W	O	Hf	O	Pe	Pe	.	RGPGG	————
Af11	644: Toma	NcM	O	O	Hf	Q	Qp	Qp	.	CEPCG	————
Af13	672: Igbira	NcK	D	O	H	.	.	Qp	.	CGACG	RG.HG
Af14	700: Sherbro	NcA	.	.	Sf	.	*	*	.	CGPCG	RGMHG
Af15	705: Kpelle	NcM	W	O	H	E	Pp	Pp	F	CGPCG	RGPGG
Af19	919: Efik	NcB	W	O	Sf	E	Qe	Cp	.	QGPGG	————
Af20	920: Ibibio	NcB	W	O	S	P	Pp	Pp	.	QGPGG	————
Af22	922: Itsekiri	NcK	D	O	Hf	S	.	Pe	F	QEAGG	————
Af23	923: Afikpo	NcK	W	O	Hf	O	*	*	V	REAGG	————
Af24	924: Edo	NcK	D	O	H	P	Pp	Pp	.	QGAGG	————
Af25	925: Isoko	NcK	W	O	Hf	S	Pp	.	.	QGPGG	————
Af28	928: Gbari	NcK	.	.	Sf	P	*	*	V	CGACG	————
Af32	932: Egba	NcK	D	O	Hf	.	Pe	Qe	.	RGAGG	————
Af33	933: Ekiti	NcK	D	O	Sf	.	Qe*	Qe*	.	QGAGG	————
Af36	936: Ewe	NcK	D	O	Sf	E	Pp	Np	F	RGPGG	————
Af42	942: Fanti	NcK	D	O	Hf	E	Np	Np*	.	QGP.G	————
Af43	943: Ga	NcK	.	.	Sf	Q	Qp	Qp	.	RGAGG	————
Af49	949: Sapo	NcK	O	O	I	P	.	Pp	F	REMGM	————
Af51	951: Gagu	NcM	O	O	O	Q	Pp	Pp	.	CGACG	————
Af52	952: Guro	NcM	O	O	Sf	Q	Qp	Qp	F	RG.GG	CGACG
Af54	954: Gbande	NcM	O	O	Sf	Q	P.	P.	F	CGPCG	————
Af56	956: Ngere	NcM	.	O	Sf	P	Pp	Pp	F	CGMCG	————
Af57	957: Temne	NcA	.	O	Sf	.	Qp	Pe	.	CGPCG	————
Ag1	12: Bambara	NcM	D	D	Hf	Q	Qp	Qp	.	QGAFE	CGACG
Ag2	13: Yatenga	NcG	Cd	D	Hf	.	Qp	Qp	.	CGACG	————
Ag3	113: Dogon	NcG	W	D	Hf	Q	Qp	Qp	.	QGAFE	————
Ag4	114: Tallensi	NcG	W	O	If	S	Qp*	Qp*	A	CGACG	CGAFE
Ag5	213: Birifor	NcG	O	.	If	.	Qp	Np	.	QGAFE	————
Ag6	214: Futajalonke	NcA	D	D	Sf	.	Qp	Pe	F	CGACG	CGRBG
Ag7	312: Bozo	NcM	O	D	Sf	.	Qp	De	.	QGAFE	CGRDG
Ag8	313: Coniagui	NcA	O	D	O	N	Np	Np	F	CGMCG	————
Ag9	645: Malinke	NcM	D	D	Hf	Q	Qp	Qp	.	CGACG	————
Ag10	673: Konkomba	NcG	O	O	I	O	Qp	Qp	.	CGPCG	————
Ag11	674: Lobi	NcG	O	O	If	.	Ce	Mp*	.	RGAFE	————
Ag12	675: Nankanse	NcG	O	O	I	Q	Qp	Qp	.	CGACG	CGAFE
Ag13	706: Kasena	NcG	.	O	Sf	P	Qp	Pp	.	CGPFP	CGPCG
Ag16	961: Banyun	NcA	O	O	O	P	Pe	Pe	F	CGMCG	————
Ag18	963: Bijogo	NcA	O	O	Sf	N	Np	Np	F	CGPCG	————
Ag19	964: Diola	NcA	O	O	O	Q	Qp	Qp	F	EGPHG	————
Ag21	966: Bassari	NcA	O	O	O	N	Np	Np	F	CGSCG	————
Ag22	967: Serer	NcA	Dc	D	Hf	Q	Np	Pe*	F	CGMCG	————
Ag25	970: Soninke	NcM	D	D	H	.	Pe	De	V	QGAFE	CGACG
Ag26	971: Susu	NcM	.	D	Sf	.	Qp	Pe	.	CGACG	RGAFE
Ag27	972: Diula	NcM	W	.	Sf	.	De	De	.	QGAFE	————
Ag30	975: Bobo	NcG	O	D	S	Q	Qp	Qp	.	RGAFE	————
Ag31	976: Minianka	NcG	O	D	H	Q	Qp	Qp	V	RGAFE	————
Ag32	977: Senufo	NcG	O	D	H	.	Qp	Qp	F	CGACG	RGAFE
Ag41	986: Kusasi	NcG	O	O	.	Q	*	*	.	CGACG	————

TABLE A. *Continued*

1	3	7	12	14	16	19	20	22	24	25	27
Ag47	992: Mossi	11025	B	Q	Pa	S	S	O	O	N	D
Ag48	993: Basari	01027	Bs	Ẽp	P	C	S	O	O	.	.
Ag49	994: Kabre	01126	St	Q	P	S	L	O	O	O	.
Ah1	14: Katab	21115	T	Fq	Pa	Cs	L	O	O	N	H
Ah2	115: Jukun	01126	B	En	D	A	O	O	R	S	H
Ah3	116: Tiv	12115	X*	Eq	Va	C	Pl	O	R	S	H
Ah4	215: Mambila	00028	Xt	En	Va	S	O	O	Rk	N	H
Ah7	315: Matakam	00019	B	Fn	P	Cs	O	O	O	O	O
Ah8	353: Wute	11116	B	Fq	Pa	S	Pl	O	O	O	.
Ah9	610: Anaguta	11017	X	Ep	P	S	L	O	O	O	H
Ah11	998: Basa	01126	X	Eq	P	.	S	O	O	N	.
Ah14	1001: Kamuku	00127	Bs	Q	P	S	S	O	O	.	.
Ah15	1002: Reshe	00325	Bs	Fq	P	A	Sl	O	O	O	H
Ah19	1006: Kadara	01027	St	Fq	Pa	S	S	O	O	O	O
Ah20	1007: Kagoro	01027	B	Fq	Pa	Cs	Ms	O	O	O	H
Ah30	1017: Longuda	00037	Bs	Eq	uAv	S	O	Sl	O	O	C
Ah31	1018: Mumuye	01027	Bs	Eq	uPa	S	Sl	O	O	O	H
Ah33	1020: Yungur	01036	Bs	Fq	uP	S	Sl	O	O	O	H
Ah36	1023: Gude	00028	B	Fq	uP	S	L	O	O	S	.
Ah38	1025: Kapsiki	00028	B	Q	P	C	L	O	O	O	.
Ah39	1026: Podokwo	00028	Bs	Q	P	C	S	O	O	.	.
Ai1	15: Banda	02017	Xb	S	P	C	L	O	O	O	O
Ai3	117: Azande	12106	Bs	Q	Vn	A	S	O	O	O	D
Ai5	217: Mamvu	11017	B	Q	P	C	L	O	O	.	H
Ai6	218: Shilluk	11125	Bs	Q	P	S	S	O	O	N	D
Ai7	316: Baya	11116	B	Q	P	C	L	O	O	N	.
Ai8	317: Dilling	11035	Bs	Q	uPn	S	P	O	O	C	D
Ai9	646: Masa	01315	B	Fq	P	C	Sl	O	O	N	H
Ai10	647: Otoro	02026	B	Q	Pn	S	Sl	O	O	O	H
Ai11	702: Mangbetu	02116	B	Q	Vn	A	L	O	O	O	H
Ai12	1027: Fali	11026	Bs	Q	P	S	L	O	O	O	.
Ai14	1029: Mbum	03214	B	Fq	P	.	L	O	O	.	.
Ai15	1030: Mundang	00145	B	Q	P	S	S	O	O	.	.
Ai21	1036: Bagirmi	10125	B	Q	P	.	L*	O	O	.	.
Ai22	1037: Sara	01036	B	Q	P	C	L	O	O	.	.
Ai23	1038: Bwaka	00019	B	Q	P	Cs	L	O	O	O	.
Ai26	1041: Ngbandi	01216	B	Q	Pa	C	S	O	O	.	O
Ai28	1043: Popoi	02017	B	Q	P	S	L	O	O	N	.
Ai29	1044: Lendu	01036	B	N	P	E	Sl	O	O	O	.
Ai30	1045: Lese	00226	Bx	Q	P	C	S	O	O	.	.
Ai32	1047: Lugbara	10045	Bs	Eq	P	C	S	O	O	N	.
Ai33	1048: Madi	01234	Bs	Eq	P	Cs	Sl	O	O	.	.
Ai35	1050: Bongo	21115	Bs	Q	P	C	S	O	O	O	.
Ai36	1051: Jur	01126	B	Q	P	C	S	O	O	N	.
Ai38	1053: Korongo	01036	B	N	uAv	A	O	Sl	O	O	D
Ai39	1054: Mesakin	01036	B	N	uAv	A	O	So	O	N	I
Ai40	1055: Moro	01036	Bd	Eq	P	S	L	O	O	N	D
Ai41	1056: Tira	01036	Bs	Q	uPn	S	Sl	O	O	N	D
Ai42	1057: Tullishi	01036	B	N	P	A	Lo	Sl	O	O	H*
Ai43	1058: Nyima	01036	Bs	Q	P	A	P	O	O	O	D
Ai44	1059: Anuak	01216	B	Q	Pa	C	Sl	O	O	O	.
Ai46	1061: Koma	01216	X	N	P	C	Sl	O	O	O	.
Ai47	1062: Mao	11116	X	Q	P	C	S	O	O	O	.
Aj1	17: Teso	01036	B	Q	P	S	S	O	O	N	H

TABLE B. *Continued*

1	3	28	30	31	32	34	35	36	37	38	39
Ag47	992: Mossi	Ec	N	7	33	A	S	.	4	.	Bm
Ag48	993: Basari	Ir	V	.	31	.	.	5	0	.	Bm
Ag49	994: Kabre	Ic	H	.	30	A	.	.	0	P	Bo
Ah1	14: Katab	Ic	V	4	40	B	.	5	9	P	So
Ah2	115: Jukun	Ec	V	.	40*	.	Q	.	5	.	So
Ah3	116: Tiv	Er	N	4	41	O	Q	4	4	A	So
Ah4	215: Mambila	Ic	H	5	40	.	.	.	.	A	So
Ah7	315: Matakam	Ic	H	.	40	A	.	*	0	A	So
Ah8	353: Wute	Ec	V	3	41	.	.	.	4	A	So
Ah9	610: Anaguta	Ec	H	4	30	B	S	5	5	P	So
Ah11	998: Basa	Ec	H	.	31	A	.	.	0	.	So
Ah14	1001: Kamuku	Ic	N	.	.	A	A	5	0	P	So
Ah15	1002: Reshe	Ic	V	.	32	.	.	5	4	.	So
Ah19	1006: Kadara	Ic	V	.	41	A	.	.	4	.	So
Ah20	1007: Kagoro	Ic	V	.	41	A	.	4	9	.	So
Ah30	1017: Longuda	Ic	H	.	30	.	.	.	0	R	Bo
Ah30	1018: Mumuye	Ic	V	4	41	.	.	.	0	.	Bo
Ah33	1020: Yungur	Ic	H	.	41	.	.	.	0	.	Bo
Ah36	1023: Gude	Ic	V	.	30	A	.	.	9	A	So
Ah38	1025: Kapsiki	Ic	V	.	31	A	.	.	0	A	So
Ah39	1026: Podokwo	Ic	V	3	21	A	.	.	0	A	Bm
Ai1	15: Banda	Ec	N	.	30	.	.	.	5	.	O
Ai3	117: Azande	Ec	N	3	32	B	S	4	4	P	O
Ai5	217: Mamvu	Et	V	2	20	A	.	.	5	.	So
Ai6	218: Shilluk	Ec	H	5	31	A	.	4	0	P	Bm
Ai7	316: Baya	Er	V	4	30	.	.	.	4	.	So
Ai8	317: Dilling	Ic	H	.	31	.	.	.	5	P	Bm
Ai9	646: Masa	Jc	N	4	30	A	.	.	0	T	Bm
Ai10	647: Otoro	Ic	H	.	31	.	.	.	0	P	Bm
Ai11	702: Mangbetu	Et	N	.	22	.	.	.	4	T	So
Ai12	1027: Fali	Ec	H	.	40	A	.	4	0	P	So
Ai14	1029: Mbum	Ec	N	3	31	A	.	.	5	R	So
Ai15	1030: Mundang	Ec	V	.	31	A	.	.	5	P	Bm
Ai21	1036: Bagirmi	Ec	V	7	23	C	.	.	9	.	Bm
Ai22	1037: Sara	Ec	N	.	20	.	.	.	0	P	Bm
Ai23	1038: Bwaka	Er	V	.	31	A	A	.	5	P	So
Ai26	1041: Ngbandi	Er	V	.	20	A	.	.	0	.	So
Ai28	1043: Popoi	Et	V	.	31	.	.	.	4	P	So
Ai29	1044: Lendu	Ec	V	.	21	A	.	.	4	A	Bm
Ai30	1045: Lese	Et	V	.	21	A	A	5	5	A	Sm
Ai32	1047: Lugbara	Ec	H	.	31	A	.	.	0	P	Bm
Ai33	1048: Madi	Ec	N	.	31	A	.	.	0	P	Bm
Ai35	1050: Bongo	Ec	N	.	21	A	.	.	0	P	So
Ai36	1051: Jur	Ec	N	4	21	.	.	.	4	T	Bm
Ai38	1053: Korongo	Ec	H	.	30	.	.	.	0	R	Bm
Ai39	1054: Mesakin	Ec	H	.	31	.	.	.	0	R	Bm
Ai40	1055: Moro	Ic	H	.	40	.	.	.	0	.	Bm
Ai41	1056: Tira	Ic	H	.	31	.	.	.	0	P	Bm
Ai42	1057: Tullishi	Ec	H	.	31	.	.	.	0	.	Bm
Ai43	1058: Nyima	Ic	H	.	30	.	.	.	6	P	Bm
Ai44	1059: Anuak	Ic	V	4	21	.	.	.	0	P	Sm
Ai46	1061: Koma	Ec	V	.	20	.	.	.	0	.	Sm
Ai47	1062: Mao	Ec	V	.	21	A	.	.	5	A	Bm
Aj1	17: Teso	Ec	N	.	31	A	.	.	0	.	qBm

TABLE C. *Continued*

1	3	42	44	46	48	50	52	54	56	58	60	62
Ag47	992: Mossi	Mc	M	M	G	P	M	F	M	M	M	E
Ag48	993: Basari	Mc	Mc	.	F	.	M	.	M	M	.	N
Ag49	994: Kabre	Mc	F	M	F	.	.	.	M	.	.	G
Ah1	14: Katab	O	O	.	O	O	M	.	M	.	Eb	N
Ah2	115: Jukun	Mc	F	.	F	.	.	.	M	M	Eb	N
Ah3	116: Tiv	Mc	M	P	F	O*	N	F	M	N	.	D
Ah4	215: Mambila	Mc	.	.	.	.	.	O	O	O	.	N
Ah7	315: Matakam	Mc	O	P	Fc	O	M	O	M	O	.	D
Ah8	353: Wute	Mc	.	.	P	.	.	G	M	E	E	G
Ah9	610: Anaguta	M	F	D	F	O	M	D	M	M	M	D
Ah11	998: Basa	Mc	P	.	F	.	.	M	.	M	E	D
Ah14	1001: Kamuku	Mc	P	P	P	.	.	.	M	.	.	.
Ah15	1002: Reshe	.	.	.	.	.	.	.	M	.	.	N
Ah19	1006: Kadara	.	.	.	M	.	.	.	M	G	M	N
Ah20	1007: Kagoro	.	.	.	O	.	M	.	M	M	E	N
Ah30	1017: Longuda	Mc	.	.	.	.	.	.	M	.	M	N
Ah31	1018: Mumuye	Mc	.	.	.	.	.	.	M	.	.	G
Ah33	1020: Yungur	Mc	.	.	.	.	.	.	M	.	.	E
Ah36	1023: Gude	.	O	P	F	.	M	.	M	.	.	E
Ah38	1025: Kapsiki	Mc	O	P	F	.	.	.	M	.	.	E
Ah39	1026: Podokwo	Mc	O	P	F	O	M	F	M	.	Mb	E
Ai1	15: Banda	Mc	O	.	F	.	.	M	G	.	G	
Ai3	117: Azande	Mc	M	O	F	M	M	G	M	G	O	G
Ai5	217: Mamvu	Mc	O	P	P	O	.	.	M	O	.	G
Ai6	218: Shilluk	Mc	O	P	F	M	D	F	M	.	M	E
Ai7	316: Baya	Mc	.	.	.	.	.	E	M	E	F	G
Ai8	317: Dilling	.	.	.	.	.	.	G	M	O	N	E
Ai9	646: Masa	Mc	.	.	F	Mc	.	.	M	E	M	E
Ai10	647: Otoro	Mc	O	.	.	O	.	.	M	O	N	E
Ai11	702: Mangbetu	Mc	.	.	.	.	.	F	M	N	.	G
Ai12	1027: Fali	.	.	.	.	.	.	.	M	.	Eb	E
Ai14	1029: Mbum	Mc	P	O	F	.	.	.	.	D	.	.
Ai15	1030: Mundang	Mc	M	.	P	P	.	.	.	M	.	G
Ai21	1036: Bagirmi	Mc	M	.	.	.	.	F	.	M	.	.
Ai22	1037: Sara	.	.	.	.	.	.	.	M	.	.	E
Ai23	1038: Bwaka	Mc	O	.	F	.	.	.	M	D	.	G
Ai26	1041: Ngbandi	Mc	O	.	F	P	.	.	M	.	.	G
Ai28	1043: Popoi	Mc	.	.	.	.	.	M	M	N	.	G
Ai29	1044: Lendu	Mc	O	.	F	.	.	F	M	M	M	E
Ai30	1045: Lese	Mc	O	.	F	P	.	.	M	M*	.	G
Ai32	1047: Lugbara	Mc	.	.	F	.	M	.	.	.	M	E
Ai33	1048: Madi	Mc	.	.	.	M	M	.	.	.	M	N
Ai35	1050: Bongo	Mc	.	.	F	.	M	E	M	M	.	G
Ai36	1051: Jur	Mc	M	.	F	.	N	.	M	E	M	G
Ai38	1053: Korongo	.	.	.	.	O	.	.	M	.	N	D
Ai39	1054: Mesakin	.	.	.	.	O	.	.	M	.	N	D
Ai40	1055: Moro	.	.	.	.	O	.	.	M	.	N	D
Ai41	1056: Tira	.	.	.	.	O	.	.	M	.	N	E
Ai42	1057: Tullishi	.	.	.	.	O	.	.	M	.	N	D
Ai43	1058: Nyima	.	.	.	.	O	.	F	M	O	N	G
Ai44	1059: Anuak	.	.	.	P	P	.	.	M	.	.	E
Ai46	1061: Koma	.	.	.	.	.	.	.	M	M	.	E
Ai47	1062: Mao	O	O	P	F	.	M	.	M	.	.	.
Aj1	17: Teso	.	.	.	.	.	.	.	M	N	M	G

TABLE D. *Continued*

1	3	64	67	69	71	73	74	76	78	80–84	85–89
Ag47	992: Mossi	NcG	D	D	H	P	Pp	Pp	.	CGACG	——
Ag48	993: Basari	NcG	O	O	H	S	Pe	Pe	F	CGACG	——
Ag49	994: Kabre	NcG	O	O	S	I	Qp	Qp	.	CGACG	——
Ah1	14: Katab	NcB	O	O	Sf	S	Pe	Pe	.	CGACG	——
Ah2	115: Jukun	NcB	D	O	If	Q	Pe*	Pe*	.	CGACG	——
Ah3	116: Tiv	NcB	O	O	Hf	O	O	Pe	A	CGACG	——
Ah4	215: Mambila	NcB	O	O	Sf	N	.	Pe*	A	CGMCG	——
Ah7	315: Matakam	AaD	O	D	O	E	Pe	Pe	.	CGACG	——
Ah8	353: Wute	NcB	D	O	H	.	Qp	Qp	.	CGPCG	——
Ah9	610: Anaguta	NcB	O	O	Sf	C	Pe	Pe	F	CGABG	——
Ah11	998: Basa	NcB	.	.	Sf	.	Qe	Qe	.	CGACG	——
Ah14	1001: Kamuku	NcB	O	O	Sf	.	Qe	Qe	V	CGMCG	——
Ah15	1002: Reshe	NcB	W	O	.	S	Qp	Qp	F	CGACG	RPP.G
Ah19	1006: Kadara	NcB	O	O	Sf	Q	Pe	Pe	F	EGACG	——
Ah20	1007: Kagoro	NcB	O	O	Sf	.	Pe	Pe	P	EGACG	CGACG
Ah30	1017: Longuda	NcE	O	O	.	O	Np	Np	.	CGACG	——
Ah31	1018: Mumuye	NcE	O	O	S	Q	Pp	Qp	E	CGMCG	——
Ah33	1020: Yungur	NcE	O	O	S	.	Qp	Qp	.	CGMCG	CGACG
Ah36	1023: Gude	AaD	D	.	O	Q	Pe	Pe	.	CGACG	——
Ah38	1025: Kapsiki	AaD	O	O	S	Q	Qp	Qp	.	CGACG	——
Ah39	1026: Podokwo	AaD	O	O	O	E	Pe	Pe	V	CGSCG	——
Ai1	15: Banda	NcE	O	O	I	Q	Pp	Qe	.	CGACG	——
Ai3	117: Azande	NcE	D	O	If	Q	Qp	Qp	A	CGACG	——
Ai5	217: Mamvu	CnC	O	O	Sf	.	.	.	V	CGGCG	——
Ai6	218: Shilluk	CnE	Cd	O	Hf	E	Pp	Pp	P	C.ACG	——
Ai7	316: Baya	NcE	O	O	H	P	Pp	Pp	P	CGACG	CGRDG
Ai8	317: Dilling	CnN	O	O	Hf	.	Pu*	Pe	.	CGACG	——
Ai9	646: Masa	NcE	O	O	.	.	Pp	Pp	.	CGPCG	——
Ai10	647: Otoro	Ko	W	O	If	O	Pe	Pe	F	CGPCG	——
Ai11	702: Mangbetu	CnC	D	O	I	Q	.	Pp	.	RGGGG	——
Ai12	1027: Fali	NcE	O	O	Sf	Q	Pu	.	F	CGACG	——
Ai14	1029: Mbum	NcE	.	.	.	P	.	.	V	CGMCG	——
Ai15	1030: Mundang	NcE	.	O	S	P	P.	P.	.	CGACG	——
Ai21	1036: Bagirmi	CnC	D	.	H	.	.	.	.	CGACG	RGAFE
Ai22	1037: Sara	CnC	O	O	S	.	Q.	Q.	.	CGMCG	——
Ai23	1038: Bwaka	NcE	O	O	Sf	P	Pe	Pe	F	RGWGG	CGPCG
Ai26	1041: Ngbandi	NcE	O	O	H	P	Pp	Pp	.	CGPCG	CGBCG
Ai28	1043: Popoi	CnC	O	O	S	A	Qp	Pe	.	CG.CG	RG.GG
Ai29	1044: Lendu	CnC	O	O	.	P	Pp	Pe	V	CGRBG	——
Ai30	1045: Lese	CnC	O	D*	.	P	Pe	Pe	P	CGWCG	——
Ai32	1047: Lugbara	CnC	O	O	If	P	.	.	.	CGPCG	——
Ai33	1048: Madi	CnC	O	O	.	P	Pe	Pe	F	CGPCG	——
Ai35	1050: Bongo	CnC	O	O	O	I	.	.	V	CGMCG	——
Ai36	1051: Jur	CnE	O	O	Sf	E	Qp*	Qp*	.	CPPCG	——
Ai38	1053: Korongo	Ko	W	O	.	.	*	*	.	CGACG	——
Ai39	1054: Mesakin	Ko	W	O	S	.	*	*	.	CGACG	——
Ai40	1055: Moro	Ko	W	O	S	O	Qp	Qp	.	CEACG	——
Ai41	1056: Tira	Ko	O	O	S	.	Pe	Pe	.	CGACG	——
Ai42	1057: Tullishi	Ko	O	O	S	Q	*	Qp	.	CGACG	——
Ai43	1058: Nyima	CnN	O	O	H	.	Pp	Pp	.	CGWCG	——
Ai44	1059: Anuak	CnE	D	.	.	Q	.	.	.	CGPCG	——
Ai46	1061: Koma	Km	O	O	S	Q	.	.	.	CGPCG	——
Ai47	1062: Mao	Km	O	O	.	Q	Qp	Qp	V	CGRBG	CGMCG
Aj1	17: Teso	CnE	O	O	If	.	Pp	Pp	.	CGRBG	CG.CG

TABLE A. *Continued*

1	3	7	12	14	16	19	20	22	24	25	27
Aj2	119: Masai	01090	B	Q	Pn	A	S	O	O	N	O
Aj3	120: Nuer	00154	B	Fq	uVu	C	S	O	O	N	D
Aj4	219: Lango	01045	B	Gq	P	A	S	O	O	O	O
Aj5	220: Turkana	21034	B	Fq	Pn	E	S	O	O	N	D
Aj6	318: Luo	01126	B	Fs	Pn	Cs	S	O	O	N	D*
Aj7	319: Nandi	00055	B	N	Pn	A	S	O	K	O	O
Aj8	354: Bari	01045	Bs	Q	uPn	C	S	O	O	N	O
Aj9	648: Kipsigis	01045	B	Q	P	A	Sl	O	O	O	I
Aj11	677: Dinka	01153	B	Eq	bP	S	S	O	O	N	D
Aj12	678: Lotuko	02134	B	Q	uP	S	S	O	O	O	E*
Aj15	1065: Kuku	01036	Bs	Q	P	C	S	O	O	O	.
Aj16	1066: Mondari	01225	B	N	P	C	S	O	O	.	.
Aj17	1067: Alur	01225	B	Fq	P	Cs	S	O	O	N	D
Aj18	1068: Bodi	02053	B	Gq	.	.	S	O	O	.	.
Aj19	1069: Didinga	02044	Bs	Q	Pn	A	S	O	O	.	.
Aj20	1070: Suri	01135	B	Q	P	A	S	O	O	.	.
Aj21	1071: Jie	00046	B	Eq	uP	A	Lo	O	O	O	.
Aj23	1073: Plains Suk	01063	B	Q	Pn	C	S	O	O	N	I
Aj24	1074: Topotha	11053	B	Q	P	.	S	O	O	.	.
Aj26	1076: Hill Suk	01036	B	Q	P	A	S	O	O	O	I*
Ca1	18: Konso	00046	O	Gq	Pn	A	Ms	O	O	O	O
Ca2	19: Somali	00091	B	Fq	P	C	Pl	O	O	N	D
Ca3	121: Tigrinya	00037	D	M	oP	A	L	O	K	N	D
Ca4	221: Iraqw	00055	B	N	Pn	.	S	L*	O	.	C
Ca5	320: Bisharin	00082	B	N	uP	C	Po	O	O	Qa	D
Ca6	649: Afar	10180	B	Fq	P	C	So	O	O	Q*	D
Ca7	679: Amhara	00136	O	Em	Vu	E	O	O	O	B	E*
Ca8	707: Gurage	00046	B	F.	P	C	P	O	O	.	D
Ca11	841: Arusi	01054	B	Q	P	.	L	O	O	O	S
Ca12	842: Gibe	01036	B	Ñ	P	.	L	O	O	.	.
Ca13	843: Macha	01036	B	N	P	S	Sl	O	K	N	.
Ca14	844: Burji	01027	B	Q	P	E	S	O	O	.	.
Ca15	845: Darasa	01027	T	Q	P	A	So	O	O	.	.
Ca16	846: Sidamo	01036	B	Q	P	A	So	O	O	.	.
Ca17	847: Tsamai	01036	B	Q	P	.	S	O	O	.	.
Ca19	849: Banna	01054	B	Eq	P	Cs	M	O	O	.	.
Ca23	853: Bako	00037	B	Q	P	.	S	O	O	.	.
Ca28	858: Basketo	00037	B	Ñ	P	.	S	O	O	O	.
Ca29	859: Janjero	00028	B	N	P	.	S	O	O	.	.
Ca30	860: Kafa	11026	B	P	P	.	S	O	O	O	E*
Ca31	861: Falasha	00037	O	M	Vn	.	O	O	B	.	.
Ca32	862: Barea	10027	Bs	Q	uNu	.	O	S	O	N	.
Ca33	863: Kunama	11026	Bs	N	uN	.	O	S	O	N	.
Ca39	1090: Jimma	00037	B	Fp	P	.	S	O	O	N	E*
Cb2	21: Wolof	00136	B	Fq	Pa	C	L	L	O	Cc	H
Cb3	122: Songhai	00235	B	N	Pn	A	Lo	O	O	Q	I
Cb4	222: Hasania	00055	B	P	uP	A	Po	O	O	Qa	D
Cb5	321: Buduma	10441	B	P	P	.	So	O	O	Q	I
Cb6	355: Tera	01117	St	Eq	uPa	S	L	O	O	Č	I
Cb7	680: Bolewa	11026	B	Q	P	A	Lo	O	O	C	I*
Cb8	681: Bororo Ful.	00082	B	Q	V	E	O	O	B	O	H
Cb9	682: Kanawa	10027	B	Fq	Pn	S	Lo	O	O	Qa	I
Cb17	875: Fur	00136	B	En	O*	E	O	L	O	Õ	H
Cb18	876: Kanembu	00136	Gd	Ep	V	A	O	O	B	Q	.
Cb19	877: Kanuri	10126	B	Q	Vn	A	O*	O	B*	T*	.

TABLE B. *Continued*

1	3	28	30	31	32	34	35	36	37	38	39
Aj2	119: Masai	O	B	2	31	.	Q	3	5	T	Bm
Aj3	120: Nuer	Ec	S	.	30	C	.	4	0	P	Bm
Aj4	219: Lango	Ec	V	3	30	B	.	5	0	T	Bm
Aj5	220: Turkana	Ec	S	.	20	B	.	4	0	.	Bm
Aj6	318: Luo	Ic	N	3	31	A	Q	2	0	P	Bm
Aj7	319: Nandi	Ic	N	.	21	A	.	2	6	T	Bm
Aj8	354: Bari	Et	N	.	20	A	.	.	0	P	Bm
Aj9	648: Kipsigis	Jc	N	.	32	A	.	.	5	T	Bm
Aj11	677: Dinka	Ec	S	.	31	A	.	.	0	P	Bm
Aj12	678: Lotuko	Ec	V	5	31	B	.	.	0	T	Bm
Aj15	1065: Kuku	Ic	N	.	31	A	.	.	0	P	Bm
Aj16	1066: Mondari	Ec	T	.	30	.	.	.	0	P	Bm
Aj17	1067: Alur	Ec	H	.	31	A	.	.	0	P	Bm
Aj18	1068: Bodi	Ec	H	.	21	A	.	4	0	P	Bm
Aj19	1069: Didinga	Ec	S	.	32	.	.	.	4	.	Bm
Aj20	1070: Suri	Ec	V	.	21	A	.	.	.	.	Bm
Aj21	1071: Jie	Ec	T	.	31	B	.	.	0	P	Bm
Aj23	1073: Plains Suk	Ec	S	.	31	A	.	.	5	P	Bm
Aj24	1074: Topotha	Ec	T	.	31	A	.	.	0	P	Bm
Aj26	1076: Hill Suk	Ic	N	.	21	A	.	.	5	.	Bm
Ca1	18: Konso	Ic	V	.	31	.	.	.	7	T	Bm
Ca2	19: Somali	Ic	B	1	32	C	P	2	4	T	Cm
Ca3	121: Tigrinya	Ic	V	7	32	C	.	.	1	.	pBm
Ca4	221: Iraqw	Ic	N	3	31	.	.	.	9	.	Bm
Ca5	320: Bisharin	Jc	S	.	31	C	.	.	4	.	Cm
Ca6	649: Afar	Cc	S	3	32	C	.	.	5	.	Cm
Ca7	679: Amhara	Ic	H	8	33	C	Q	4*	1	A	pBm
Ca8	707: Gurage	Jr	V	.	30	A	.	.	4	.	Bm
Ca11	841: Arusi	Ec	T	.	22	A	.	.	9	.	.pBm
Ca12	842: Gibe	Ic	N	.	23	C	.	.	2	.	pBm
Ca13	843: Macha	Ic	N	.	3*	.	.	.	7	.	pBm
Ca14	844: Burji	Ir	N	.	.	A	.	.	7	.	Bm
Ca15	845: Darasa	Ir	N	.	22	.	.	.	7	.	Bm
Ca16	846: Sidamo	Ir	N	.	21	A	.	.	7	.	Bm
Ca17	847: Tsamai	Jc	N	.	21	.	.	.	5	.	Bm
Ca19	849: Banna	Ec	H	.	31	A	.	.	5	P	Bm
Ca23	853: Bako	Ic	N	.	22	A	.	4	0	.	Bm
Ca28	858: Basketo	Ir	N	.	21	A	.	.	0	.	Bm
Ca29	859: Janjero	Ir	N	.	23	B	.	.	9	.	pBm
Ca30	860: Kafa	Ic	N	.	34	A	.	.	1	.	pBm
Ca31	861: Falasha	Ic	V	.	2*	C	.	.	1	A	pBm
Ca32	862: Barea	Ec	V	.	20	.	.	.	2	P	pBm
Ca33	863: Kunama	Ec	V	.	20	.	.	.	3	P	pBm
Ca39	1090: Jimma	Ic	N	.	33	C	.	.	9	.	pBm
Cb2	21: Wolof	Ec	V	8*	32	C	S	4	4	A	Bm
Cb3	122: Songhai	Ic	V	7	33	C	.	2	4	.	Bm
Cb4	222: Hasania	Ec	S	.	.	C	.	.	9	.	Bm
Cb5	321: Buduma	Ec	N	.	21	.	.	.	5	.	Bm
Cb6	355: Tera	Ec	V	.	41	.	.	.	4	A	Eo
Cb7	680: Bolewa	Ec	V	.	32	C	.	.	9	P	Bo
Cb8	681: Bororo Ful.	Ec	T	2	20	.	.	.	4	A	Bm
Cb9	682: Kanawa	Ec	V	8	32	C	.	.	4	A	Bo*
Cb17	875: Fur	Ic	V	.	33	C	.	.	5	P	Bm
Cb18	876: Kanembu	Ic	V	.	31	C	.	.	4	.	Bm
Cb19	877: Kanuri	Ic	V	7	33	C	.	.	9	A	Bm

TABLE C. *Continued*

1	3	42	44	46	48	50	52	54	56	58	60	62
Aj2	119: Masai	Mc	O	P	F	O	.	O	M	O	Db	O
Aj3	120: Nuer	O	O	.	O	O	.	F	M	N	N	E
Aj4	219: Lango	Mc	.	.	.	.	.	O	M	O	M	G
Aj5	220: Turkana	.	.	F	O	O	E	F	M	M	D	F
Aj6	318: Luo	Mc	O	P	F	O	.	O	M	D	M	E
Aj7	319: Nandi	Mc	O	F	Fc	O	D	.	M	O	D	G
Aj8	354: Bari	Mc	O	.	P	.	.	O	Mc	Mc	N	D
Aj9	648: Kipsigis	Mc	O	P	F	O	M	.	M	.	D	D
Aj11	677: Dinka	Mc	.	.	.	.	.	.	M	M	N	E
Aj12	678: Lotuko	Mc	.	.	.	.	.	.	M	F	N	D
Aj15	1065: Kuku	Mc	M*	.	F	.	M	.	M	M	M	D
Aj16	1066: Mondari	Mc	.	P	P	P	.	.	M	M	N	D
Aj17	1067: Alur	Mc	O	.	F	P	M	.	M	.	M	D
Aj18	1068: Bodi	O	.	M	.	.	.	.	M	O	D	D
Aj19	1069: Didinga	Mc	.	.	.	.	.	.	M	O	M	G
Aj20	1070: Suri	Mc	.	.	.	.	.	.	M	O	M	.
Aj21	1071: Jie	O	.	F	O	.	.	.	M	O	N	G
Aj23	1073: Plains Suk	O	.	.	.	O	.	F	E	M	O	D	G
Aj24	1074: Topotha	Mc	.	.	F	.	.	.	M	O	N	G
Aj26	1076: Hill Suk	Mc	.	.	F	.	.	E	M	O	D	G
Ca1	18: Konso	Mc	M	Mc	Fc	O	.	.	M	O	Mb	E
Ca2	29: Somali	Mc	Mc	Mc	O	O	G	O	Mc	O	D	*
Ca3	121: Tigrinya	Mc	.	.	.	.	.	.	M	O	N	N
Ca4	221: Iraqw	Mc	.	P	.	.	.	O	O	O	M	M
Ca5	320: Bisharin	.	.	P	.	.	.	.	M	O	M	F
Ca6	649: Afar	Mc	.	.	.	F	.	.	.	.	D	*
Ca7	679: Amhara	Mc	Mc	Mc	Fc	.	M	.	Mc	M	D	N
Ca8	707: Gurage	Mc	.	.	.	.	.	.	Mc.	.		N
Ca11	841: Arusi	Mc	.	P	P	.	M	.	M	O	D	N
Ca12	842: Gibe	Mc	P	Mc	P	.	N	.	M	O	N	M
Ca13	843: Macha	Mc	.	Mc	P	.	N	.	M	O	N	M
Ca14	844: Burji	Mc	M	Mc	Fc	O	.	.	M	O	D	M
Ca15	845: Darasa	Mc	P	Mc	.	.	.	.	M	O	D	E
Ca16	846: Sidamo	Mc	P	Mc	Fc	.	.	.	M	O	D	E
Ca17	847: Tsamai	O	O	P	O	.	M	.	M	O	N	E
Ca19	849: Banna	Mc	O	.	O	O	M	.	M	O	M	D
Ca23	853: Bako	Mc	O	Mc	Fc	O	.	.	M	O	M	E
Ca28	858: Basketo	O	O	Mc	G	.	.	.	O	O	M	N
Ca29	859: Janjero	Mc	P	Mc	Pc	.	.	.	.	O	.	.
Ca30	860: Kafa	Mc	M	Mc	Fc	.	.	.	M	Mc*	N	.
Ca31	861: Falasha	Mc	M	M	F	.	.	.	.		M	M
Ca32	862: Barea	O	O	P	F	.	.	.	.		M	E
Ca33	863: Kunama	O	O	P	F	.	.	.	.		N	E
Ca39	1090: Jimma	Mc	Mc	Mc	Fc	.	.	.	Mc	.	D	M
Cb2	21: Wolof	Mc	Mc	Mc	Fc	O	M	G	M	M	M	N
Cb3	122: Songhai	Mc	Mc	Fc	Fc	Mc	D	O	Mc	Mc	.	N
Cb4	222: Hasania	.	.	.	.	.	.	O	M	O	N	N
Cb5	321: Buduma	Mc	.	.	.	.	.	O	.	.	.	.
Cb6	355: Tera	Mc	.	.	.	.	.	O	M	D	.	E
Cb7	680: Bolewa	Mc	P	.	.	.	.	.	M	.	.	E
Cb8	681: Bororo Ful.	.	.	.	.	.	.	O	O	O	N	.
Cb9	682: Kanawa	Mc	M	.	P	.	.	O	.	O	D	N
Cb17	875: Fur	Mc	.	.	Fc	.	.	.	M	G	D	E
Cb18	876: Kanembu	Mc	M	.	Fc	.	.	.	M	.	.	N
Cb19	877: Kanuri	Mc	P	.	.	.	.	.	.	.	D	E

TABLE D. *Continued*

1	3	64	67	69	71	73	74	76	78	80–84	85–89
Aj2	119: Masai	CnE	O	D	O	O	Pe	Pe	F*	EGRRP	————
Aj3	120: Nuer	CnE	O	E	O	O	Pe	Pe	.	CGPCG	CGRDG
Aj4	219: Lango	CnE	W	O	If	P	Pp	Pp	.	CGPDG	CP..G
Aj5	220: Turkana	CnE	O	O	O	O	Pe	Pe	.	CGRDH	SGREG
Aj6	318: Luo	CnE	W	O	O	P	Pp	Pp	F*	CSPCG	————
Aj7	319: Nandi	CnE	O	O*	O	S	Pp	Pp	.	CGPCG	————
Aj8	354: Bari	CnE	W	De	O	P	Pe	Pe	P	CGPCG	————
Aj9	648: Kipsigis	CnE	O	D	O	O	Pe	Pe	F	CGPCG	————
Aj11	677: Dinka	CnE	O	O	S	.	.	Pe	.	CPPCG	————
Aj12	678: Lotuko	CnE	W	D	O	P	.	.	A	CG.CG	————
Aj15	1065: Kuku	CnE	E	D	I	P	Pp	Pp	.	CGMDG	————
Aj16	1066: Mondari	CnE	W	O	O	P	O	.	.	CP.CG	————
Aj17	1067: Alur	CnE	D	O	S	P	Pp	Pp	V	CGPCG	CGRBG
Aj18	1068: Bodi	CnE	.	.	.	Q	Pp	Pp	V	CGRBG	————
Aj19	1069: Didinga	CnE	O	.	S	P	Pp	Pp	F	CG.CG	————
Aj20	1070: Suri	CnE	.	D	Sf	P	.	.	.	CGRBG	————
Aj21	1071: Jie	CnE	W	O	O	.	.	Pe	P	CGPCG	————
Aj23	1073: Plains Suk	CnE	O	O	O	O	Pp	Pp	P	CGRDG	————
Aj24	1074: Topotha	CnE	.	O	.	P	Pe	Pe	F	CGRBG	CGRDG
Aj26	1076: Hill Suk	CnE	O	.	O	C	Qp	Qp	.	CGWCG	————
Ca1	18: Konso	AaC	O	D	O	P	Pp	.	.	CGWCG	CSSFE
Ca2	19: Somali	AaC	W	D	Hf	E	De	De	P	CGRDM	CGACG
Ca3	121: Tigrinya	AaS	Cd	D	Hf	A	Pe	Pe	.	CGACG	————
Ca4	221: Iraqw	AaC	W	.	.	O	Pe	Pe	.	CGPCG	RSWFE
Ca5	320: Bisharin	AaC	O	.	O	O	.	Pe	.	CGACG	————
Ca6	649: Afar	AaC	W	O	H	.	.	.	V	CGRDM	RGACG
Ca7	679: Amhara	AaS	C	D	Hf	A	Pe	Pe	V	CGPCG	————
Ca8	707: Gurage	AaS	.	D	.	.	Pp	Pp	.	CGWCG	————
Ca11	841: Arusi	AaC	O	D	S	E	Pp	Pp	V	CGRDG	CGOCG
Ca12	842: Gibe	AaC	D	D	H	.	Pp	Pp	V	CGPCG	————
Ca13	843: Macha	AaC	.	D	Hf	P	Pp	Pp	.	CG.CG	————
Ca14	844: Burji	AaC	O	D	If	P	.	.	V	CG.CG	————
Ca15	845: Darasa	AaC	.	D	.	P	Pe	Pe	.	CGWCG	————
Ca16	846: Sidamo	AaC	.	D	.	.	Pp	Pp	V	CGRBG	————
Ca17	847: Tsamai	AaC	O	O	.	.	.	.	E	CGWCG	————
Ca19	849: Banna	AaC	O	O	.	P	.	.	E	CGWCG	————
Ca23	853: Bako	AaC	.	D	.	P	Pp	Pp	.	CGPCG	CGMCG
Ca28	858: Basketo	AaC	D	D	.	.	Pp	Pp	.	CGPCG	————
Ca29	859: Janjero	AaC	D	D	Hf	.	.	O	.	CGPCG	————
Ca30	860: Kafa	AaC	D	D	H	.	Pp	Pp	V	CGPCG	EGPHG
Ca31	861: Falasha	AaS*	W	O	O	A	.	.	V	CGPCG	————
Ca32	862: Barea	CnE	O	O	I	O	Mp	Mp	F	CGRBG	————
Ca33	863: Kunama	CnK	O	O	I	O	Mp	Mp	F	CGRBG	CGGCG
Ca39	1090: Jimma	AaC	C	D	H	O	Pe	Pe	.	CGACG	————
Cb2	21: Wolof	NcA	Cd	D	Hf	Q	De	De	P	CGMCG	————
Cb3	122: Songhai	Xy	Ce	D	Hf	Q	De	De	P	EGRRM	QGAFE
Cb4	222: Hasania	AaS	W	.	S	.	De	De	.	RGFGF	————
Cb5	321: Buduma	AaD	O	D	Sf	O	Pe	Pe	.	CGRBG	————
Cb6	355: Tera	AaD	D	O	S	.	De	De	.	CGACG	————
Cb7	680: Bolewa	AaD	D	O	H	.	.	.	.	CGACG	RGAFE
Cb8	681: Bororo Ful.	NcA	W	.	Sf	I	O	Pe˙	F	CGRBG	————
Cb9	682: Kanawa	AaD	Dc	O˙	Hf	.	Pp	De	.	CGACP	RGAFE
Cb17	875: Fur	Xy	D	D	Sf	P	Pu	Pu	F*	CGMCG	CGSCG
Cb18	876: Kanembu	Ka	D	D	Hf	.	Pe	De	.	CGRBG	————
Cb19	877: Kanuri	Ka	D	D	S	.	De	De	E	CGPCG	CGMCG

TABLE A. *Continued*

1	3	7	12	14	16	19	20	22	24	25	27
Cb21	1079: Djafun	00091	B	Q	uP	A	L	O	O	Cc	I
Cb23	1081: Tukulor	00145	B	Ep	P	.	S	O	O	Q	.
Cb24	1082: Wodaabe	00091	B	Q	oP	D	So	O	O	Qa	.
Cb26	1084: Zazzagawa	10036	Bd	F̃q	P	S	Lo	O	O	Qc	I*
Ccl	22: Regeibat	01072	B	Fn	P	C	Po	O	O	Qa	D
Cc2	23: Teda	20035	B	Fq	uP	E	Sl	O	O	N	I
Cc3	123: Siwans	00037	B	Fn	P	D	So	O	O	Q	D
Cc4	223: Mzab	00019	B	M	Pn	S	Lo	O	O	.	.
Cc5	650: Antessar	01016	Bd	M	Va	A	O	Lo	O	Qc	I
Cc9	880: Ahaggaren	11053	B	M	uAu	A	O	Lo	O	Q	.
Cc10	881: Asben	00064	B	N	vAn	A	O	So	O	Q	.
Cc16	887: Chaamba	01072	B	P	P	.	So	O	O	Qa	D
Cc17	888: Delim	02152	B	Fn	P	A	So	O	O	Qa	D
Cc20	891: Zenaga	00073	B	M	P	.	So	O	O	Qa	.
Cd1	24: Barabra	00136	B	N	uP	A	So	O	O	Qa	D
Cd2	124: Egyptians	00136	B	Fn	uP	D	Po	O	O	Qa	D
Cd3	125: Riffians	01135	B	En	Pn	C	Sl	O	O	T	.
Cd4	224: Kabyle	00037	B	Fn	P	S	So	O	O	Q	.
Cd5	322: Shluh	10036	B	Fm	P	S	L	O	O	.	.
Cd6	876: Anc. Egyptians	00127	B	M	Nv	.	O	O	B	Q	.
Cd11	897: Guanche	00226	B	Em	V	.	O	Lo	O	Q	.
Cd12	898: Algerians	00037	B	Fn	P	S	So	O	O	Qa	D
Ce1	25: Gheg	00046	B	Fp	P	E	S	O	K	Cm	E
Ce4	225: Basques	00235	D	Gm	Bn	A	O	O	B	.	E
Ce5	611: Neapolitans	00118	O	M	Nu	D	O	O	K	S	E
Ce6	652: Spaniards	00037	O	M	N	A	O	O	B	Q	E
Ce7	708: Greeks	00136	D	M	Vn	A	O	O	K	N	E
Cf1	27: New England	00136	O	M	Nv	A	O	O	K	Q	E
Cf3	226: Tristan	10324	O	M	N	D	O	O	K	.	E
Cf4	356: Brazilians	01126	O	M	Nv	A	O	O	B	O	E
Cf5	1133: Fr. Canadians	00127	D	M	Nv	A	O	O	K	N	E
Cg1	28: Dutch	00136	O	Fm	Bn	A	O	O	K	Q	E
Cg2	29: Icelanders	02341	D	Fm	Vn	A	O	O	K	.	D
Cg3	128: Irish	01045	D	Gm	Vn	A	O	O	K	N	E
Cg4	129: Lapps	02260	O	M	Vu	E	O	O	K	S	E
Ch1	30: Serbs	00046	D	Fm	Pn	S	L	O	O	.	H
Ch2	130: Hutsul	01144	D	M	vN	D	O	O	K	.	E
Ch3	228: Czechs	00037	D	Gm	Vn	A	O	O	K	S	E
Ch4	323: Cheremis	00235	D	M	N	A	O	O	B	N	.
Ch5	357: Bulgarians	00028	O	Fm	Vn	A	O	O	B	.	D
Ch6	685: Byelorussians	00136	D	Gm	Bn	A	O	O	K	S	E
Ch7	686: Ukrainians	00136	D	Gm	Vn	D	O	O	K	N	E
Ch8	1106: Hungarians	00127	G	Em	Vn	D	O	O	K	N	E
Ch9	1134: Lithuanians	00145	D	Fm	Vn	A	O	O	K	O	E
Ci1	31: Kalmyk	01171	G	Em	Pn	C	Ps	O	O	N	O
Ci2	32: Khevsur	01135	Bd	N	oP	C	S	O	O	O	.
Ci3	131: Kumyk	00037	Bd	N	Nv	D	O	O	K	.	E
Ci4	229: Cherkess	01045	B	Fp	Pn	A	S	O	O	.	E
Ci5	653: Turks	00145	B	Gn	Vn	D	O	O	K	D	D
Ci6	908: Osset	01054	B	En	P	Cs	S	O	O	T	.
Ci7	909: Chechen	00055	B	Fp	P	C	S	O	O	.	.
Ci10	912: Armenians	00037	Bd	Em	Vu	A	O*	O	B	O	E
Ci11	913: Kurd	00145	B	N	P	D	So	O	K	Qa	Z*
Cj1	33: Syrians	00046	B	Fn	Pn	A	Lo	O	O	Qa	D
Cj2	132: Rwala	11080	B	Q	P	A	Po	O	K	Qa	D

TABLE B. *Continued*

1	3	28	30	31	32	34	35	36	37	38	39
Cb21	1079: Djafun	Cc	B	.	.	.	.	.	4	P	Bm
Cb23	1081: Tukulor	Ec	V	.	31	C	.	.	2	.	Bm
Cb24	1082: Woodabe Ful.	Cc	B	2	31	C	.	5	5	P	Bm
Cb26	1084: Zazzagawa	Jc	V	8	33	C	.	4	4	P	Bm*
Cc1	22: Regeibat	Jt	S	.	43	C	.	.	4	A	pCm
Cc2	23: Teda	Jt	S	.	31	C	.	.	5	.	Cm
Cc3	123: Siwans	Jt	X	6	41	C	P	.	4	.	Bm
Cc4	223: Mzab	Jt	V	7	30	C	.	.	3	A	Sm
Cc5	650: Antessar	Jc	B	.	31	C	.	.	4	.	Cm
Cc9	880: Ahaggaren	Jt	B*	.	33	C	.	.	3	A	Cm
Cc10	881: Asben	Jc	B*	.	32	C	.	.	9	A	Cm
Cc16	887: Chaamba	Jt	S	2	22	C	.	.	4	P	Cm
Cc17	888: Delim	Jt	B	.	33	C	.	.	4	.	pCm
Cc20	891: Zenaga	Ic	S	.	32	C	.	.	9	.	Cm
Cd1	24: Barabra	Jt	V	2	30*	C	P	.	4	.	Bm
Cd2	124: Egyptians	Jc	V	8	43	C	S	2	3	A	pBm
Cd3	125: Riffians	Ic	V	7	31	C	.	2	1	A	pBm
Cd4	224: Kabyle	Ic	V	5	43	C	.	.	9	A	pBm
Cd5	322: Shluh	Jc	H	.	41	C	.	.	9	A	pBm
Cd6	867: Anc. Egyptians	Jc	V	8	24	O	S	.	.	A	pBm
Cd11	897: Guanche	Ec	V	.	32	.	.	.	.	.	Sm
Cd12	898: Algerians	Jc	V	8	4*	C	.	.	4	A	pBm
Ce1	25: Gheg	Ic	N	4	32	C	.	.	0	A	pBm
Ce4	225: Basques	Ic	N	.	.	C	.	.	0	A	pBm
Ce5	611: Neapolitans	Ic	X	8	23	C	S	0	0	A	pBm
Ce6	652: Spaniards	Ic	V	8	23	C	S	.	0	A	pBm
Ce7	708: Greeks	Ic	V	8	23	C	.	.	0	A	pBm
Cf1	27: New England	Ic	X	8	23	C	S	1	0	A	pBm
Cf3	226: Tristan	Ir	V	3	20	C	.	.	0	A	pBm
Cf4	356: Brazilians	Ic	V	8	24	C	.	.	0	A	pBm
Cf5	1133: Fr. Canadians	Ic	V	8	23	C	S	.	0	A	pBm
Cg1	28: Dutch	Ic	V	8	33	C	S	.	0	A	pBm
Cg2	29: Icelanders	Cc	V	.	.	.	.	.	0	A	.
Cg3	128: Irish	Ir	N	8	22	C	S	.	0	A	pBm
Cg4	129: Lapps	O	B	1	20	C	A	2	0	A	Dm
Ch1	30: Serbs	Ic	X	8	33	C	S	.	0	A	pBm
Ch2	130: Hutsul	Ic	N	7	.	C	B*	.	0	A	pBm
Ch3	228: Czechs	Ic	V	8	23	C	S	.	0	A	pBm
Ch4	323: Cheremis	Ic	H	5	31	C	.	.	.	.	pBm
Ch5	357: Bulgarians	Ic	V	8	33	C	.	1	0	A	pBm
Ch6	685: Byelorussians	Ir	V	7	34	C	S	.	0	A	pBm
Ch7	686: Ukrainians	Ic	V	8	34	C	.	.	0	A	pBm
Ch8	1106: Hungarians	Ic	V	8	33	C	S	.	0	A	pBm
Ch9	1134: Lithuanians	Ic	V	8	33	C	S	.	0	A	pBm
Ci1	31: Kalmyk	Cc	S	.	43	.	.	.	.	A	Bm
Ci2	32: Khevsur	Ic	V	.	20	.	.	.	.	.	pBm
Ci3	131: Kumyk	Ic	V	.	.	C	.	.	9	.	pBm
Ci4	229: Cherkess	Ic	H	.	31	C	.	.	9	S	pBm
Ci5	653: Turks	Ic	V	8	23	C	S	.	9	A	pBm
Ci6	908: Osset	Ic	V	.	31	C	.	.	0	.	pBm
Ci7	909: Chechen	Ic	V	.	.	C	.	.	9	.	pBm
Ci10	912: Armenians	Ic	V	8	33	C	.	.	0	.	pBm
Ci11	913: Kurd	Jc	T	.	32	C	.	.	4	A	pBm
Cj1	33: Syrians	Jc	V	8	32	C	S	.	2	A	pBm
Cj2	132: Rwala	O	B	.	31	C	A	.	3	A	Cm

TABLE C. *Continued*

1	3	42	44	46	48	50	52	54	56	58	60	62
Cb21	1079: Djafun	.	.	.	.	.	.	F	M	O	D	O
Cb23	1081: Tukulor	Mc	Mc	Mc	.	.	.	.	M	M	M	N
Cb24	1082: Wodaabe	.	.	P	.	.	.	O	O	O	N	.
Cb26	1084: Zazzagawa	Mc	D	Mc	M	.	M	.	M	M	N	N
Cc1	22: Regeibat	Mc	F	P	.	O	F	.	M	Mc	N	M
Cc2	23: Teda	Mc	O	Mc	P	O	.	F	M	O	D	E
Cc3	123: Siwans	O*	F	Mc	F	O	.	O	O	O	M	M
Cc4	223: Mzab	Mc	P	P	.	.	.	O	O	O	N	M
Cc5	650: Antessar	Mc	.	Mc	.	O	.	.	M	O	M	*
Cc9	880: Ahaggaren	Mc	O	F	F	O	F	F	M	O	M	*
Cc10	881: Asben	Mc	.	.	.	.	.	.	M	O	M	*
Cc16	887: Chaamba	.	F	Mc	P	O	.	F	M	O	M	*
Cc17	888: Delim	Mc	F	Mc	.	O	F	.	M	Mc	N	M
Cc20	891: Zenaga	Mc	.	P	.	O	.	.	O	M	M	M
Cd1	24: Barabra	Mc	.	.	.	P	.	.	O	M	E	M
Cd2	124: Egyptians	Mc	Mc	Mc	Mc	P	.	O	O	Mc	N	N
Cd3	125: Riffians	Mc	D	Mc	D	M	M	O	M	M	D	M
Cd4	224: Kabyle	Mc	.	.	.	P	.	F	O	O	.	E
Cd5	322: Shluh	Mc	.	Mc	.	O	.	F	M	.	M	N
Cd6	867: Anc. Egyptians	Mc	Mc	.	Mc	P	.	.	M	.	M	N
Cd11	897: Guanche	O	.	.	.	O	.	.	M	M	.	D
Cd12	898: Algerians	Mc	P	P	P	.	.	.	.	.	D	M
Ce1	25: Gheg	Mc	F	Mc	D	P	M	F	O	O	N	E
Ce4	225: Basques	Mc	.	.	.	.	.	O	O	M	M	M
Ce5	611: Neapolitans	Mc	Ii	N	Ii	M	M	O	M	D	D	D
Ce6	652: Spaniards	Mc	Ii	Mc	Ii	P	M	O	M	M	M	N
Ce7	708: Greeks	Mc	Ii	.	Ii	P	Mc	O	O	M	Mc	D
Cf1	27: New England	Mc	Ii	Ii	Ii	Mc	Mc	O	M	Mc	M	M
Cf3	226: Tristan	M	O	M	O	M	M	M	M	M	D	M
Cf4	356: Brazilians	Mc	Ii	M	F	.	M	.	M	M	N	N
Cf5	1133: Fr. Canadians	Mc	Ii	Ii	Ii	P	.	.	M	M	D	N
Cg1	28: Dutch	Mc	Ii	Ii	Ii	Ii	Mc	O	O	Mc	N	N
Cg2	29: Icelanders	M	.	.	.	.	.	O	M	M	.	N
Cg3	128: Irish	Mc	.	.	.	.	M	O	M	O	N	N
Cg4	129: Lapps	O	F	F	O	O	M	F	M	E	E	O
Ch1	30: Serbs	Mc	F	P	Mc	P	Mc	O	M	O	G	E
Ch2	130: Hutsul	Mc	F	M	P	.	M	O	M	.	D	N
Ch3	228: Czechs	Mc	Ii	Ii	Ii	P	Mc	O	M	O	F	E
Ch4	323: Cheremis	Mc	.	P	.	.	M	.	M	.	.	D
Ch5	357: Bulgarians	Mc	F	P	P	P	M	O	M	M	E	E
Ch6	685: Byelorussians	Mc	Ii	.	P	P	.	.	M	M	E	N
Ch7	686: Ukrainians	Mc	Ii	.	P	P	.	F	M	M	G	N
Ch8	1106: Hungarians	Mc	F	.	P	.	.	O	.	.	.	N
Ch9	1134: Lithuanians	Mc	Ii	P	P	P	.	.	M	Mc	G	N
Ci1	31: Kalmyk	Mc	.	F	.	O	E	F	M	O	N	M
Ci2	32: Khevsur	Mc	.	.	.	.	.	.	M	M	N	G
Ci3	131: Kumyk	Mc	F	.	P	.	O	.	O	.	.	.
Ci4	229: Cherkess	Mc	.	.	.	.	.	O	M	O	M	N
Ci5	653: Turks	Mc	P	P	P	P	.	.	M	M	N	N
Ci6	908: Osset	Mc	.	P	.	.	.	.	M	.	.	G
Ci7	909: Chechen	Mc	F	P	.	.	.	.	M	.	.	N
Ci10	912: Armenians	Mc	P	.	.	.	.	.	M	.	D	N
Ci11	913: Kurd	Mc	Nc	P	F	O	Mc	O	M	M	N	N
Cj1	33: Syrians	Mc	Ii	P	F	.	N	O	M	O	N	N
Cj2	132: Rwala	Mc	F	F	.	O	F	F	M	O	M	O

TABLE D. *Continued*

1	3	64	67	69	71	73	74	76	78	80–84	85–89
Cb21	1079: Djafun	NcA	O	O	S	.	O	Pp	.	CGRBG	————
Cb23	1081: Tukulor	NcA	D	D	Hf	I	Pp	De	F	CGACG	————
Cb24	1082: Wodaabe Ful.	NcA	O	O	.	P	O	Pe	F	CGRDG	————
Cb26	1084: Zazzagawa	AaD	Cd	D	Sf	Q	De	De	P	CGACG	————
Cc1	22: Regeibat	AaS	Ce	Cd	H	E	De	De	.	RGF.F	————
Cc2	23: Teda	Ka	D	D	If	S	De	De	V	EGSCG	RGFRF
Cc3	123: Siwans	AaB	W	.	Hf	O	De	De	E	RGSFE	————
Cc4	223: Mzab	AaB	D	E	Sf	O	.	.	V	QGSFE	————
Cc5	650: Antessar	AaB	E	Ed	Hf	E	.	Pe	F	RGHHH	CGRBG
Cc9	880: Ahaggaren	AaB	E	D	H	N	Np	De	P	EGAFE	RGAFE
Cc10	881: Asben	AaB	E	D	H	N	Mp	De	.	RGMRH	CGRBM
Cc16	887: Chaamba	AaS	E	D	Hf	P	.	.	.	EGFRF	RGSFE
Cc17	888: Delim	AaS	E	D	H	.	De	De	.	RGF.F	————
Cc20	891: Zenaga	AaS	E	D	H	E	Pp	De	.	*	————
Cd1	24: Barabra	CnN	W	.	H	.	De	De	.	QGAFE	CGSCM
Cd2	124: Egyptians	AaS	Ce	C	Sf	E	De	De	V	RGSFE	————
Cd3	125: Riffians	AaB	W	DeO	O	O	Pe	Pe	P	QGSFE	————
Cd4	224: Kabyle	AaB	O	.	If	E	Pe	De	.	RGPGT	————
Cd5	322: Shluh	AaB	O*	O*	O*	E	De	De	V	RESFE	————
Cd6	867: Anc. Egyptians	AaE	C	.	H	P	Pp	Ce	F	QGSFE	————
Cd11	897: Guanche	AaB	D	D	O	M	Me	Me	.	RGSFE	————
Cd12	898: Algerians	AaS	Ce	D	H	O	De	De	V	QGSFE	RGA.G
Ce1	25: Gheg	IeA	O	.	O	P	Pe	Pe	V	REWGW	RESGT
Ce4	225: Basques	Xx	C	O	O	.	Cp	Ce	.	R....	————
Ce5	611: Neapolitans	IeR	C	O	O	E	De	Ce	P	RESFS	RGSFS
Ce6	652: Spaniards	IeR	C	.	O	A	Ce	Ce	V	RESGT	————
Ce7	708: Greeks	IeH	C	O	O	E	Ce	Ce	.	RGSHT	————
Cf1	27: New England	IeG	C	O	O	E	Ce	Ce	P	REWGW	————
Cf3	226: Tristan	IeG	O	O	O	O	Ce	Ce	P	RESGG	————
Cf4	356: Brazilians	IeR	C	E	Hf	E	Ce	Ce	P	RGAGT	————
Cf5	1133: Fr. Canadians	IeR	C	O	O	E	Pq	.	V	REWGW	————
Cg1	28: Dutch	IeG	C	O	O	E	Ce	Ce	T	RESGT	————
Cg2	29: Icelanders	IeG	Ew	O	H	.	Pe	Pe	.	R....	————
Cg3	128: Irish	IeC	C	O	O	.	Pq	Pq	V	RGSGG	————
Cg4	129: Lapps	UrF	W	O	O	.	Pu	Ce	A	RGFGF	————
Ch1	30: Serbs	IeS	C	O	O	E	.	.	V	QEPHT	————
Ch2	130: Hutsul	IeS	W	O	O	.	Pe	Pe	F	RGPHG	————
Ch3	338: Czechs	IeS	C	O	O	.	Pe	Pe	.	RG...	————
Ch4	323: Cheremis	UrF	E	O	O	.	Cu	Cu	.	RGWGG	————
Ch5	357: Bulgarians	IeS	C	O	O	.	De	De	.	RGAHT	————
Ch6	685: Byelorussians	IeS	C	.	O	.	Pe	Pe	.	RGWGG	————
Ch7	686: Ukrainians	IeS	C	O	O	E	Pu	Pe	.	RG...	————
Ch8	1106: Hungarians	UrF	C	O	O	.	.	.	V	RG...	————
Ch9	1134: Lithuanians	IeB	C	D*O	O	C	Pe	Pe	.	RG...	————
Ci1	31: Kalmuk	AlM	D	O	.	P	O	Pe	.	CGFDF	————
Ci2	32: Khevsur	Gr	O	O	O	O	Pe	Pe	.	RESFE	————
Ci3	131: Kumyk	AlT	.	.	.	.	.	.	.	RESFE	————
Ci4	229: Cherkess	Ak	D	O	Sf	P	De	De	.	RGP.G	————
Ci5	653: Turks	AlT	C	.	O	E	Ce	Ce	V	RG...	————
Ci6	908: Osset	IeP	D	.	H	P	Pe	Pe	.	QGSFE	————
Ci7	909: Chechen	Cl	.	.	.	.	.	.	.	RGSFE	————
Ci10	912: Armenians	IeM	W	.	O	E	Pe	De	.	.....	————
Ci11	913: Kurd	IeP	D	O	O	P	Pe	.	V	RGSFE	RGFGF
Cj1	33: Syrians	AaS	Ec	.	O	E	.	.	.	QEADP	QEAGG
Cj2	132: Rwala	AaS	W	D	H	.	O	Pe	V	RGFGF	————

TABLE A. *Continued*

1	3	7	12	14	16	19	20	22	24	25	27
Cj3	230: Hebrews	01136	B	Fp	P	.	Po	O	O	Q	E
Cj4	413: Babylonians	00226	Td	M	B	.	O	O	B	.	.
Cj5	414: Mutair	01090	B	N	P	D	So	O	O	Qa	D
Cj7	417: Lebanese	00127	O	M*	Pn	D	Lo	O	O	S*	D
Cj8	914: Druze	00019	B	Fm	P	S	Lo	O	O	Qa	D
Cj10	1091: Madan	20323	B	Fq	P	S	So	O	O	Qa	D
Ea1	34: Sindhi	00235	Bd	Fn	P	D	Lo	O	O	Q	D
Ea2	133: Pathan	00037	B	N	P	A	Po	O	K	Qa	H
Ea3	231: Hazara	00055	Bd	Fn	P	A	Po	O	O	Qa	D
Ea4	232: Kohistani	11044	B	N	P	S	Po	O	O	.	D
Ea5	324: Nuri	01036	B	Fq	P	A	S	O	O	O	.
Ea6	358: Basseri	01081	Bs	N	Pn	D	Po	O	O	Qa	.
Ea7	709: Moghol	00046	B	Fn	P	D	So	O	O	Q	D*
Ea8	1107: Bakhtiari	01081	B	.	P	C	So	O	O	.	D
Ea9	1135: Iranians	00037	B	En	Vn	A	Lo	O	O	Qa	D
Eb1	35: Kazak	01081	Bd	Fp	P	C	Ps	O	O	N	O
Eb2	36: Monguor	00136	B	Fn	P	S	S	O	O	C	.
Eb3	134: Khalka	01081	Bd	Gm	Pn	A	Sl	O	K	N	O
Eb7	687: Chahar	01081	B	Em	P	A	Sl	O	O	E	O
Ec1	37: Gilyak	23500	B	N	P	S	S	O	O	Mm	I
Ec2	38: Yakut	12241	Gs	Fq	uP	C	P	O	O	T	S
Ec3	135: Chukchee	02350	S	Gq	uVu	A	O	O	B	Q	E
Ec4	136: Yurak	03340	Bd	Fn	P	E	P	O	O	Tm	E*
Ec5	235: Koryak	11530	S	En	uVu	A	O	O	B	S	E
Ec6	236: Yukaghir	15400	Sx	Gn	uUv	E	O	O	B	S	.
Ec7	325: Ainu	23401	O	Fn	Vu	D	O*	L	O	T	D*
Ec8	360: Ket	03610	B	M	Vn	.	S	O	O	.	.
Ec9	1108: Goldi	03412	B	Fn	P	.	S	O	O	E	.
Ec10	1109: Ob Ostyak	03430	B	N	P	A	S	O	O	N	O
Ed1	39: Koreans	00226	O	Gm	Pn	E	S	O	O	O	E
Ed2	40: Lolo	01036	B	N	oP	C	P	O	O	Cm	D
Ed3	137: Manchu	00127	Bx	Em	P	C	S	O	O	C	I
Ed4	138: Miao	01126	B	Fn	P	S	S	O	K	Cc	H
Ed5	237: Japanese	00217	O	Gm	Vn	A	O	O	K	Q	E
Ed6	238: Min Chinese	00127	B	Fn	P	D	Sl	O	O	Ě	H
Ed7	326: Okinawans	00226	Td	Gm	Pn	A	So	O	K	S	E
Ed8	361: Minchia	00127	B	Fn	P	D	Lo	O	O	Q	D*
Ed9	710: Li	01117	B	Gn	oP	E	So	O	O	.	.
Ed10	1110: Shantung	00127	D	Fm	P	S	S	O	O	T	D
Ee1	41: Abor	02224	Bs	N	Vn	A	Ms	O	O	M	.
Ee2	139: Burusho	00046	Td	Fn	P	A	S	O	O	O	H
Ee3	140: Lepcha	01036	B	Fn	P	E	S	O	O	N	H
Ee4	239: Tibetans	00046	Db	Go	P	A	S	O	O	T	E
Ee5	327: Dard	01036	B	Ep	P	A	S	O	O	O	D
Ee6	630: Sherpa	00055	D	O	P	A	S	O	O	S	O
Ef1	42: Santal	01117	B	Fn	P	E	S	O	O	O	D
Ef5	327: Bhil	11125	B	Fn	P	E	S	O	O	N	D
Ef6	362: Oraon	00127	B	Fn	P	E	S	O	O	O	H
Ef7	612: Pahari	00046	B	Fn	P	A	S	O	K	O	H
Ef8	1092: Kashmiri	10126	B	Fn	P	A	Po	O	O	Q	H
Ef9	1136: Gujarati	00127	Bd	N	P	T	P	O	O	Čc	H
Eg1	43: Chenchu	81010	B	M	B	E	P	O	O	Cm	I
Eg2	44: Tamil	00226	D	Fn	P	A	L	O	O	Cc	I
Eg3	142: Maria Gond	21025	B	Er	P	C	P	O	O	Cc	I
Eg4	143: Toda	10090	T	O	P	C	S	S	O	Cc	I

TABLE B. *Continued*

1	3	28	30	31	32	34	35	36	37	38	39
Cj3	230: Hebrews	Jc	V	.	32	C	.	.	1	.	pBm
Cj4	413: Babylonians	Jc	V	8	23	O	.	.	.	.	pBm
Cj5	414: Mutair	O	B	.	31	C	.	.	4	.	Cm
Cj7	417: Lebanese	It	V	8	33	C	.	.	.	.	pBm
Cj8	914: Druze	Ic	V	5	31	C	A	2	5	A	pBm
Cj10	1091: Madan	Jc	V	7	4*	C	.	.	9	.	pBm
Ea1	34: Sindhi	Jc	V	8	33	C	.	.	9	A	pBm
Ea2	133: Pathan	Jc	V	5	42	C	.	.	3	.	pBm
Ea3	231: Hazara	Jc	T	3	31	C	.	.	9	A	pBm
Ea4	232: Kohistani	Jc	T	.	31	C	.	.	3	A	pBm
Ea5	324: Nuri	Jc	V	5	31	*	.	.	.	A	pBm
Ea6	358: Basseri	Cc	B	5	21	C	S	.	2	A	Sm
Ea7	709: Moghol	Jc	H	3	3*	C	.	.	3	A	pBm
Ea8	1107: Bakhtiari	Jc	B	.	32	C	.	.	9	.	Bm
Ea9	1135: Iranians	Jc	V	8	34	C	S	.	9	A	pBm
Eb1	35: Kazak	C	S	2	33	C	S	.	4	P	Em*
Eb2	36: Monguor	Ic	H	.	31	.	.	.	0	A	pBm
Eb3	134: Khalka	C	S	1	33	.	.	.	0	A	pBm
Eb7	687: Chahar	C	T	3	32	O	.	.	0	A	pBm
Ec1	37: Gilyak	O	S	2	20	A	.	.	0	A	O
Ec2	38: Yakut	Cc	S	2	32	B	S	.	0	A	Bm
Ec3	135: Chukchee	O	B	1	30	B	C	1	0	A	Do
Ec4	136: Yurak	O	B	1	30	B	.	2	0	A	Do
Ec5	235: Koryak	O	T	3	30	B	A	2	0	A	Do
Ec6	236: Yukaghir	O	S	1	30	.	.	1	0	A	O
Ec7	325: Ainu	Ec	T	1	31	O	A	2	0	A	O
Ec8	360: Ket	O	S	2	20	.	.	.	0	.	Do
Ec9	1108: Goldi	Ec	V	.	31	.	.	.	0	.	P
Ec10	1109: Ob Ostyak	O	S	.	30	.	.	.	0	A	Do
Ed1	39: Koreans	Jc	V	8	32	O	S	.	0	A	pBo
Ed2	40: Lolo	Ic	V	3	30	O	.	.	0	A	pBo
Ed3	137: Manchu	Ic	V	.	4*	.	.	.	0	.	pBo
Ed4	138: Miao	Jc	H	.	41	.	.	.	0	A	Bo
Ed5	237: Japanese	Jc	X	8	34	.	S	1	0	A	pBm
Ed6	238: Min Chinese	Jc	V	8	34	.	C	1	0	A	pBo
Ed7	326: Okinawans	Ir	V	8	32	O	C	.	0	A	pBo
Ed8	361: Minchia	Jc	V	5	41	O	.	.	0	A	pBm
Ed9	710: Li	Ic	V	3	32	O	B	.	0	A	pBo
Ed10	1110: Shantung	Ir	V	8	44	.	S	.	0	A	pBo
Ee1	41: Abor	Ec	V	3	30	O	A	.	0	T	Bo
Ee2	139: Burusho	Jc	V	4	41	C	Q	5	9	A	pBm
Ee3	140: Lepcha	Ic	N	3	31	B	A	0	0	A	pBm
Ee4	239: Tibetans	Jc	V	7	34	O	.	.	0	O	pBm
Ee5	327: Dard	Ic	T	5	32	O	S	1	0	A	pBm
Ee6	630: Sherpa	Ic	T	4	32	O	.	.	0	A	pBm
Ef1	42: Santal	Jc	V	.	31	A	.	.	0	A	pBo
Ef5	327: Bhil	Ic	N	2	31	B	A	2	0	A	pBm
Ef6	362: Oraon	Ic	V	.	41	.	.	.	0	T	pBm
Ef7	612: Pahari	Ic	V	8	44	O	.	.	0	A	pBm
Ef8	1092: Kashmiri	Jc	V	8	43	C	A	2	3	A	pBm
Ef9	1136: Gujarati	Ic	V	8	33	O	.	.	0	A	pBm
Eg1	43: Chenchu	Cc	T	1	30	O	O	1	0	A	Bm
Eg2	44: Tamil	Jc	V	8	43	.	.	.	0	A	pBm
Eg3	142: Maria Gond	Ec	V	2	31	B	.	1	0	T	So
Eg4	143: Toda	O	T	1	31	O	A	2	0	A	Bm

TABLE C. *Continued*

1	3	42	44	46	48	50	52	54	56	58	60	62
Cj3	230: Hebrews	Mc	P	.	.	.	.	O	M	M	N	M
Cj4	413: Babylonians	Mc	P	P	P	P	.	.	.	.	M	M
Cj5	414: Mutair	Mc	F	.	.	O	F	O	M	O	M	O
Cj7	417: Lebanese	Mc	Ii*	.	P	P	Mc	.	.	M	.	M
Cj8	914: Druze	Mc	O	Mc	F	O	M	E	M	O	N	N
Cj10	1091: Madan	Mc	Mc	.	.	Mc	M	N	.	M	G	N
Ea1	34: Sindhi	Mc	P	Mc	P	.	.	.	Mc	.	M	M
Ea2	133: Pathan	Mc	Mc	.	P	.	.	O	O	O	N	M
Ea3	231: Hazara	Mc	P	F	P	.	N	O	O	O	N	N
Ea4	232: Kohistani	Mc	Mc	P	Mc	.	M	E	M	O	D	D
Ea5	324: Nuri	Mc	Mc	M	.	O	Mc	.	M	O	M	G
Ea6	358: Basseri	Mc	F	P	O	O	E	F	M	O	N	.
Ea7	709: Moghol	Mc	F	.	.	O	M	.	O	O	N	M
Ea8	1107: Bakhtiari	Mc	D	.	.	O	Mc	.	M	O	N	M
Ea9	1135: Iranians	Mc	D	P	P	.	Mc	O	O	.	D	N
Eb1	35: Kazak	Mc	F	P	O	O	F	O	M	O	N	E
Eb2	36: Monguor	Mc	Mc	P	O	O	.	O	M	M	D	E
Eb3	134: Khalka	Mc	O	M	O	O	N	O	M	O	D	M
Eb7	687: Chahar	Mc	.	M	.	O	M	.	M	O	D	M
Ec1	37: Gilyak	Mc	O	F	O	P	M	F	M	M	O	O
Ec2	38: Yakut	Mc	Mc	F	F	M	M	F	M	M	N	F
Ec3	135: Chukchee	Mc	O	F	P	P	D	F	M	M	N	O
Ec4	136: Yurak	O	O	F	O	P	F	F	M	M	O	O
Ec5	235: Koryak	Mc	O	F	P	M	.	F	M	N	M	O
Ec6	236: Yukaghir	O	.	.	.	.	.	.	M	M	O	O
Ec7	325: Ainu	O	F	E	O	M	N	F	M	D	O	F
Ec8	360: Ket	.	.	.	.	.	.	.	M	M	M	O
Ec9	1108: Goldi	.	.	.	.	.	.	O	M	D	.	F
Ec10	1109: Ob Ostyak	.	.	P	F	P	.	.	M	M	M	O
Ed1	39: Koreans	Mc	F	P	M	P	M	O	M	M	N	E
Ed2	40: Lolo	Mc	P	P	O	.	M	O	M	O	E	E
Ed3	137: Manchu	Mc	P	.	P	.	.	F	O	F	N	N
Ed4	138: Miao	Mc	F	.	P	.	M	O	M	M	F	N
Ed5	237: Japanese	Mc	Ii	.	Ii	P	Mc	O	O	Mc	M	E
Ed6	238: Min Chinese	Mc	P	.	P	.	.	.	O	M	G	M
Ed7	326: Okinawans	Mc	G	.	N	Mc	N	O	O	M	D	E
Ed8	361: Minchia	Mc	F	P	.	M	Mc	O	O	M	.	E
Ed9	710: Li	O	F	M	F	O	.	.	M	M	D	D
Ed10	1110: Shantung	Mc	P	.	P	.	.	O	O	.	M	E
Ee1	41: Abor	Mc	F	O	P	O*	M	G	M	E	N	N
Ee2	139: Burusho	Mc	Mc	P	P	O	N	O	O	O	M	E
Ee3	140: Lepcha	O	F	P	O	O	M	F	M	O	E	E
Ee4	239: Tibetans	Mc	Mc	P	.	P	.	O	M	Mc	D	E
Ee5	327: Dard	Mc	Mc	Pc	Pc	O*	M	O	M	O	N	G
Ee6	630: Sherpa	Mc*	F	N	.	O	Mc	O	.	O	N	D
Ef1	42: Santal	Mc	Mc	.	P	.	D	F	M	M	N	E
Ef5	327: Bhil	Mc	O	P	P	P	M	G	M	E	N	N
Ef6	362: Oraon	.	.	.	.	.	M	F	M	N	N	D
Ef7	612: Pahari	Mc	Mc	.	O	.	Mc	.	O	M	G	N
Ef8	1092: Kashmiri	Mc	Mc	Ec	Mc	Mc	Mc	G	M	Mc	M	N
Ef9	1136: Gujarati	Mc	Ec	Mc	Mc	.	.	O	O	F	N	E
Eg1	43: Chenchu	O	O	O	O	O*	N	E	M	M	N	M
Eg2	44: Tamil	Mc	Mc	Mc	Mc	.	Mc	O	O	.	M	N
Eg3	142: Maria Gond	O	O	.	O	M	D	G	M	M	N	D
Eg4	143: Toda	O	O	.	O	O	M	F	O	O	M	O

TABLE D. *Continued*

1	3	64	67	69	71	73	74	76	78	80–84	85–89
Cj3	230: Hebrews	AaS	W	O	I	.	.	Pe	V	.....	
Cj4	413: Babylonians	AaS	C	O	H	.	Pe	Pe	V	RGAFE	
Cj5	414: Mutair	AaS	.	O	H	.	De	De	V	RGFFF	————
Cj7	417: Lebanese	AaS	C	O	O	E	Pe	Pe	.	RGSFE	RGSHT
Cj8	914: Druze	AaS	O	O	H	A	De	De	V	RGSFE	————
Cj10	1091: Madan	AaS	D	D	Hf	A	Pe	.	.	RGMRM	————
Ea1	34: Sindhi	IeI	E	C	.	.	Pe	.	V	RGA..	————
Ea2	133: Pathan	IeP	C	D	Sf	I	De	De	.	RGSFE	————
Ea3	231: Hazara	IeP*	W	D	S	P	Pp	Pp	V	QEAFE	CESFG
Ea4	232: Kohistani	IeI	E	C	.	O	De	De	.	RGSFE	————
Ea5	324: Nuri	IeI	W	D	H	P	Pe	Pe	.	QGAFE	————
Ea6	358: Basseri	IeP	W	D	O	P	O	Pe	V	RGFFF	RGFGF
Ea7	709: Moghol	AlM	W	D	.	C	Pe	De	V	RGAGP	RGFRF
Ea8	1107: Bakhtiari	IeP	D	.	H	P	.	.	.	RGFFF	————
Ea9	1135: Iranians	IeP	Ec	.	Hf	A	.	.	V	RGA..	————
Eb1	35: Kazak	AlT	D	O	Hf	.	O	Pu	P	CGFDF	QGAFE
Eb2	36: Monguor	AlM	D	.	S	P	Pe	Pe	A	RGA.G	————
Eb3	134: Khalka	AlM	D	O	Hf	P	Pe	Pe	.	CGFCF	————
Eb7	687: Chahar	AlM	Dw	O	Hf	.	O	.	.	RGA.T	————
Ec1	37: Gilyak	Xx	O	O	O	Q	O	Pe	P	RSWFE	RPWGG
Ec2	38: Yakut	AlT	W	O	Sf	E	Qp	Pe	F	RSRHE	CGRCB
Ec3	135: Chukchee	Lu	W	O	If	I	O	Pe	F	CGHCH	CGRCG
Ec4	136: Yurak	UrS	W	O	O	.	.	.	E	CGRCG	————
Ec5	235: Koryak	Lu	W	O	If	S	P.	Pe	V	PSWFE	CSRCW
Ec6	236: Yukaghir	Xx	O	O	If	S	O	Pu	.	CGRCG	RGWHW
Ec7	325: Ainu	Xx	O	O	O	P	.	Pe	F	RGGGG	————
Ec8	360: Ket	Xx	O	O	O	O	O	Pu	.	RSEFE	CGRCB
Ec9	1108: Goldi	AlG	O	O	S	.	.	.	.	CGBCH	————
Ec10	1109: Ob Ostyak	UrU	W	O	Sf	.	.	De	.	CGRCB	RSW.E
Ed1	39: Koreans	Xx	C	D	Hf	S	Pp	Pp	P	REWHG	QEWHG
Ed2	40: Lolo	Tb	D	.	H	P	Pe	Pe	F	RG..W	————
Ed3	137: Manchu	AlG	W	O	If	E	Pu	Pu	.	RGA.W	————
Ed4	138: Miao	My	O	O	O	A	Pe	Pe	.	REWGT	————
Ed5	237: Japanese	Jr	C	D	O	E	Pp	Pp	V	REWHG	REWHT
Ed6	238: Min Chinese	Si	C	O	If	A	Pe	Pe	.	R....	————
Ed7	326: Okinawans	Jr	Dc	O	O	E	Pp	Pp	P	REWHG	REWHT
Ed8	361: Minchia	Tb*	W	O	O	E	Pe	Pe	V	QESGT	RGSGG
Ed9	710: Li	Tk	W	O	.	P	Pe	Pe	F	RPWRG	————
Ed10	1110: Shantung	Si	C	O	.	A	Pe	Pe	.	RG...	————
Ee1	41: Abor	Tb	W	O	H	O	Pu	Pe	F	RPWGG	————
Ee2	139: Burusho	Xx	C	D	.	.	.	.	V	RGFSE	————
Ee3	140: Lepcha	Tb	W	.	Hf	P	Pe	Pe	F	RGMGG	RPMGG
Ee4	239: Tibetans	Tb	C	.	S	E	Pq	Pq	V	RGSFE	————
Ee5	327: Dard	IeI	D	C	H	.	Pe	Pe	.	RGSFE	————
Ee6	630: Sherpa	Tb	W	De	Hf	C	Pe	Pe	F	RGSGW	*
Ef1	42: Santal	MkM	O	O	O	P	Pe	Pe	V	QGAGG	————
Ef5	327: Bhil	IeI	C	C	O	P	Pe	Pe	P	RGPGW	CGRBG
Ef6	362: Oraon	Dr	.	C	If	E	Pe	Pe	.	RGPGG	————
Ef7	612: Pahari	IeI	C	C	O	E	Pe	Pe	E	RGSGG	————
Ef8	1092: Kashmiri	IeI	C	C	.	.	Pe	Pe	E	RESGG	————
Ef9	1136: Gujarati	IeI	C	C	.	.	Pe	Pe	E	RG...	————
Eg1	43: Chenchu	Dr	O	O	O	C	Pe	Pe	F	CGMCG	CGRCG
Eg2	44: Tamil	Dr	C	C	O	.	.	Pe	.	GRPGG	————
Eg3	142: Maria Gond	Dr	W	C*	O	P	O	O	F	RGPGG	————
Eg4	143: Toda	Dr	O	O	O	C	O	Pe	F	RGRRG	————

TABLE A. *Continued*

1	3	7	12	14	16	19	20	22	24	25	27
Eg5	242: Coorg	01126	O	Fm*	P	T	S	O	O	Cc	I
Eg6	243: Kerala	00136	O*	En	O*	A	O	S	O	Cm	I
Eg7	329: Hill Bhuiya	11125	B	M	P	C	S	O	O	C	H
Eg8	363: Kol	10027	B	Fn	P	E	O	O	R*	O	H
Eg9	654: Baiga	11206	B	P	P	C	S	O	O	C	I
Eg10	688: Telugu	00037	D	Fn	P	A	S	O	O	Cm	I
Eg13	1137: Muria Gond	12115	Bs	Fn	P	A	P	O	O	Cc	I
Eh1	45: Andamanese	42400	O	M	B	A	O	O	B	O	E*
Eh2	46: Merina	00127	T	N	V	A	Po	E	O	C*	H
Eh3	144: Tanala	00226	T	Fq	P	T	Sl	E	O	Cc	I*
Eh4	145: Vedda	43300	T	Fm	Mn	C	O	S	O	Cp	I
Eh5	244: Nicobarese	11215	O	N	Uv	A	O	O	B	S	E
Eh6	245: Sinhalese	00136	D	M*	Vu	A	O	O	Q*	Cm	I
Eh7	613: Antandroy	20143	B	Q*	Pu	D	Lo	O	O	S	H
Eh8	614: Sakalava	00154	O	Eq	P	C	L	O	O	O	H
Ei1	47: Garo	00118	O	Gn	Ma	A	O	M	O	Cm	I
Ei2	48: Lhota	11125	Bs	P	uPn	S	Ps	O	O	Mm	O
Ei3	146: Burmese	00226	D	M*	Uv	D	O	O	K	Q	H
Ei4	147: Lakher	02116	B	N	P	A	So	O	O	Em	O
Ei5	246: Kachin	11026	B	Fn	Pn	S	Sl	O	O	Mm	I*
Ei6	247: Purum	01027	Sd	Gn	uP	A	Sl	O	O	Mm	S
Ei7	364: Karen	01216	O	M	U	A	O	O*	B	S	E
Ei8	365: Khasi	11125	O	Em	M	S	O	Sl	O	C	I
Ei9	417: Mogh	01126	B	N	P	A	S	O	O	Cc	I*
Ei10	418: Chakma	01126	B	N	Pn	C	Sl	O	O	N	D
Ei11	419: Aimol	02125	Sb	N	P	A	Ml	O	O	Mm	Z*
Ei13	421: Angami	01126	T	M	P	S	Ms	O	O	.	O
Ei14	422: Ao	01126	T	M	P	S	P	O	O	O	O
Ei16	424: Sema	01225	B	N	P	S	S	O	O	Mm	O
Ei18	426: Palaung	00028	B	N	Vn	D	O	O	B	.	E
Ei19	711: Chin	02116	B	N	Pn	A	Sl	O	O	M	O
Ej1	49: Lamet	12025	Bs	N	uPn	S	S	O	O	Mm	O
Ej2	50: Mnong Gar	10225	G	N	M	S	O	S	O	Mm*	C
Ej3	148: Semang	43300	O	N	uV	E	O	O	B	O	H
Ej4	149: Annamcse	00226	T	Fp	P	S	S	O	O	O	H
Ej5	248: Cambodians	10216	B	N*	uNb	A	O	O	K	Q	E
Ej6	249: Selung	11800	O	N	uNv	A	O	O	B	.	E
Ej7	330: Akha	12115	O	N	P	A	L	O	O	O	I*
Ej8	366: Malays	00226	B	Fn	uVn	A	O	O	K	Q	H
Ej9	367: Siamese	00217	T	Gn	Un	A	O	O	K	Q	H
Ej10	456: Rhade	01018	D	En	M	S	O	P	O	C	C
Ej11	712: Cham	00118	T	Gn	M	A	O	L	O	O	H
Ej12	1094: Lawa	00118	B	Gm	Pu	S	L	O	O	Mm	.
Ej13	1112: Muong	01225	B	Fn	uP	C	S	O	O	N	.
Ej14	1138: Senoi	11206	O	En	B	A	O	O	K	O	H
Ia1	51: Atayal	02116	B	Gm	Vu	A	Lo	O	R	N	H
Ia2	52: Sagada	00037	G	M	B	A	O	O	Kr	S	E
Ia3	150: Ifugao	02116	B	M	B	A	O	O	Kr	N	H
Ia4	151: Subanun	00019	Bs	N	uBn	A	O	O	K	Q	H
Ia5	250: Hanunoo	10117	S	N	Uv	A	O	O	K	Ň	E
Ia6	331: Paiwan	02116	B	Gn	Vu	D	O	O	Rk	N	H
Ia7	368: Tagbanua	01117	St*	N	Uv	D	O	O	K	N	E
Ia9	1095: Ami	01117	O*	Fm	M	S	O	Sl	O	N	E
Ia10	1096: Bunun	03016	B	Fm	P	S	P	O	O	N	H*
Ia11	1097: Puyuma	01117	O	M	Uv	D	O	O	R	N	E

TABLE B. *Continued*

1	3	28	30	31	32	34	35	36	37	38	39
Eg5	242: Coorg	Ic	H	3	42	O	A	2	0	A	pBm
Eg6	243: Kerala	Jc	N	8	42	.	.	.	0	R	pBm
Eg7	329: Hill Bhuiya	Er	W	2	21	A	A	*	0	T	pBo
Eg8	363: Kol	Ic	V	.	31	.	.	.	0	A	pBo
Eg9	654: Baiga	Ec	W	2	20	.	.	1	0	T	O
Eg10	688: Telugu	Jc	V	8	43	O	.	.	0	A	pBm
Eg13	1137: Muria Gond	Ec	V	.	3.	A	A	5	0	T	pBo
Eh1	45: Andamanese	O	S	1	20	O	A	.	0	T	O
Eh2	46: Merina	Jc	V	7	33	.	A	.	2	A	Bo
Eh3	144: Tanala	Jc	V	3	41	A	Q	1	3	A	Bm
Eh4	145: Vedda	O	S	1	30	O	Õ	1	0	A	O
Eh5	244: Nicobarese	Ht	H	1	30	.	A	.	0	A	P
Eh6	245: Sinhalese	Jc	V	8	33	.	.	.	0	A	pBm
Eh7	613: Antandroy	Ec	T	.	21	A	Q	.	5	A	Bm
Eh8	614: Sakalava	Er*	H	4	33	A	.	.	5	A	Bm
Ei1	47: Garo	Ec	V	3	31	A	O	.	0	P	Bo
Ei2	48: Lhota	Ec	V	.	30	O	A	.	0	T	Bo
Ei3	146: Burmese	Jc	V	8	23	O	.	.	0	A	pBo
Ei4	147: Lakher	Ec	V	.	31	C	Q	.	0	S	Bo
Ei5	246: Kachin	Ec	V	3	41	B	.	.	0	A	Bo
Ei6	247: Purum	Ec	V	2	30	O	.	2	0	S	qBo
Ei7	364: Karen	Jc	V	.	30	A	O	.	0	.	Bo
Ei8	365: Khasi	Ec	V	2	41	A	A	.	0	T	Bo
Ei9	417: Mogh	Ec	V	.	31	.	.	.	.	.	qBo
Ei10	418: Chakma	Ec	V	.	21	.	.	.	0	A	qBm
Ei11	419: Aimol	Ec	V	2	30	A	.	.	0	T	Bo
Ei13	421: Angami	Jc	V	6	30	O	C	.	0	T	Bo
Ei14	422: Ao	Ec	V	5	20	B	.	.	0	T	Bo
Ei16	424: Sema	Ec	V	4	30	A	.	.	0	S	Bo
Ei18	426: Palaung	Ec	V	2	21	O	.	.	0	.	Bo
Ei19	711: Chin	Ec	V	.	31	O	.	.	0	A	Bo
Ej1	49: Lamet	Ec	V	2	30	O	.	.	0	T	Bo
Ej2	50: Mnong Gar	Ec	W	3	30	O	.	.	0	A	Bo
Ej3	148: Semang	O	B	1	20	B	A	4	0	A	O
Ej4	149: Annamese	Jc	V	8	34	O	S	4*	0	A	pBo
Ej5	248: Cambodians	Jc	V	8	23	O	.	.	0	A	pBo
Ej6	249: Selung	O	B*	.	20	.	.	.	0	A	O
Ej7	330: Akha	Ec	W	4	20	O	.	.	0	.	Bo
Ej8	366: Malays	Jc	V	.	32	C	.	.	9	A	pBo
Ej9	367: Siamese	Jc	V	8	34	O	S	.	0	A	pBo
Ej10	456: Rhade	Ec	H	.	30	O	.	2	0	A	Bo
Ej11	712: Cham	Jc	H	5	32	O	.	.	0	.	pBo
Ej12	1094: Lawa	Ec	V	4	31	O	.	.	0	A	pBo
Ej13	1112: Muong	Jc	N	.	32	O	.	.	0	A	pBo
Ej14	1138: Senoi	Ec	W	2	30	O	O	4	0	A	O
Ia1	51: Atayal	Ec	V	3	31	O	A	.	0	A	P
Ia2	52: Sagada	Jc	V	6	30	O	A	2	0	P	pBo
Ia3	150: Ifugao	Jc	H	3	30	O	.	.	0	S	P
Ia4	151: Subanun	Ec	N	1	20	O	.	.	0	A	P
Ia5	250: Hanunoo	Ec	H	3	20	.	.	.	0	A	Bo
Ia6	331: Paiwan	Ec	V	4	31	O	A	.	0	R	P
Ia7	368: Tagbanua	Ec	V	.	20	.	.	.	0	A	Bo
Ia9	1095: Ami	Jc	V	5	30	O	.	.	0	T	pBo
Ia10	1096: Bunun	Ec	N	.	30	A	.	.	0	.	P
Ia11	1097: Puyuma	Jc	V	5	20	.	.	.	0	T	pBo

TABLE C. *Continued*

1	3	42	44	46	48	50	52	54	56	58	60	62
Eg5	242: Coorg	Mc	.	.	.	O	M	O	M	M	.	M
Eg6	243: Kerala	Mc	.	.	.	.	.	O	M	Mc	N	N
Eg7	329: Hill Bhuiya	.	O	.	P	.	M	F	M	N	M	E
Eg8	363: Kol	Mc	O	.	.	O	N	G	O	O	N	N
Eg9	654: Baiga	.	.	.	P	.	.	F	M	E	O	E
Eg10	688: Telugu	Mc	Pc	Mc	Mc	.	Mc	O	Mc	M	D	N
Eg13	1137: Muria Gond	O	O	.	O	O	N	G	M	M	D	N
Eh1	45: Andamanese	O	O	O	F	M	G	G	M	D	O	O
Eh2	46: Merina	Mc	F	O	.	.	Mc	E	M	G	M	G
Eh3	144: Tanala	Mc	F	M	O*	M	M	O	M	N	M	D
Eh4	145: Vedda	O	O	P	E	O	.	D	M	M	O	O
Eh5	244: Nicobarese	Mc	O	.	Fc	M	M	F	M	M	F	M
Eh6	245: Sinhalese	Mc	.	.	D	P	.	.	.	.	.	N
Eh7	613: Antandroy	Mc	F	.	O	O	M	.	M	G	M	E
Eh8	614: Sakalava	Mc	F	P	O	P	M	O	M	N	M	E
Ei1	47: Garo	O	F	O	F	O*	M	E	M	D	D	D
Ei2	48: Lhota	Mc	F	O	F	.	M	O	M	M	M	N
Ei3	146: Burmese	Mc	F	.	Mc	M	Mc	O	Mc	Mc	M	N
Ei4	147: Lakher	Mc	F	O	F	.	M	O	M	M	D	E
Ei5	246: Kachin	Mc	.	.	P	.	M	F	M	O	G	N
Ei6	247: Purum	Mc	F	O	O	.	.	O	M	O	D	E
Ei7	364: Karen	O	F	.	O	.	M	N	M	E	.	E
Ei8	365: Khasi	Mc	F	P	Fc	P	M	F	M	E	N	G
Ei9	417: Mogh	O	F	.	O	.	M	O	M	N	N	D
Ei10	418: Chakma	O	F	.	O	.	M	.	M	N	N	D
Ei11	419: Aimol	Mc	F	.	F	O	M	.	M	M	.	E
Ei13	421: Angami	Mc	F	O	P	O	.	O	M	N	.	E
Ei14	422: Ao	Mc	F	O	F	O	M	O	M	M	.	E
Ei16	424: Sema	Mc	F	.	F	O	.	O	M	M	.	E
Ei18	426: Palaung	Mc	F	.	.	.	M	O	O	O	N	E
Ei19	711: Chin	Mc	F	.	M	.	.	.	M	N	.	E
Ej1	49: Lamet	O	O	.	O	.	N	F	M	M	D	E
Ej2	50: Mnong Gar	Mc	F	.	F	.	N	F	M	E	E	O
Ej3	148: Semang	O	O	O	O	O*	F	D	M	M	O	O
Ej4	149: Annamese	Mc	Pc	.	Pc	M	Mc	.	.	N	.	N
Ej5	248: Cambodians	Mc	F	.	P	.	M	.	.	N	F	E
Ej6	249: Selung	O	O	.	.	M	.	O	M	N	O	O
Ej7	330: Akha	Mc	F	.	.	.	.	E	M	E	E	G
Ej8	366: Malays	Mc	F	.	P	M	M	.	M	M	N	E
Ej9	367: Siamese	Mc	G	.	P	Mc	N	O	E	M	E	E
Ej10	456: Rhade	Mc	F	M	O	O	E	F	M	M	E	N
Ej11	712: Cham	Mc	F	.	.	.	.	O	O	.	.	N
Ej12	1094: Lawa	Mc	F	.	.	.	M	O	M	E	N	D
Ej13	1112: Muong	Mc	F	.	Pc	.	Mc	F	M	N	.	D
Ej14	1138: Senoi	O	O	O	O	O*	.	D	M	D	O	D
Ia1	51: Atayal	Mc	F	P	P	.	M	M	M	M	F	G
Ia2	52: Sagada	Mc	F	O	O	O	M	O	M	E	Nb	E
Ia3	150: Ifugao	Mc	F	O	D	.	.	.	.	G	.	G
Ia4	151: Subanun	.	.	.	.	.	M	M	M	.	.	E
Ia5	250: Hanunoo	Mc	F	.	.	O	.	G	M	N	N	G
Ia6	331: Paiwan	Mc	F	P	P	.	.	.	M	M	F	G
Ia7	368: Tagbanua	Mc	.	.	.	.	.	.	M	N	.	E
Ia9	1095: Ami	Mc	F	.	P	.	.	.	M	M	N	E
Ia10	1096: Bunun	Mc	O	.	P	.	.	.	M	O	F	G
Ia11	1097: Puyuma	Mc	F	P	P	.	.	.	M	M	N	G

TABLE D. *Continued*

1	3	64	67	69	71	73	74	76	78	80–84	85–89
Eg5	242: Coorg	Dr	C	C	Hf	P	Pe	Pe	V	RGSHG	————
Eg6	243: Kerala	Dr	C	C	O	N	.	.	.	QEAGT	REAGG
Eg7	329: Hill Bhuiya	MkM	.	.	O	P	.	Pe	F	RGWGG	————
Eg8	363: Kol	MkM	.	C	O	C	Pe	Pe	.	RGAGG	————
Eg9	654: Baiga	McM	O	O	O	.	.	Pe	F	RGWGG	————
Eg10	688: Telugu	Dr	C	C	O	.	Pe	Pe	P	RGPGG	RGSGT
Eg13	1137: Muria Gond	Dr	O	O	O	.	.	.	F	RGPGG	————
Eh1	45: Andamanese	Xy	O	O	O	C	O	.	F	RGOSG	————
Eh2	46: Merina	Mp	D	O	Hf	A*	Ce	Ce	F	RGMGG	RGAGG
Eh3	144: Tanala	Mp	D	O	Hf	E	Pe	Ce	F	REMGG	————
Eh4	145: Vedda	IeI	O	O	O	.	Pe	Pe	P	*	RG.GG
Eh5	244: Nicobarese	MkK	O	O	O	C	O	Ce	F	CPRBG	RP.GG
Eh6	245: Sinhalese	IeI	C	C	O	.	Ce	Ce	F	RGPGG	RGAGT
Eh7	613: Antandroy	Mp	D	O	Hf	Q	Pp	Pe	V	RGWGG	RGGSG
Eh8	614: Sakalava	Mp	D	O	Hf	Q	.	.	F	RGMGG	————
Ei1	47: Garo	Tb	W	O	Sf	M	O	M*	A	REMGG	————
Ei2	48: Lhota	Tb	W	O	Hf	Q	Pe	Pe	.	REWGG	————
Ei3	146: Burmese	Tb	C	O	Sf	A	Ce	Ce	P	RPWGG	————
Ei4	147: Lakher	Tb	D	O	H	P	Pp	Pp	A	RPMGG	————
Ei5	246: Kachin	Tb	D	O	Sf	P	Pu	Pu	A	REMGG	————
Ei6	247: Purum	Tb	W	O	.	O	Pu	Pu	V	RPWGG	————
Ei7	364: Karen	Tb	W	O	If	P	Ce	Ce	.	RPWGG	————
Ei8	365: Khasi	McK	C	.	O	M	N.	N.	.	EEWGG	————
Ei9	417: Mogh	Tb	.	.	.	.	Pp	Pp	.	RPWGG	————
Ei10	418: Chakma	IeI	.	O	Hf	.	Pe	Pe	.	RPWGG	————
Ei11	419: Aimol	Tb	W	O	O	E	Pp	Pp	A	RPWGG	————
Ei13	421: Angami	Tb	W	O	I	P	Pe	Pe	P	RGWGG	————
Ei14	422: Ao	Tb	W	O	Hf	O	Qe	Qe	F	RPMGG	————
Ei16	424: Sema	Tb	De	O	O	.	Pe	Pe	V	RPWGG	————
Ei18	426: Palaung	MkK	W	O	.	Q	.	.	F	RPWGG	————
Ei19	711: Chin	Tb	D	O	H	P	Pu	Pu	.	RPWGG	————
Ej1	49: Lamet	MkK	W	O	O	P	O	Pe	F	RPWSW	————
Ej2	50: Mnong Gar	MkC	W	O	I	O	.	Ce	.	EGWGG	————
Ej3	148: Semang	MkS	O	O	O	P	O	Ce	P	RGRSG	————
Ej4	149: Annamese	Am	C	O	Sf	E	Ce	Ce	V	QEPGG	QESGT
Ej5	248: Cambodians	MkC	Cd	O	Sf	E	Pe	Ce	V	RPWGG	————
Ej6	249: Selung	Mp	O	O	O	.	.	.	.	*	————
Ej7	330: Akha	Tb	O	O	O	Q	Pp	Pe	F	RPWHG	————
Ej8	366: Malays	Mp	D	O	If	.	Pe	Ce	V	RPMGG	————
Ej9	367: Siamese	Tk	C	O	Hf	E	Ce	Ce	V	RPWGG	REWGT
Ej10	456: Rhade	Mp	W	O	O	M	*	.	.	RPWGG	————
Ej11	712: Cham	Mp	D	O*	.	E	Nu*	Nu*	.	RPWGG	————
Ej12	1094: Lawa	MkK	D	O	.	S	.	.	P	RPWGG	————
Ej13	1112: Muong	Am	De	O	O	P	Pp	.	.	RPWGG	————
Ej14	1138: Senoi	MkS	O	O	O	O	O	O	F	RPWGG	————
Ia1	51: Atayal	Mp	O	O	If	E	Pu	Pu	V	RGWGG	————
Ia2	52: Sagada	Mp	W	O	O	O	Ce	Ce	F	REWHG	————
Ia3	150: Ifugao	Mp	W	O	Hf	O	Cp	Cp	F	RPMHG	————
Ia4	151: Subanun	Mp	O	O	O	O	O	Ce	.	RPGGG	————
Ia5	250: Hanunoo	Mp	O	O	O	O	O	Ce	.	REWHG	————
Ia6	331: Paiwan	Mp	D	O	O	P	Cp	Cp	.	RGS.S	————
Ia7	368: Tagbanua	Mp	D	O	If	O	Ce	Ce	.	R....	————
Ia9	1095: Ami	Mp	O	O	.	E	M.	M.	.	RP.GG	————
Ia10	1096: Bunun	Mp	O	O	.	P	P.	P.	.	RGWGG	————
Ia11	1097: Puyuma	Mp	D	O	.	C	.	.	.	RG.GG	————

TABLE A. *Continued*

1	3	7	12	14	16	19	20	22	24	25	27
Ia12	1098: Sugbuhanon	00217	B	M	N	A	O	O	B	O	E
Ia13	1099: Tawi-Tawi	00802	B	M	B	A	O	O	K	Q	E
Ia14	1100: Yami	00415	O	M	V	A	O*	O	K	O	E
Ia16	1139: Kalinga	02116	O	M	Un	A	O	O	K	S	E
Ib1	53: Iban	00226	O	Gm	B	A	O	O	K	Q	E
Ib2	54: Javanese	00127	T	Gn	uUv	A	O	O	Kr	Q	E
Ib3	152: Balinese	00136	T	Fn	Vu	D	O	O	R*	Qa	H
Iv4	153: Batak	00127	B	Fn	Pu	A	S	O	O	Mm	S
Ib5	251: Dusun	01225	B	N	Vu	D	O	O	Kr	N	E
Ib6	252: Minangkabau	00127	O	En	Om	S	O	Ps	O	Cc	H
Ib7	369: Mentaweians	01216	S	M	Vu	S	O	O	S*	T*	E*
Ib8	1114: Kubu	33202	St	N	uB	.	O	O	B	N	.
Ic1	55: Macassarese	00226	B	N	Bn	S	O	O	R	Q	E
Ic2	154: Alorese	20017	Bd	N	Vu	E	So	O	K	N	H
Ic3	155: Belu	00037	B	Ep	M	S	O	L	O	Mm	H*
Ic5	254: Toradja	02026	B	Em	U	A	O	O	B	S	H
Ic6	332: Tanimbarese	11215	Bs	Fn	uP	A	L	O	O	Cm	H
Ic7	1115: Ili-Mandiri	01315	Bx	Fn	Pu	S	S	O	O	Cm	.
Ic8	1116: Kei	11215	B	En	Pu	.	S	O	O	Mm	.
Ic9	1117: Sumbanese	01027	G	Gn	P	C	S	O	O	Mm	.
Ic10	1118: Tobelorese	11206	B	Em	Vu	E	O	O	B	O	.
Ic11	1140: Ambonese	00316	B	M	Vn	S	L	O	K	N	.
Id1	56: Aranda	64000	D	R	P	C	M	M	O	Rr	I
Id2	156: Murngin	53200	S	R	uP	C	M	M*	O	Mm	S
Id3	157: Tiwi	53200	Bs	Fp	Vu	A	O	P	O	Ss	I
Id4	255: Dieri	73000	X	R	V	E	O	M	O	Rr	I
Id5	256: Kariera	35200	X	R	P	C	M	M*	O	Cc	I
Id6	333: Wikmunkan	44200	D	R	P	C	M	O	O	Mm*	I
Id8	1141: Tasmanians	44200	O*	N	.	E	.	.	.	.	.
Id9	1142: Wongaibon	33400	X	N	P	C	M	M	O	Rr	I
Ie1	57: Kapauku	01126	B	Fp	P	C	Ps	O	O	Ss	I
Ie2	58: Wantoat	02017	X	Q	P	C	Sl	O	K*	Cc	I
Ie3	158: Arapesh	21016	O	P	P	S	Ml	O	O	O	O
Ie4	159: Wogeo	20215	G	P	P	T	L	M	O	S*	I
Ie5	247: Keraki	01117	X	P	P	C	M	O	O	O	I
Ie6	258: Waropen	31312	G	En	P	S	Sl	O	O	Mm	I
Ie7	334: Enga	01027	B	N	Pu	Cs	Ps	O	O	O	I
Ie8	371: Purari	41212	B	P	P	S	M	O	O	N	H
Ie9	457: Orokaiva	21215	B	N	P	S	S	O	O	C	I
Ie10	631: Motu	10405	Bs	F.	Pu	S	L	O	K	N	H
Ie11	632: Kakoli	11017	Gb	Gn	P	C	P	O	O	R	I
Ie12	655: Kwoma	32014	B	P	P	Cs	L	O	O	S	O
Ie13	656: Kiwai	12205	X	En*	P	S	L	O	O	S	I
Ie14	657: Miriam	00316	X	N	P	C	S	O	O	N	I
Ie15	690: Abelam	21016	Bx	N	P	S	S	O	O	O	I
Ie16	691: Kutubu	41014	B	Ep	Op*	A	P	O	O	O	I
Ie17	713: Siane	11017	B	*	Op*	Cs	P	O	O	O	I
Ie18	1101: Kimam	21106	Xb	Fn	Vu	S	L*	O	K	N	H
Ie19	1119: Marindanim	12214	X	M*	Op	S	Ms	O	O	N	Z*
Ie20	1143: Koita	12115	B	N	P	A	S	O	O	N	H
Ie21	1144: Mailu	10315	G	Fm	P	S	L	O	O	.	H*
Ie22	1145: Mekeo	11116	B	Fp	P	S	P	O	O	O	H
Ie23	1146: Muju	11125	B	Fn	P	C	L	O	O	O	I
Ie24	1147: Koiari	12016	B	P	P	S	L	O	O	O	H
Ie25	1148: Mafulu	01117	B	P	bP	S	L	O	O	O	.

TABLE B. *Continued*

1	3	28	30	31	32	34	35	36	37	38	39
Ia12	1098: Sugbuhanon	Jc	V	8	24	C	.	2	0	A	pBo
Ia13	1099: Tawi-Tawi	Hr	B*	4	20	.	.	.	9	A	So
Ia14	1100: Yami	Er	V	4	20	.	.	.	0	.	So
Ia16	1139: Kalinga	Jc	H	.	21	A	O*	.	0	T	Bo
Ib1	53: Iban	Ec	V	.	30	O	A	.	0	A	P
Ib2	54: Javanese	Jc	V	8	24	C	.	2	5	A	pBo
Ib3	152: Balinese	Jc	V	.	32	.	.	.	0	A	pBo
Ib4	153: Batak	Jc	V	.	30	C	.	.	.	P	pBo
Ib5	251: Dusun	Ec	V	4	30	A	.	.	0	A	qBo
Ib6	252: Minangkabau	Jc	X	.	40	.	.	.	9	P	pBo
Ib7	369: Mentaweians	Hr	V	.	30	.	.	.	0	.	P
Ib8	1115: Kubu	Hr	B	.	20	.	.	.	0	A	O
Ic1	55: Macassarese	Jc	N	3	33	C	A	2	4	A	pBo
Ic2	154: Alorese	Ec	X	3	32	A*	.	3	0	A	P
Ic3	155: Belu	Ec	H	.	41	.	.	.	9	A	Bo
Ic5	254: Toradja	Ec	V	.	31	.	.	.	0	A	Bo
Ic6	332: Tanimbarese	Er	V	.	31	.	.	.	0	P	P
Ic7	1115: Ili-Mandiri	Ec	V	5	42	.	A	.	0	A	So
Ic8	1116: Kei	Hr	V	.	30	.	.	.	0	.	P
Ic9	1117: Sumbanese	Jc	X	.	21	.	.	.	5	A	pBo
Ic10	1118: Tobelorese	Ec	V	.	32	.	.	.	0	.	P
Ic11	1140: Ambonese	Ec	V	6	3.	C	.	.	9	A	P
Id1	56: Aranda	O	B	1	20	O	A	1	5*	P	O
Id2	156: Murngin	O	B	1	20	O	O	1	4	T	O
Id3	157: Tiwi	O	B	3	30	A	A	.	0	S	O
Id4	255: Dieri	O	B	1	21	O	A	.	4*	P	O
Id5	256: Kariera	O	B	1	20	.	.	.	0	P	O
Id6	333: Wikmunkan	O	B	1	20	.	.	.	0	.	O
Id8	1141: Tasmanians	O	B	1	20	O	O	4*	0	.	O
Id9	1142: Wongaibon	O	B	.	20	.	.	.	0	.	O
Ie1	57: Kapauku	Er	V	2	31	A	.	1	0	R	P
Ie2	58: Wantoat	Hr	V	2	30	O	A	5	0	T	P
Ie3	158: Arapesh	Hr	H	.	20	O	.	3	0	A	P
Ie4	159: Wogeo	Hr	V	2	30	O	.	5	5	T	P
Ie5	247: Keraki	Hr	T	2	30	O	A	3	0	T	P
Ie6	258: Waropen	Ht	V	.	40	.	.	.	.	.	P
Ie7	334: Enga	Er	N	4	40	.	.	.	0	P	P
Ie8	371: Purari	Ht	V	.	40	.	.	.	0	T	P
Ie9	457: Orokaiva	Hr	V	2	30	O	.	4	0	A	P
Ie10	631: Motu	Er	V	5	40	O	.	4	0	R	P
Ie11	632: Kakoli	Ir	N	4	30	A	P	5	0	P	P
Ie12	655: Kwoma	Hr	H	.	30	O	A	5	0*	O	P
Ie13	656: Kiwai	Hr	V	.	30	.	.	.	0	A	O
Ie14	657: Miriam	Hr	V	.	20	.	.	.	0	.	P
Ie15	690: Abelam	Hr	V	.	30	O	.	3	0	.	P
Ie16	691: Kutubu	Hr	V	.	40	.	.	.	0	T	P
Ie17	713: Siane	Hr	W	4	30	O	.	5*	.	T	P
Ie18	1101: Kimam	Ir	N	4	40	.	C	2*	0	T	P
Ie19	1119: Marindanim	Hr	H	4	40	O	.	2	0	T	P
Ie20	1143: Koita	Hr	V	.	30	O	.	.	0	R	P
Ie21	1114: Mailu	Hr	V	.	40	.	.	.	0	T	P
Ie22	1145: Mekeo	Hr	V	4	30	.	.	.	0	T	P
Ie23	1146: Muju	Hr	N	1	30	O	.	.	0	.	P
Ie24	1147: Koiari	Hr	V	.	30	.	.	3	0	.	P
Ie25	1148: Mafulu	Hr	H	.	30	O	A	.	0	T	P

TABLE C. *Continued*

1	3	42	44	46	48	50	52	54	56	58	60	62
Ia12	1098: Sugbuhanon	Mc	F	.	F	M	.	.	M	N	.	E
Ia13	1099: Tawi-Tawi	O	O	.	O	M	M	O	O	N	.	G
Ia14	1100: Yami	Mc	F	.	P	P	.	F	M	N	F	D
Ia15	1139: Kalinga	Mc	F	O	F	O	M	E	M	N	E	D
Ib1	53: Iban	Mc	F	O	F	M	M	E	M	N	N	E
Ib2	54: Javanese	Mc	F	O	E	O*	N	E	O	E	E	G
Ib3	152: Balinese	Mc	P	.	P	P	.	.	O	M	N	M
Ib4	153: Batak	Mc	F	.	F	P	.	O	M	.	N	E
Ib5	251: Dusun	.	P	.	P	P	.	M	M	D	D	D
Ib6	252: Minangkabau	Mc	F	.	P	P	.	.	.	M	.	E
Ib7	369: Mentaweians	O	O	O	O	P	.	O	M	N	.	D
Ib8	1114: Kubu	O	O	.	O	O	.	.	M	.	O	.
Ic1	55: Macassarese	Mc	F	.	P	P	M	O	O	M	N	N
Ic2	154: Alorese	Mc	O	.	.	.	M	G	M	O	M	G
Ic3	155: Belu	Mc	P	.	P	P	.	.	M	.	N	D
Ic5	254: Toradja	Mc	O*	O	P	P	.	.	M	.	.	E
Ic6	332: Tanimbarese	Mc	P	.	P	P	.	M	M	M	G	G
Ic7	1115: Ili-Mandiri	Mc	F	.	O	P	.	.	.	.	D	N
Ic8	1116: Kei	O	O	.	O	P	.	.	M	.	.	.
Ic9	1117: Sumbanese	Mc	.	.	P	P	.	.	M	.	.	G
Ic10	1118: Tobelorese	O	O	.	O	P	.	.	M	D	.	E
Ic11	1140: Ambonese	Mc	P	.	P	P	.	.	.	.	.	.
Id1	56: Aranda	O	O	O	O	O	F	F	M	O	O	O
Id2	156: Murngin	O	O	O	O	M	G	G	M	N	O	O
Id3	157: Tiwi	O	O	.	O	M	.	F	M	D	O	O
Id4	255: Dieri	O	O	O	O	.	.	F	M	M	O	O
Id5	256: Kariera	O	O	O	O	.	.	F	M	M	O	O
Id6	333: Wikmunkan	O	O	O	O	.	.	F	M	D	O	O
Id8	1141: Tasmanians	O	O	O	O	O*	F	F	M	F	O	O
Id9	1142: Wongaibon	O	O	O	O	.	.	F	M	.	O	O
Ie1	57: Kapauku	O	O	O	O	M	M	O	M	F	F	D
Ie2	58: Wantoat	O	O	.	O	O	.	O	M	O	F	D
Ie3	158: Arapesh	O	O	O	.	.	.	M	M	O	F	N
Ie4	159: Wogeo	O	O	O	O	M	M	G	O	N	.	D
Ie5	247: Keraki	O	O	O	O	M	M	O	M	D	F	E
Ie6	258: Waropen	O	.	.	.	.	.	N	M	M	M	G
Ie7	334: Enga	O	O	O	O	.	.	O	M	O	F	G
Ie8	371: Purari	O	O	.	O	M	M	D	M	G	F	N
Ie9	457: Orokaiva	O	O	O	F	M	.	E	M	N	E	G
Ie10	631: Motu	O	O	O	G	M	M	.	M	N	E	E
Ie11	632: Kakoli	O	O	O	O	O	M	D	M	O	F	G
Ie12	655: Kwoma	O	O	O	P	M	M	E	M	F	G	E
Ie13	656: Kiwai	O	O	.	.	P	.	D	M	N	O	E
Ie14	657: Miriam	O	O	.	.	P	.	.	M	N	.	G
Ie15	690: Abelam	O	O	O	F	.	M	.	M	.	F	D
Ie16	691: Kutubu	O	O	.	O	.	.	N	M	D	F	G
Ie17	713: Siane	O	O	.	O	O	M	B	M	O	F	G
Ie18	1101: Kimam	O	O	O	O	M	.	D	M	G	.	N
Ie19	1119: Marindanim	O	O	O	O	M	M	D	M	F	F	G
Ie20	1143: Koita	O	O	O	P	P	.	.	M	N	.	G
Ie21	1144: Mailu	O	O	.	F	M	.	.	M	D	.	E
Ie22	1145: Mekeo	O	O	O	O	O	.	.	.	E	.	E
Ie23	1146: Muju	O	O	.	O	P	.	.	M	N	F	D
Ie24	1147: Koiari	O	O	O	O	.	.	.	M	.	.	D
Ie25	1148: Mafulu	O	O	O	O	O	.	.	M	M	F	D

TABLE D. *Continued*

1	3	64	67	69	71	73	74	76	78	80–84	85–89
Ia12	1098: Sugbuhanon	Mp	C	O	O	E	Ce	Ce	.	RPWGG	————
Ia13	1099: Tawi-Tawi	Mp	W	O	O	P	.	.	.	*	RP.GG
Ia14	1100: Yami	Mp	O	O	O	O	Pe	Pe	.	RGWGG	RSGGG
Ia16	1139: Kalinga	Mp	W	O	O	C	Cp	Cp	F	RPWGG	————
Ib1	53: Iban	Mp	O	O	Hf	C	Ce	Ce	P	RPGGG	————
Ib2	54: Javanese	Mp	C	O	O	E	Ce	Ce	V	RGMGG	RGMHT
Ib3	152: Balinese	Mp	D	C	Hf	Q	.	.	.	Q.PGG	————
Ib4	153: Batak	Mp	W	O	Sf	P	Pe	Pe	F	RP.GG	————
Ib5	251: Dusun	Mp	W	O	O	C	Ce	Ce	F	RPWGG	————
Ib6	252: Minangkabau	Mp	D	O	Hf	N	O	Ne	.	RPWGG	————
Ib7	369: Mentaweians	Mp	O	O	O	O	N*	.	F	RP..G	————
Ib8	1114: Kubu	Mp	O	O	O	.	.	Ce	F	REWFG	————
Ic1	55: Macassarese	Mp	Dc	O	Hf	P	.	.	P	RPG.G	————
Ic2	154: Alorese	Mp	W	O	If	.	.	.	P	RP...	————
Ic3	155: Belu	Mp	D	E	Hf	N	O	*	.	RGWGG	————
Ic5	254: Toradja	Mp	W	O	Sf	E	Ce	Ce	.	RG.GG	RP.GG
Ic6	332: Tanimbarese	Mp	D	O	If	P	Pe	Pe	.	RPOGG	————
Ic7	1115: Ili-Mandiri	Mp	D	O	Hf	.	Pe	Pe	.	RGWHG	————
Ic8	1116: Kei	Mp	O	O	H	P	Pp	Pp	.	RP...	————
Ic9	1117: Sumbanese	Mp	D	O	H	P	Pp	Pp	.	RP.HG	————
Ic10	1118: Tobelorese	Pa	O	O	H	E	De	De	.	RP...	————
Ic11	1140: Ambonese	Mp	D	O	Hf	P	Pe	Pe	.	RG.GG	————
Id1	56: Aranda	Au	O	O	O	P	O	Pp	E	RGRSG	————
Id2	156: Murngin	Au	O	O	O	P	O	.	E	RGRRB	SGREB
Id3	157: Tiwi	Au	O	O	O	P	O	.	E	*	————
Id4	255: Dieri	Au	O	O	O	P	O	.	.	.....	————
Id5	256: Kariera	Au	O	O	O	.	O	.	.	.....	————
Id6	333: Wikmunkan	Au	O	O	O	.	O	.	.	.....	————
Id8	1141: Tasmanians	Xy	O	O	O	C	O	.	.	SGREB	CGRBG
Id9	1142: Wongaibon	Au	O	O	O	P	O	.	.	.....	————
Ie1	57: Kapauku	Pa	W	O	O	I	.	.	A	RGWGG	————
Ie2	58: Wantoat	Pa	O	O	O	I	Pe	Pe	.	RGWGG	————
Ie3	158: Arapesh	Pa	O	O	O	O	Pe	Pe	E	RE.GG	————
Ie4	159: Wogeo	Mp	O	O	O	P	Pe	Pe	A	RGGGG	————
Ie5	247: Keraki	Pa	O	O	O	O	Op	Pe	E	EGBGB	RGOGB
Ie6	258: Waropen	Mp	O	O	If	S	.	.	.	RP.HG	————
Ie7	334: Enga	Pa	O	O	O	O	Pe	Pe	V	R..GG	————
Ie8	371: Purari	Pa	O	O	O	I	Pe	Pe	.	RPWGG	————
Ie9	457: Orokaiva	Pa	O	O	O	C	.	.	A	RPWHG	————
Ie10	631: Motu	Mp	W	O	O	P	Dp	Dp	A	RPGHG	————
Ie11	632: Kakoli	Pa	Ow	O	O	C	Pe	Pq	A	EGBRG	————
Ie12	655: Kwoma	Pa	O	O	O	O	Pe	Pe	A	RGWGG	————
Ie13	656: Kiwai	Pa	O	O	O	O	.	.	.	R....	————
Ie14	657: Miriam	Pa	O	O	O	O	.	.	.	.....	————
Ie15	690: Abelam	Pa	O	O	O	O	.	Pp	.	RGRGG	————
Ie16	691: Kutubu	Pa	O	O	O	.	P.	P.	V	RG..G	RP..G
Ie17	713: Siane	Pa	W	O	O	I	Pp	O	F	CGWCG	————
Ie18	1101: Kimam	Pa	O	O	O	.	Pe	O	P	CGRBG	RGGGG
Ie19	1119: Marindanim	Pa	O	O	O	O	.	.	V	RGWGG	————
Ie20	1143: Koita	Pa	D	O	O	P	Pe	Ce	F	RPGGG	————
Ie21	1144: Mailu	Pa	O	O	O	.	Pe	Pe	.	RPGGG	————
Ie22	1145: Mekeo	Pa	D	O	O	P	Pe	.	.	RPGGG	————
Ie23	1146: Muju	Pa	O	O	O	I	Pe	Pe	.	RPWGG	————
Ie24	1147: Koiari	Pa	W	O	O	I	Ce	O	V	RPWGG	————
Ie25	1148: Mafulu	Pa	W	O	O	P	Pe	Pe	F	RPWGG	————

TABLE A. *Continued*

1	3	7	12	14	16	19	20	22	24	25	27
Ie26	1149: Ngarawapum	12016	Xb	N	P	S	L	O	O	Rr	I
Ie27	1150: Banaro	21115	X	M	P	S	S	O	O	C	H
Ia28	1151: Busama	11116	X	N	V	S	L	L	O	C	.
Ie29	1152: Manam	00316	O	N	Pn	S	L	O	O	O*	H
Ie30	1153: Mimika	41401	X	Fm	Mv	A	O	Sl	O	.	H
If1	59: Palauans	00415	B	N	vAv	S	O	Ps	S	N	H
If2	60: Trukese	00505	O	Em	Mv	S	O	S	O	S	C
If3	160: Majuro	00415	O	Em	B	S	O	S	K	C	I
If4	161: Ifaluk	00415	O	Em	B	S	O	S	K	N	H
If5	259: Ponapeans	00316	O	N	Ma	A	O	S	O	Cc	C
If6	260: Yapese	00415	O	Fm	Pa	S	L	S	O	S	C
If7	372: Onotoa	10504	B	N*	Vu	S	O	O	Rk	N	H
If8	427: Chamorro	00127	O	M	N	A	O	O	B	N	E
If9	428: Ulithians	00415	S	M	Vu	D	O	L	O	S	C
If11	430: Kusaians	00415	O	N	Vn	A	O	Sl	O	C	H
If12	431: Bikinians	00415	O	Fm	M	S	O	S	O	Cc	I
If13	432: Nauruans	00406	O	Fn	M	A	O	S	K	Cc	I
If14	633: Makin	01414	Gs	N	Vu	S	O	O	R	N	H
If15	692: Carolinians	00505	O	Em	M	S	O	S	O	N	H
Ig1	61: Siuai	21025	B	N	vAu	S	O	S	O	Cm	H
Ig2	62: Trobrianders	10315	G	N	Av	S	O	P	O	D	C
Ig3	162: Kurtatchi	11215	B	S	B	E	O	S	K	N	I
Ig4	163: Lesu	01414	B	N	M	S	O	M	O	S*	I
Ig5	261: Dobuans	00316	G	M	C*	C	O	S	O	O	I
Ig6	262: Ulawans	01306	B	N	V	S	O	O	R	O	H
Ig7	335: Lakalai	21214	Bx	Fr	vDn	S	O	P	K	Cc	I
Ig9	373: Manus	00910	G	N	Pn	S	L	L	O	Rr	Z*
Ig10	615: Usiai	20026	G	Q	P	S	L	L	O	R	C
Ig11	693: Rossel	31303	B	N	Vu	A	O	S	O	O	C
Ig12	1102: Choiseulese	11116	B*	N	Vu	S	O	O	Rk	O	H
Ig13	1154: Aua	01504	O	R*	O*	S	O	Lo	O	Q	.
Ig14	1155: Dahuni	01316	G	En	D*	A	O	S	O	O	H
Ih1	63: Mota	00316	B	R	A	S	O	Ms	O	C	C
Ih2	64: Seniang	01315	B	R	P	C	P	O	O	N	C
Ih3	164: Bunlap	10117	Xb	N	P	S	S	M	O	N*	I
Ih4	165: Lau	00415	G	Fr	oPu	C	Ps	O	O	Cc	I
Ih5	263: Ajie	00316	X	.	P	C	Ps	O	O	Cc	I
Ih6	337: Rotumans	00217	O	M	Ma	S	O	L	K	S	H
Ih7	374: Lifu	10315	Bs	Eq	P	C	L	O	O	N	H
Ih8	394: Vanua Levu	01306	G	Fn	Pu	S	L	M	O	S	I
Ih9	1156: Santa Cruz	01315	B	Fn	Vn	A	O	Ps	O	C	H*
Ih10	1157: Tannese	00217	B	N	P	C	L	O	O	Cc	I
Ii1	65: Samoans	00316	G	En	B	S	O	S	O	N	H
Ii2	66: Tikopia	00505	G	Q	P	A	Sl	O	K	S	H
Ii3	166: Pukapukans	00415	G	M	P	S	So	Sl	K	N	H*
Ii4	264: Ellice	00514	G	Fn	Vu	S	O	O	S	O	H
Ii5	265: Ontong-Java	00505	O	En	Uv	A	O	O	S	N	H
Ii6	375: Tokelau	00604	O	En	Uv	S	O	O	R	N	O
Ii7	1103: Kapingamarangi	00415	O	Fn	vB	A	O	O	K	N	H
Ii8	1120: Futunans	00316	O	Fn	bVu	.	O	O	R	S	H
Ii9	1121: Niueans	00505	O	N	Vu	S	O	O	R	S	H
Ii12	1124: Tongans	00316	O	N	Va	S	O	O	R*	O	H
Ii13	1125: Uveans	00406	O	N	Vu	.	O	O	S	N	H
Ij1	67: Mangaians	00406	O	Fr	Vu	E	O	O	S	N	H
Ij2	167: Maori	22204	G	Fp	Vu	S	O	O	Rk	S	H

TABLE B. *Continued*

1	3	28	30	31	32	34	35	36	37	38	39
Ie26	1149: Ngarawapum	Hr	V	3	40	.	.	4	0	T	P
Ie27	1150: Banaro	Hr	H	.	30	.	.	.	0	.	P
Ie28	1151: Busama	Hr	V	.	30	O	.	.	0	T	P
Ie29	1152: Manam	Hr	H	.	30	O	.	.	0	T	P
Ie30	1153: Mimika	Ht	T	3	30	.	.	.	0	.	O
If1	59: Palauans	Hr	V	.	42	O	C*	.	0	A*	P
If2	60: Trukese	Ht	H	3	30	O	C	4	0	T*	P
If3	160: Majuro	Ht	V	.	31	O	A	1	0	A	P
If4	161: Ifaluk	Ht	V	2	31	O	Q*	3	0	A	P
If5	259: Ponapeans	Hr	N	1	32	O*	.	2	0	.	P
If6	260: Yapese	Ht	N	.	31	.	.	5	0	T	P
If7	372: Onotoa	Hr	V	4	31	.	.	.	.	A	P
If8	427: Chamorro	Ec	V	5	21	C	.	1	0	A	Bm
If9	428: Ulithians	Ht	V	2	31	.	.	.	0	T	P
If11	430: Kusaians	Ht	N	.	32	A*	.	.	0	P	P
If12	431: Bikinians	Ht	V	3	31	.	.	.	0	.	P
If13	432: Nauruans	Ht	N	4	31	.	.	.	0	.	O
If14	633: Makin	Ht	X	4	31	A	A	1	4	P	P*
If15	692: Carolinians	Hr	H	.	30	.	.	3	0	T	P
Ig1	61: Siuai	Hr	H	.	30	O	.	5	0	A	P
Ig2	62: Trobrianders	Hr	V	3	21	O	A	4	0	T	P
Ig3	162: Kurtatchi	Hr	H	3	30	O	A	4	0	T	P
Ig4	163: Lesu	Hr	H	4	30	O	A	5	4	T	P
Ig5	261: Dobuans	Hr	V	.	30	.	.	4	.	P	P
Ig6	262: Ulawans	Hr	H	3	30	O	C	.	0	T	P
Ig7	335: Lakalai	Hr	H	3	40	.	.	.	0	T	P
Ig9	373: Manus	Ct	V	3	30	O	A	.	0	R	P
Ig10	615: Usiai	Hr	V	2	30	O	A	.	0	T	P
Ig11	693: Rossel	Ht	V	1	30	A	.	4	0	.	P
Ig12	1102: Choiseulese	Hr	H	.	30	O	.	.	.	T	P
Ig13	1154: Aua	Hr	V	.	31	.	.	.	.	T	O
Ig14	1155: Dahuni	Hr	H	4	40	O	.	3	9	T	P
Ih1	63: Mota	Hr	V	.	30	O	A	.	0	T	P
Ih2	64: Seniang	Hr	V	.	20	.	A	.	0	T	P
Ih3	164: Bunlap	Hr	V	2	30	O	A	4	3	T	P
Ih4	165: Lau	Hr	V	2	32	O	A	4	5	T	P
Ih5	263: Ajie	Jr	V	.	31	.	.	.	.	.	P
Ih6	337: Rotumans	Hr	V	.	31	.	.	.	.	A	P
Ih7	374: Lifu	Hr	V	.	31	.	.	.	.	T	P
Ih8	394: Vanua Levu	Hr	V	2	41	O	.	.	5	.	P
Ih9	1156: Santa Cruz	Hr	V	.	40	.	.	.	.	T	P
Ih10	1157: Tannese	Hr	V	.	21	.	.	.	9	T	P
Ii1	65: Samoans	Hr	V	2	42	A	C	4	4	A	P
Ii2	66: Tikopia	Hr	H	5	31	O	A	.	5	A	O
Ii3	166: Pukapukans	Ht	V	3	31	A	A	1	0	A*	P
Ii4	264: Ellice	Ht	V	.	31	.	A	2	.	T	P
Ii5	265: Ontong-Java	Ht	T	.	40	O	.	.	.	A	O
Ii6	375: Tokelau	Ht	V	.	31	.	.	5	5	T	O
Ii7	1103: Kapingamarangi	Hr	V	.	31	O	.	3	0	T	P
Ii8	1120: Futunans	Hr	V	.	31	O	A	.	5	T	P
Ii9	1121: Niueans	Hr	V	4	31	O	A	.	5	.	O
Ii12	1124: Tongans	Hr	V	.	32	O	C	2	5	A	P
Ii13	1125: Uveans	Hr	V	.	32	O	C	.	5	T	P
Ij1	67: Mangaians	Hr	N	.	41	O	A	.	6	A	O
Ij2	167: Maori	Er	V	.	41	A	A	.	0	.	O

TABLE C. *Continued*

1	3	42	44	46	48	50	52	54	56	58	60	62
Ie26	1149: Ngarawapum	O	O	O	O	O	.	.	M	.	.	N
Ie27	1150: Banaro	O	O	.	.	.	M	M	M	.	.	F
Ie28	1151: Busama	O	O	.	F	M	M	.	M	M	.	G
Ie29	1152: Manam	O	O	.	.	M	M	.	M	N	.	G
Ie30	1153: Mimika	O	O	.	O	P	.	D	M	D	O	.
If1	59: Palauans	O	F	.	F*	M	M	O	O	N	.	G
If2	60: Trukese	O	F	O	O	M	M	O	O	D	F	N
If3	160: Majuro	O	O	O	O	M	M	O	O	N	.	N
If4	161: Ifaluk	O	F	O	O	Mc	M	F	O	N	F	D
If5	259: Ponapeans	O	F	O	O	Mc	N	O	O	N	.	N
If6	260: Yapese	O	F	O	.	Mc	M	O	O	N	F	G
If7	372: Onotoa	O	O	O	O	M	M	E	O	N	O	E
If8	427: Chamorro	Mc	O	O	O	M	Mc	O	O	M	.	E
If9	428: Ulithians	O	.	O	O	M	M	.	.	M	.	G
If11	430: Kusaians	O	F	O	O	M	M	O	O	D	.	M
If12	431: Bikinians	O	O	O	O	P	.	O	O	D	M	M
If13	432: Nauruans	O	O	O	O	P	.	O	M	D	O	E
If14	633: Makin	O	O	O	O	M	M	O	Mb	N	E	G
If15	692: Carolinians	O	F	O	.	M	M	O	O	M	.	F
Ig1	61: Siuai	O	O	O	G	O	N	G	M	D	G	E
Ig2	62: Trobrianders	O	O	O	P	M	N	F	M	N	F	D
Ig3	162: Kurtatchi	O	O	O	F	M	M	G	M	N	F	G
Ig4	163: Lesu	O	O	O	O	M	M	O	M	N	F	G
Ig5	261: Dobuans	O	O	.	.	P	.	O	M	N	.	E
Ig6	262: Ulawans	O	O	O	O	Mc	M	O	M	N	F	E
Ig7	335: Lakalai	O	O	.	.	M	M	N	M	D	F	E
Ig9	373: Manus	O	O	.	P	M	M	F	O	N	G	O
Ig10	615: Usiai	O	O	O	O	O	M	N	M	O	G	G
Ig11	693: Rossel	O	O	O	O	M	M	N	M	M	.	G
Ig12	1102: Choiseulese	O	O	.	P	.	.	.	M	.	.	D
Ig13	1154: Aua	O	.	.	.	M	.	.	M	N	O	N
Ig14	1155: Dahuni	O	O	O	F	M	M	.	M	D	.	D
Ih1	63: Mota	O	O	.	O	M	.	O	O	N	N	.
Ih2	64: Seniang	O	O	O	O	M	.	O	M	N	N	E
Ih3	164: Bunlap	O	O	.	O	P	.	.	.	.	M	N
Ih4	165: Lau	O	O	O	F	M	M	G	M	D	M	G
Ih5	263: Ajie	O	O	.	.	.	.	.	.	.	.	G
Ih6	337: Rotumans	O	O	.	.	P	.	O	O	D	.	M
Ih7	374: Lifu	O	O	.	.	P	M	N	O	N	.	F
Ih8	394: Vanua Levu	O	O	O	.	.	M	F	M	G	E	N
Ih9	1156: Santa Cruz	O	Mc	.	O	Mc	M	.	M	N	E	G
Ih10	1157: Tannese	O	O	.	.	P	.	.	M	.	.	E
Ii1	65: Samoans	O	O	O	O	M	Mc	O	O	D	E	G
Ii2	66: Tikopia	O	O	O	O	Mc	M	O	O	D	O	D
Ii3	166: Pukapukans	O	O	O	O	M	M	N	O	D	E	F
Ii4	264: Ellice	O	O	O	O	Mc	N	O	O	D	.	N
Ii5	265: Ontong-Java	O	M	O	O	Mc	D	O	O	M	O	G
Ii6	375: Tokelau	O	O	O	O	P	.	O	O	D	O	M
Ii7	1103: Kapingamarangi	O	F	O	O	M	M	O	M	N	.	F
Ii8	1120: Futunans	O	O	O	O	Mc	M	.	.	G	F	M
Ii9	1121: Niueans	O	O	O	O	M	M	.	O	D	O	E
Ii12	1124: Tongans	O	O	O	O	M	M	.	.	N	M	N
Ii13	1125: Uveans	O	O	O	O	Mc	Mc	.	O	D	F	M
Ij1	67: Mangaians	O	O	O	O	M	M	O	O	N	O	F
Ij2	167: Maori	O	P	.	O	M	Mc	N	M	N	O	N

TABLE D. *Continued*

1	3	64	67	69	71	73	74	76	78	80–84	85–89
Ie26	1149: Ngarawapum	Pa	O	O	O	C	Pe	.	.	CGRBG	———
Ie27	1150: Banaro	Pa	O	O	O	O	O	O	.	R....	———
Ie28	1151: Busama	Mp	W	O	O	I	M.	P.	V	RPMGG	———
Ie29	1152: Manam	Mp	O	O	O	P	Pp	.	.	RP...	———
Ie30	1153: Mimika	Pa	O	O	O	.	.	.	.	RGMGG	———
If1	59: Palauans	Mp	Dw	O	O	N	Np	Pe	F	RPGGG	REWGG
If2	60: Trukese	Mp	O	O	O	N	Pe*	Pe	F	RGGHG	———
If3	160: Majuro	Mp	D	O	O	N	*	Pe*	F	RGGGG	RPWGG
If4	161: Ifaluk	Mp	O	O	O	N	*	*	F	RGWGG	RGMGG
If5	259: Ponapeans	Mp	D	O	O	N	Ne	Ne	F	REMGG	———
If6	260: Yapese	Mp	C*	C*	O	N	Qp	Pe	F	REMGG	———
If7	372: Onotoa	Mp	W	O	If	E	De	Ce	V	REMGG	———
If8	427: Chamorro	Mp	O	O	O	E	Ce	Ce	V	RPWGG	———
If9	428: Ulithians	Mp	O	O	O	N	*	Ce	.	RG..G	———
If11	430: Kusaians	Mp	D	O	O	.	.	.	F	RE.GG	———
If12	431: Bikinians	Mp	O	O	O	O	.	.	.	RG...	———
If13	432: Nauruans	Mp	D	O	O	.	.	.	.	.....	———
If14	633: Makin	Mp	D	O	O	S*	De	Pe	V	RGOGG	REOGG
If15	692: Carolinians	Mp	O	O	O	.	.	.	F	RGGGG	RPWGG
Ig1	61: Siuai	Pa	W	O	O	I	N*	Ce	P	RPGGG	RGGGG
Ig2	62: Trobrianders	Mp	D	O	O	M	Me	Me	F	RGWGG	———
Ig3	162: Kurtatchi	Mp	Dw	O	O	M	*	*	A	RGRRG	RPWGG
Ig4	163: Lesu	Mp	O	O	O	I	.	Me	.	RGWGG	———
Ig5	261: Dobuans	Mp	O	O	O	O	M*	M*	F	RPMGG	———
Ig6	262: Ulawans	Mp	O	O	O	P	Ce	Ce	V	RGWGG	———
Ig7	335: Lakalai	Mp	W	O	O	C	.	Ce	.	R....	———
Ig9	373: Manus	Mp	W	O	O	O	O	O	V	RP.GG	———
Ig10	615: Usiai	Mp	O	O	O	.	.	.	.	R....	———
Ig11	693: Rossel	Pa	W	O	O	P	.	.	.	RGRRG	RGOGG
Ig12	1102: Choiseulese	Mp	W	O	I	P	P.	P.	P	.....	———
Ig13	1154: Aua	Mp	O	O	If	P	M	M	F	RPWGG	———
Ig14	1155: Dahuni	Mp	W	O	O	M	Me	O	.	RPWGG	———
Ih1	63: Mota	Mp	W	O	O	S	Me	Me	.	RGWGG	———
Ih2	64: Seniang	Mp	W	O	O	P	.	.	.	RGWGG	———
Ih3	164: Bunlap	Mp	W	O	O	O	O	Qp	V	RGWGG	REWGG
Ih4	165: Lau	Mp	W	O	O	Q	.	Pe	A	RGGGG	———
Ih5	263: Ajie	Mp	O	O	O	P	.	.	.	CEBCG	RGGGG
Ih6	337: Rotumans	Mp	D	O	O	Q	.	.	P	R....	———
Ih7	374: Lifu	Mp	D	O	Sf	P	Pe	Pe	.	CGRBG	———
Ih8	394: Vanua Levu	Mp	O	O	O	.	*	.	P	RGPHG	———
Ih9	1156: Santa Cruz	Pa	W	O	I	I	.	.	V	.....	———
Ih10	1157: Tannese	Mp	D	O	O	P	Pe	Pe	.	.....	———
Ii1	65: Samoans	Mp	D	O	O	P	.	.	F	EEMGG	———
Ii2	66: Tikopia	Mp	D	O	O	P	Pe	.	A	RGRGG	———
Ii3	166: Pukapukans	Mp	O	O	O	P	.	.	F	RG.GG	———
Ii4	264: Ellice	Mp	D	O	O	.	Qp	Qp	F	REMGG	———
Ii5	265: Ontong-Java	Mp	W	O	O	Q	*	.	.	RGMGG	———
Ii6	375: Tokelau	Mp	O	O	O	Q	*	Ce	F	RG.GG	———
Ii7	1103: Kapingamarangi	Mp	D	O	O	P	Ce	Ce	F	RGMGG	———
Ii8	1120: Futunans	Mp	D	O	O	E	*	.	F	EGWGG	———
Ii9	1121: Niueans	Mp	D	O	O	.	.	Pe	F	RGMGG	———
Ii12	1124: Tongans	Mp	D	O	O	P	Q	*	P	EEMGG	———
Ii13	1125: Uveans	Mp	D	O	O	Q	*	.	F	EEWGG	———
Ij1	67: Mangaians	Mp	D	O	O	Q	.	.	P	RGWGG	———
Ij2	167: Maori	Mp	D	O	If	P	Pp	.	F	RGWGB	RGGGG

TABLE A. *Continued*

1	3	7	12	14	16	19	20	22	24	25	27
Ij3	168: Marquesans	00415	G	O	Vn	A	O	O	K	Cc*	H
Ij4	266: Manihikians	00505	O	Fn	Vu	.	O	O	B*	Q	H
Ij5	267: Raroians	10504	O	En	Bn	A	O	O	Rk	.	H
Ij6	376: Hawaiians	10405	O	En	B	S	O	O	Rk	S	H
Ij7	658: Mangarevans	00604	O	N	Vu	A	O	O	R	S	H
Ij8	659: Tahitians	00415	O	N*	B	A	O	O	R	O	H
Ij9	1126: Easter	01207	O	Fn	Vu	.	O	O	R	O	H
Na1	68: Nabesna	26200	Ts	M*	uUv	A	O	P	O	Cc	I
Na2	69: Tareumiut	03700	O	Fp	B	A	O	O	K	N	I
Na3	169: Copper Eskimo	04600	S	M	Nv	D	O	O	B	S	E
Na4	170: Kaska	14500	S	Em	M	S	O	M	O	Mm	C
Na5	268: Naskapi	17200	Ox	Fn	B	A	O	O	B*	Cc	I
Na6	269: Nunivak	13600	O	Fn	uVn	A	O	O	Q	Q	I
Na7	338: Attawapiskat	13600	S	N	uVu	A	O	O	Q*	Cc	I
Na8	377: Ingalik	14500	O	N	Uv	A	O	O	B	S	H
Na9	458: Aleut	13600	S	Ep	uV	A	O	O	Q	Qm	I
Na10	459: Chugach	02800	O	.	uV	A	O	O	B	C	E
Na11	460: Sivokakmeit	02800	S	Gm	uP	S	L	O	K	T	I
Na12	461: Nunamiut	17200	S	Gn	uB	A	O	O	K	N	E
Na13	462: Baffinland	02800	St	Gr	uN	A	O	O	B	.	.
Na14	463: Polar Eskimo	14500	O	N	Bn	A	O	O	B	.	E
Na15	464: Dogrib	23500	O	N	uV	A	O	O	K	.	H
Na16	465: Satudene	14500	O	N	uVu	A	O	O	B	.	.
Na17	466: Slave	15400	S	R	uVu	A	O	O	K	O	H
Na19	468: Carrier	24400	Bs	Fr	uMv	A	O	P	O	Cc	I
Na20	469: Kutchin	14500	O	P	Vu	A	O	S	O	O	H
Na21	484: Caribou Eskimo	15400	B	Gp	B	A	O	O	B	N	Z*
Na22	485: Iglulik	05500	O	Fn	Vu	E	O	O	K	N	H*
Na23	486: Labrador	04600	B	Fn	uV	A	O	O	B	.	.
Na24	487: Angmagsalik	02800	O	En	Vu	A	O	O	B	O	E
Na26	489: Tanaina	14500	Sb	Fp	uVn	A	O	M	O	N	I
Na27	490: Tahltan	15400	B	N	uAb	E	O	S	O	.	.
Na28	491: Sekani	15400	S	R	uV	.	O	O	B	S	H
Na29	492: Beaver	35200	O	N	U	D	O	O	B	.	.
Na30	493: Chipewyan	06400	O	N	uV	.	O	O	B	O	H
Na31	494: Eastern Cree	25300	O	Fn	Uv	A	O	O	B*	Q*	.
Na32	495: Montagnais	26200	S	En	V	A	O	O	B*	Cm	I
Na33	496: N. Saulteaux	24400	O	Fn	Vu	A	S	O	O	Cc	I
Na34	497: Pekangekum	24400	O	Gn	uPu	C	Lo	O	Q	C	I
Na35	498: Nipigon	25300	O	Fn	uVu	.	S	O	O	C	I
Na36	499: Chippewa	22402	O	Fn	uN	A	S	O	O	Cc	I
Na37	500: Rainy River	34300	B	Fn	uB	A	S	O	O	Cc	I
Na38	501: Katikitegon	33400	O	Fn	V	E	S	O	O	C	I
Na39	502: E. Ojibwa	33400	S	N	uVu	C	S	O	O	Cc	I
Na41	504: Micmac	15400	S	M	uV	A	So	O	O	N	H
Na42	660: Potawatomi	15103	O	P	P	.	Ms	O	O	O	H
Nb1	70: Haida	22600	S	En	uA	C	O	M	O	Cp	C
Nb2	71: Twana	13600	Gb	En	V	E	O	O	K	N	H
Nb3	171: Kwakiutl	32500	Gb	Fn	Vu	E	O	O	Rk	Ss	H
Nb4	172: Yurok	41500	B	Fp	Vu	E	O	O	B	N	H
Nb5	270: Eyak	23500	S	P	uA*	A	O	M	O	C	I
Nb6	271: Tolowa	42400	B	P	Pu	C	L	O	O	E	I
Nb7	378: Tsimshian	22600	Bd	Ep	A	A	O	P	O	Cm	I
Nb8	470: Haisla	23500	G	.	uAv	A	O	S	O	Cm	I
Nb9	471: Bellacoola	22600	G	Fp	Vu	A	O	O	R	O	H

TABLE B. *Continued*

1	3	28	30	31	32	34	35	36	37	38	39
Ij3	168: Marquesans	Ht	N	2	31	O	A	1	7	A	P
Ij4	266: Manihikians	Ht	V	.	31	O	A	.	0	.	O
Ij5	267: Raroians	Ht	N	.	31	.	.	.	.	.	O
Ij6	376: Hawaiians	Jr	V	.	32	O	S	.	.	.	P
Ij7	658: Mangarevans	Ht	V	.	32	O	A	2	5	.	O
Ij8	659: Tahitians	Ht	V	.	32	O*	.	.	.	.	P
Ij9	1126: Easter	Er	V	.	21	O	.	.	.	.	O
Na1	68: Nabesna	O	S	1	20	O	C	.	0	.	O
Na2	69: Tareumiut	O	T	3	30	O	C	.	0	A	O
Na3	169: Copper Eskimo	O	S	1	20	O	C	1	0	A	O
Na4	170: Kaska	O	S	2	20	O	C	2	0	.	O
Na5	268: Naskapi	O	S	1	20	A	.	.	0	A	O
Na6	269: Nunivak	O	T	.	30	O*	A	.	0	P	O
Na7	338: Attawapiskat	O	S	2	30	O	C	.	0	A	O
Na8	377: Ingalik	O	S	.	20	A	A	.	0	.	O
Na9	458: Aleut	O	V	3	30	A	C*	2	0	A	O
Na10	459: Chugach	O	V	.	30	O	C	2	0	P	O
Na11	460: Sivokakmeit	O	V	3	40	.	A	.	0	A	Do*
Na12	461: Nunamiut	O	S	2	20	O	C	1	0	A	O
Na13	462: Baffinland	O	S	1	20	B	C	2	0	A	O
Na14	463: Polar Eskimo	O	S	1	20	O	A	5*	0	P	O
Na15	464: Dogrib	O	S	.	20	.	.	.	0	A	O
Na16	465: Satudene	O	B	.	20	A	C	.	0	.	O
Na17	466: Slave	O	S	2	20	A	C	4*	0	A	O
Na19	468: Carrier	O	T	4	30	B	C	2	0	A	O
Na20	469: Kutchin	O	S	1	21	O	C	2	0	A	O
Na21	484: Caribou Eskimo	O	S	1	20	O	C	2	0	A	O
Na22	485: Iglulik	O	S	1	30	O	C	2	0	A	O
Na23	486: Labrador	O	S	1	30	.	C	.	0	A	O
Na24	487: Angmagsalik	O	T	1	30	O	A	4*	0	A	O
Na26	489: Tanaina	O	V	.	30	O	C	.	0	R	O
Na27	490: Tahltan	O	T	.	30	A	C	4*	0	P	O
Na28	491: Sekani	O	S	.	20	C	C	.	0	.	O
Na29	492: Beaver	O	S	1	20	O	.	.	0	.	O
Na30	493: Chipewyan	O	S	.	20	O	C	1	0	A	O
Na31	494: Eastern Cree	O	S	.	20	O	C	.	0	A	O
Na32	495: Montagnais	O	S	3	30	O	C	2	0	A	O
Na33	496: N. Saulteaux	O	S	2	30	O	C	4	0	A	O
Na34	497: Pekangekum	O	T	1*	31	.	.	.	0	A	O
Na35	498: Nipigon	O	S	2	30	A	C	.	0	A	O
Na36	499: Chippewa	Ec	S	2	30	O	C	.	0	A	O
Na37	500: Rainy River	O	S	2	30	O	C	.	0	A	O
Na38	501: Katikitegon	O	T	2	30	A	C	1	0	A	O
Na39	502: E. Ojibwa	O	S	2	20	O	C	.	0	A	O
Na41	504: Micmac	O	S	1	21	A	C	3*	0	A	O
Na42	660: Potawatomi	Ec	T	.	31	A	C	2	0	A	O
Nb1	70: Haida	O	V	.	30	O	C	5	0	R	O
Nb2	71: Twana	O	S	2	30	O	C	2	0	A	O
Nb3	171: Kwakiutl	O	V	.	31	.	C	3	0	A	O
Nb4	172: Yurok	O	V	1	30	O	C	3	0	A	O
Nb5	270: Eyak	O	V	1	31	O	C	.	0	R	O
Nb6	271: Tolowa	O	T	.	20	O	C	2	0	A	O
Nb7	378: Tsimshian	O	T	.	41	O	C	.	0	R	O
Nb8	470: Haisla	O	T	4	30	O	C	.	0	R	O
Nb9	471: Bellacoola	O	V	2	30	A	C	1	0	A	O

TABLE C. *Continued*

1	3	42	44	46	48	50	52	54	56	58	60	62
Ij3	168: Marquesans	O	O	O	O	Mc	Mc	O	O	N	F	M
Ij4	266: Manihikians	O	O	O	O	M	.	O	O	D	O	.
Ij5	267: Raroians	O	O	O	O	M	M	E	O	N	O	N
Ij6	376: Hawaiians	O	O	O	O	Mc	M	.	O	N	.	M
Ij7	658: Mangarevans	O	O	O	O	Mc	Mc	.	O	N	O	E
Ij8	659: Tahitians	O	O	O	O	Mc	.	.	O	N	.	N
Ij9	1126: Easter	O	O	O	O	M	.	.	.	N	O	N
Na1	68: Nabesna	O	O	F	O	M	D	N	M	M	O	O
Na2	69: Tareumiut	O	O	F	F	M	E	.	M	D	O	O
Na3	169: Copper Eskimo	O*	O	F	O	M	M	F	M	N	O	O
Na4	170: Kaska	O	O	F	O	M	M	F	M	E	O	O
Na5	268: Naskapi	O	O	F	O	M	F	F	M	.	O	O
Na6	269: Nunivak	O	O	G	F	M	N	F	M	N	O	O
Na7	338: Attawapiskat	O	O	F	O	M	D	F	M	N	O	O
Na8	377: Ingalik	O	O	F	F	N	N	F	M	N	O	O
Na9	458: Aleut	O	O	F	O*	P	.	F	M	M	O	O
Na10	459: Chugach	O	O	F	O	N	M	G	M	N	O	O
Na11	460: Sivokakmeit	O	O	F	F*	M	M	G	M	N	M	O
Na12	461: Nunamiut	O	O	F	O	M	N	F	M	N	F	O
Na13	462: Baffinland	O	O	F	N	M	M	.	M	M	O	O
Na14	463: Polar Eskimo	O	O	F	O	M	M	D	N	N	O	O
Na15	464: Dogrib	O	O	F	O	F	M	F	N	N	O	O
Na16	465: Satudene	O	O	F	O	D	G	.	M	M	O	O
Na17	466: Slave	O	O	F	O	M	.	F	N	N	O	O
Na19	468: Carrier	O	F	G	O	P	.	F	N	N	O	O
Na20	469: Kutchin	O	O	F	O	N	.	.	M	N	O	O
Na21	484: Caribou Eskimo	O	O	O*	O	D	D	G	M	N	O	O
Na22	485: Iglulik	O	O	G	O	M	N	O	M	N	O	O
Na23	486: Labrador	O	O	F	O	M	M	F	M	M	O	O
Na24	487: Angmagsalik	O	O	F	O	D	E	F	M	M	O	O
Na26	489: Tanaina	O	O	F	O	D	M	F	M	M	O	O
Na27	490: Tahltan	O	O	F	O	P	M	.	M	M	O	O
Na28	491: Sekani	O	O	F	O	P	.	.	M	M	O	O
Na29	492: Beaver	O	O	F	O	P	F	G	M	.	O	O
Na30	493: Chipewyan	O	O	F	O	P	.	.	M	M	O	O
Na31	494: Eastern Cree	O	O	F	O	M	F	F	M	E	O	O
Na32	495: Montagnais	O	O	F	O	N	E	F	M	E	O	O
Na33	496: N. Saulteaux	O	O	F	O	N	F	F	M	N	O	O
Na34	497: Pekangekum	O	O	F	O	M	M	.	M	M	O	O
Na35	498: Nipigon	O	O	F	O	O	F	F	M	N	O	O
Na36	499: Chippewa	O	O	F	O*	N	G	F	M	G	O	G
Na37	500: Rainy River	O	O	F	O	M	F	G	M	E	O	O
Na38	501: Katikitegon	O	O	P	F	P	F	G	M	N	O	O
Na39	502: E. Ojibwa	O	O	F	O	E	.	G	M	N	O	O
Na41	504: Micmac	O	F	P	O	N	M	.	M	N	O	O
Na42	660: Potawatomi	O	O	P	.	P	.	.	M	.	O	G
Nb1	70: Haida	O*	F	F	O	M	M	F	M	M	O	O
Nb2	71: Twana	O	F	G	O	Mc	M	F	M	N	O	O
Nb3	171: Kwakiutl	O	F	.	O	M	M	F	M	N	O	O
Nb4	172: Yurok	O	O	N	O	M	M	G	M	N	O	O
Nb5	270: Eyak	O	O	F	O	M	M	F	M	M	O	O
Nb6	271: Tolowa	O	O	P	O	M	.	G	M	M	O	O
Nb7	378: Tsimshian	O*	F	O	O	M	M	F	M	N	O	O
Nb8	470: Haisla	O	F	P	O	M	.	.	M	M	O	O
Nb9	471: Bellacoola	O	O	.	O	M	M	F	M	M	O	O

TABLE D. *Continued*

1	3	64	67	69	71	73	74	76	78	80–84	85–89
Ij3	168: Marquesans	Mp	D	O	O	P	Cp	Cp	F	REGGG	————
Ij4	266: Manihikians	Mp	D	O	O	P	.	.	F	RGMGG	————
If5	267: Raroians	Mp	O	O	O	P	Ce	Ce	F	RGOGG	————
Ij6	376: Hawaiians	Mp	De	O	Hf	P	Cp	Cp	F	REGGG	RESHG
Ij7	658: Mangarevans	Mp	D	O	O	P	Pp	Pp	F	RGGGG	————
Ij8	659: Tahitians	Mp	D	O	O	P	.	.	F	RGOGG	————
Ij9	1126: Easter	Mp	D	O	I	P	.	.	F	EGRGG	EGSFE
Na1	68: Nabesna	AtN	O	O	O	C	O	O	E	CGRDH	RGBFB
Na2	69: Tareumiut	Es	W	O	O	O	O	Pe	F	CSRDE	CGRHH
Na3	169: Copper Eskimo	Es	O	O	O	O	O	Ce	T	CGRDI	EGRGH
Na4	170: Kaska	AtN	O	O	O	O	*	Pe	F	CGRCE	RGRGG
Na5	268: Naskapi	Ag	O	O	O	S	O	Pe	F	CGRCH	————
Na6	269: Nunivak	Es	W	O	O	O	O	Pe	.	RSWHE	————
Na7	338: Attawapiskat	Ag	O	O	O	C	Pe	Pe	.	CSRCE	CGRCB
Na8	377: Ingalik	AtN	W	O	O	O	O	Pe	P	RSWDE	RGBGB
Na9	458: Aleut	Es	D	O	H	P	O	Ce	P	RSREE	————
Na10	459: Chugach	Es	D	O	Sf	P	Cp	Pe	P	RGWFB	RGWGW
Na11	460: Sivokakmeit	Es	.	O	O	.	.	.	.	PGWCG	PCHFH
Na12	461: Nunamiut	Es	W	O	O	I	O	Ce	F	CGHEH	CGRDE
Na13	462: Baffinland	Es	O	O	O	C	O	Pp	.	CGRDI	ESRDH
Na14	463: Polar Eskimo	Es	O	O	O	O	O	O	F	ESSDS	EGRCH
Na15	464: Dogrib	AtN	O	O	O	C	.	.	.	CGRCH	RGWGW
Na16	465: Satudene	AtN	O	O	O	C	O	.	F	CGRCG	RGW.E
Na17	466: Slave	AtN	O	O	O	C	O	O	A	CGRCW	RGRGW
Na19	468: Carrier	AtN	D	O	H	O	O	.	.	RGRGM	CSRCM
Na20	469: Kutchin	AtN	W	O	I	P	Pp	.	A	CGRDH	RSWGE
Na21	484: Caribou Eskimo	Es	O	O	O	S	O	O	P	EGRDI	RGRGH
Na22	485: Iglulik	Es	O	O	O	S	O	O	P	EGRDI	RGRGH
Na23	486: Labrador	Es	O	O	O	P	O	O	F	CGRDI	RGRGH
Na24	487: Angmagsalik	Es	O	O	O	O	O	Pp	F	RSSGE	SGRSH
Na26	489: Tanaina	AtN	D	O	O	P	O	O	V	RSWGB	————
Na27	490: Tahltan	AtN	W	O	H	N	.	Ne	A	RGWGB	————
Na28	491: Sekani	AtN	O	O	O	C	O	.	.	CGRCG	————
Na29	492: Beaver	AtN	O	O	O	.	O	O	E	CGRCG	————
Na30	493: Chipewyan	AtN	O	O	O	O	O	Qe	.	CGRCG	————
Na31	494: Eastern Cree	Ag	O	O	O	C	.	O	A	CGRCH	ESRDB
Na32	495: Montagnais	Ag	O	O	O	P	Pp	Pp	V	CGRCB	CGRCH
Na33	496: N. Saulteaux	Ag	O	O	O	O	.	.	.	CGRCB	————
Na34	497: Pekangekum	Ag	O	O	O	.	Pp	Pe	F	RGWGB	CGRDB
Na35	498: Nipigon	Ag	O	O	O	P	.	O	.	CGRCG	RGREB
Na36	499: Chippewa	Ag	O	O	O	P	.	.	V	EGMDB	RDRGB
Na37	500: Rainy River	Ag	O	O	O	O	Dq	Ce	A	CGRCH	————
Na38	501: Katikitegon	Ag	O	O	O	P	.	O	V	CGRCB	EGREB
Na39	502. E. Ojibwa	Ag	O	O	O	P	O	.	V	RGRGM	CGRCB
Na41	504: Micmac	Ag	O	O	O	P	.	.	V	CGRCB	————
Na42	660: Potawatomi	Ag	O	O	.	.	.	.	.	CGRDM	————
Nb1	70: Haida	Xy	D	O	Hf	N	Np	Np	A	RSWGW	————
Nb2	71: Twana	Sa	W	O	Hf	I	O	O	V	RGWSW	RGMGM
Nb3	171: Kwakiutl	Wa	D	O	Hf	P	.	Pp	V	RSWGW	————
Nb4	172: Yurok	Ri	W	O	I	I	.	Ce	.	RSWGW	————
Nb5	270: Eyak	Xy*	W	O	If	N	.	Ne	.	RGWGB	————
Nb6	271: Tolowa	AtP	W	O	I	P	O	Pe	V	RSWGW	————
Nb7	378: Tsimshian	Xy*	D	O	Hf	N	Np	Np	.	RSWGW	————
Nb8	470: Haisla	Wa	D	O	Hf	M	O	O	E	RSWGW	————
Nb9	471: Bellacoola	Sa	D	O	H	O	O	Pe	P	RSWGW	————

TABLE A. *Continued*

1	3	7	12	14	16	19	20	22	24	25	27
Nb10	472: Alkatcho	14500	S	Fp	uVu	A	O	O	R	N	H
Nb11	473: Nootka	22600	G	Fn	Vu	E	O	O	B	N	H
Nb13	475: Squamish	23500	B	Ep	V	E	O	O	B	N	H
Nb15	477: Lummi	32500	Gb	Ep	Vu	E	O	O	B	N	H
Nb16	478: Klallam	13600	G	Fr	V	E	O	O	B	N	H
Nb17	479: Puyallup	32500	Gb	Ep	Vu	A	O	O	K	S	H
Nb18	480: Quileute	13600	B	Ep	V	E	O	O	B	N	.
Nb19	481: Chinook	22600	B	Fp	V	.	O	O	B	O	.
Nb21	483: Coos	13600	Bx	Ep	Vu	A	O	O	B	O	I
Nb22	505: Tlingit	13600	Gb	Fn	A	C	O	M	O	Pp	C
Nb23	506: Bellabella	23500	G	Fn	Vu	A	O	O	R	C	H
Nb24	507: Makah	22600	Gb	Fn	V	E	O	O	R	N	H
Nb25	508: Quinault	23500	T	Fn	Vu	E	O	O	K	N	E*
Nb26	509: Cowichan	23500	B	Ep	Vu	E	O	O	B	N	H
Nb27	510: Stalo	33400	G	Fp	Vu	E	O	O	B	N	H
Nb28	511: Alsea	12700	B	Fn	Vu	E	O	O	B	O	I
Nb31	514: Tututni	32500	B	P	Pn	C	L	O	O	Mm	I
Nb32	515: Shasta	43300	B	Fn	Vu	E	O	O	B	N	I
Nb33	516: Chimariko	43300	B	Fn	B	A	O	O	B	N	E
Nb34	517: Karok	41500	B	Fn	Vu	E	O	O	B	N	H
Nb35	518: Hupa	41500	B	Fp	Vu	E	O	O	B	N	H
Nb36	519: Wiyot	41500	B	Fp	Vu	E	O	O	B	N	E*
Nb39	522: Sinkyone	43300	B	Fn	uB	A	O	O	B	N	H
Nc1	72: Nomlaki	63100	G	N	uP	C	L	O	O	O	O
Nc2	173: Tubatulabal	53200	B	M	Vu	A	O	O	B	N	H
Nc3	174: Yokuts	43300	O	Eq	uP	S	Ml	O	O	N	H
Nc4	272: Atsugewi	43300	Gb	Fr	uV	E	O	O	B	N	E
Nc5	273: Miwok	63100	O	R	P	C	Ml	O	O	O	O
Nc6	339: Diegueno	54100	B	Fs	Pu	C	S	O	O	N	I
Nc7	375: Yuki	43300	G	N	uVn	A	O	O	B	N	H
Nc8	523: Klamath	32500	Gb	Fn	Vu	A	O	O	B	N	H
Nc9	524: Modoc	53200	G	Fn	uVu	A	O	O	B	N	H
Nc10	525: Achomawi	34300	Bs	Fp	uVu	A	O	O	B	N	.
Nc11	526: Yana	52300	S	Fn	uV	A	O	O	B	N	E
Nc12	527: Maidu	53200	S	Fr	bVu	A	O	O	B	N	I
Nc13	528: Nisenan	53200	O	N	uVu	A	O	O	B	S	H
Nc14	529: Wintu	33400	O	N	Vu	E	O	O	B	N	O
Nc15	530: Coast Yuki	42400	O	Q	uB	E	O	O	B	O	H
Nc17	532: Northern Pomo	53200	O	Fp	uB	A	O	O	B	O	O
Nc18	533: Eastern Pomo	43300	O	Fn	B	A	O	O	B	S	O
Nc19	534: Southern Pomo	43300	O	Fm	U	A	O	O	B	N	C
Nc20	535: Wappo	53200	O	Fm	B	A	O	O	B	N	C
Nc22	537: Patwin	53200	B	Fn	uB	A	Lo	O	O	M	O
Nc23	538: Monachi	53200	O	N	uPu	A	Lo*	O	O	N	H
Nc24	539: Lake Yokuts	52300	O	En	uP	C	M	O	O	N	O*
Nc25	540: Wukchumni	43300	O	Fn	uP	A	L	O	O	N	H
Nc27	542: Kawaiisu	53200	B	M	uV	A	O	O	B	.	H
Nc29	544: Gabrielino	42400	O	N	uP	C	M	O	O	O	.
Nc30	545: Serrano	64000	B	Fp	P	C	M	O	O	N	I
Nc31	546: Cahuilla	64000	O*	Fn	Pu	C	M	O	O	N	I
Nc32	547: Cupeno	64000	O	N	Pu	C	M	O	O	N	I
Nc33	548: Luiseno	62200	B	R	P	C	M	O	O	I	I
Nc34	549: Kiliwa	43300	B	N	P	C	S	O	O	I	I
Nd1	73: Tenino	32500	G	Gp	Vu	E	O	O	K	N	H
Nd2	74: Southern Ute	36100	O	N	Uv	A	O	O	B	N	H

TABLE B. *Continued*

1	3	28	30	31	32	34	35	36	37	38	39
Nb10	472: Alkatcho	O	T	.	30	O	C	.	0	A	O
Nb11	473: Nootka	O	T	.	31	O	C	.	0	A	O
Nb13	475: Squamish	O	T	.	30	O	C	.	0	A	O
Nb15	477: Lummi	O	S	3	30	O	C	.	0	A*	O
Nb16	478: Klallam	O	S	2	30	O	C	.	0	.	O
Nb17	479: Puyallup	O	T	1	30	O	C	.	0	.	O
Nb18	480: Quileute	O	V	1	30	O	C	2	0	.	O
Nb19	481: Chinook	O	V	.	30	.	C	4*	0	A	O
Nb21	483: Coos	O	V	.	30	.	C	.	0	A	O
Nb22	505: Tlingit	O	T	4	30	O	C	1	0	R	O
Nb23	506: Bellabella	O	T	2	30	O	C	.	0	A	O
Nb24	507: Makah	O	T	3	30	O	C	.	0	A	O
Nb25	508: Quinault	O	S	2	30	O	C	1	0	A	O
Nb26	509: Cowichan	O	T	.	30	O	C	.	0	A	O
Nb27	510: Stalo	O	T	1	30	O*	C	.	0	A	O
Nb28	511: Alsea	O	V	.	30	.	C	.	0	P	O
Nb31	514: Tututni	O	T	.	20	.	C	.	0	.	O
Nb32	515: Shasta	O	T	1	31	O	C	.	0	A	O
Nb33	516: Chimariko	O	V	1	30	O	C	.	0	.	O
Nb34	517: Karok	O	V	.	30	O	C	2	0	.	O
Nb35	518: Hupa	O	V	2	30	O	C	4	0	.	O
Nb36	519: Wiyot	O	V	1	30	A	C	.	0	.	O
Nb39	522: Sinkyone	O	V	2	30	B	C	2	0	A	O
Nc1	72: Nomlaki	O	V	3	20	A	C	.	0	.	O
Nc2	173: Tubatulabal	O	S	1	21	O	.	2	0	.	O
Nc3	174: Yokuts	O	S	.	30	O	C	2	0	A	O
Nc4	272: Atsugewi	O	S	2	20	O	C	1	0	A	O
Nc5	273: Miwok	O	T	.	20	.	C	2	0	A	O
Nc6	339: Diegueno	O	S	3	30	O	C	3	0	A	O
Nc7	375: Yuki	O	T	2	20	A	C	2	0	A	O
Nc8	523: Klamath	O	S	1	30	O	C	2	0	A	O
Nc9	524: Modoc	O	S	1	30	O*	C	2	0	A	O
Nc10	525: Achomawi	O	S	.	30	.	C	2	0	A	O
Nc11	526: Yana	O	S	.	30	.	C	.	0	A	O
Nc12	527: Maidu	O	T	1*	31	A	C	.	0	A	O
Nc13	528: Nisenan	O	T	.	20	O	C	1*	0	A	O
Nc14	529: Wintu	O	S	2	20	A	C	2	0	P	O
Nc15	530: Coast Yuki	O	S	.	20	A	C	1	0	A	O
Nc17	532: Northern Pomo	O	S	.	30	O*	C	1	0	.	O
Nc18	533: Eastern Pomo	O	T	3	30	A	C	.	0	A	O
Nc19	534: Southern Pomo	O	S	.	30	.	C	.	0	.	O
Nc20	535: Wappo	O	S	3	30	.	C	.	0	A	O
Nc22	537: Patwin	O	S	.	30	.	C	.	0	P	O
Nc23	538: Monachi	O	S	2	20	.	C	2	0	.	O
Nc24	539: Lake Yokuts	O	S	.	30	O	C	.	0	A	O
Nc25	540: Wukchumni	O	S	.	30	.	C	2	0	P	O
Nc27	542: Kawaiisu	O	S	.	20	.	C	.	0	.	O
Nc29	544: Gabrielino	O	T	.	20	A	C	.	0	.	O
Nc30	545: Serrano	O	S	.	30	A	C	.	0	.	O
Nc31	546: Cahuilla	O	S	.	30	A	C	.	0	.	O
Nc32	547: Cupeno	O	S	.	20	.	C	.	0	.	O
Nc33	548: Luiseno	O	S	3	20	O*	C	4	0	A	O
Nc34	549: Kiliwa	O	S	.	20	O	C	.	0	A*	O
Nd1	73: Tenino	O	T	4	20	C	C	.	0	A	O*
Nd2	74: Southern Ute	C*	S	.	20	A	C	4	0	A	Eo

TABLE C. *Continued*

1	3	42	44	46	48	50	52	54	56	58	60	62
Nb10	472: Alkatcho	O	.	.	O	.	.	F	M	N	O	O
Nb11	473: Nootka	O	G	M	O	M	M	F	M	N	O	O
Nb13	475: Squamish	O	F	E	O	M	M	.	M	M	O	O
Nb15	477: Lummi	O	F	F	O	M	M	F	M	M	O	O
Nb16	478: Klallam	O	F	F	O	P	.	F	M	N	O	O
Nb17	479: Puyallup	O	F	M	O	Mc	M	G	M	N	O	O
Nb18	480: Quileute	O	.	F	O	M	.	F	M	M	O	O
Nb19	481: Chinook	O	O	F	O	P	.	F	M	M	O	O
Nb21	483: Coos	O	.	F	O	P	.	.	M	.	O	O
Nb22	505: Tlingit	O	F	F	O	M	M	F	M	M	O	O
Nb23	506: Bellabella	O	P	E	O	P	.	.	M	M	O	O
Nb24	507: Makah	O	F	F	O	M	M	F	M	M	O	O
Nb25	508: Quinault	O	P	P	O	Mc	M	F	M	M	O	O
Nb26	509: Cowichan	O	F	E	O	M	M	F	M	M	O	O
Nb27	510: Stalo	O	P	P	O	M	M	G	M	M	O	O
Nb28	511: Alsea	O	O	.	O	P	N	F	M	N	O	O
Nb31	514: Tututni	O	O	.	O	M	.	.	M	M	O	O
Nb32	515: Shasta	O	O	N	O	.	M	G	M	N	O	O
Nb33	516: Chimariko	O	O	P	O	O*	.	E	M	M	O	O
Nb34	517: Karok	O	O	P	O	P	.	G	M	M	O	O
Nb35	518: Hupa	O	O	P	O	P	.	E	M	N	O	O
Nb36	519: Wiyot	O	O	P	O	P	.	G	M	N	O	O
Nb39	522: Sinkyone	O	O	D	O	P	.	F	M	N	O	O
Nc1	72: Nomlaki	O	O	N	O	O	N	F	M	N	O	O
Nc2	173: Tubatulabal	O	O	M	F	O	N	G	M	N	O	O
Nc3	174: Yokuts	O	O	.	F	O	.	E	M	N	O	O
Nc4	272: Atsugewi	O	O	M	O	M	M	F	M	M	O	O
Nc5	273: Miwok	O	O	.	O	O	.	.	M	.	O	O
Nc6	339: Diegueno	O	O	M	P	O	.	F	M	O	O	O
Nc7	375: Yuki	O	O	M	O	O	M	G	M	N	O	O
Nc8	523: Klamath	O	O	F	O	N	N	F	M	N	O	O
Nc9	524: Modoc	O	O	E	O	P	D	F	M	M	O	O
Nc10	525: Achomawi	O	O	M	O	P	N	F	M	N	O	O
Nc11	526: Yana	O	O	M	O	P	.	G	M	M	O	O
Nc12	527: Maidu	O	O	M	O	P	N	G	M	N	O	O
Nc13	528: Nisenan	O	O	M	O	O	M	G	M	N	O	O
Nc14	529: Wintu	O	O	M	O	O	N	G	M	M	O	O
Nc15	530: Coast Yuki	O	O	P	O	O	.	G	M	N	O	O
Nc17	532: Northern Pomo	O	O	M	O	O	.	E	M	N	O	O
Nc18	533: Eastern Pomo	O	O	M	O	O	M	G	M	N	O	O
Nc19	534: Southern Pomo	O	O	M	O	O	.	.	M	.	O	O
Nc20	535: Wappo	O	O	O*	O	O	M	G	M	M	O	O
Nc22	537: Patwin	O	O	F	O	O	E	.	M	.	O	O
Nc23	538: Monachi	O	O	M	F	O	N	G	M	.	O	O
Nc24	539: Lake Yokuts	O	O	M	O	O	.	F	M	.	O	O
Nc25	540: Wukchumni	O	O	M	F	.	N	G	M	N	O	O
Nc27	542: Kawaiisu	O	O	M	.	.	.	.	M	.	O	O
Nc29	544: Gabrielino	O	O	M	O	P	.	F	M	.	O	O
Nc30	545: Serrano	O	O	M	P	O	.	.	M	.	O	O
Nc31	546: Cahuilla	O	O	M	P	O	.	.	M	M	O	O
Nc32	547: Cupeno	O	O	M	P	O	.	F	M	.	O	O
Nc33	548: Luiseno	O	O	M	P	O	.	G	M	.	O	O
Nc34	549: Kiliwa	O	O	.	F	O	.	G	M	.	O	O
Nd1	73: Tenino	O	O	P	O	M	M	G	M	N	O	O
Nd2	74: Southern Ute	O	O	F	O*	O	F	G	M	M	M	D

TABLE D. *Continued*

1	3	64	67	69	71	73	74	76	78	80–84	85–89
Nb10	472: Alkatcho	AtN	D	O	H	P	.	*	P	CSRCM	R.WGE
Nb11	473: Nootka	Wa	D	O	H	P	.	De	V	RGWGW	————
Nb13	475: Squamish	Sa	W	O	H	O	.	Pe	V	RGWSW	————
Nb15	477: Lummi	Sa	D	O	H	.	.	.	V	RGWGW	RGMSM
Nb16	478: Klallam	Sa	D	O	H	P	Pp	O	V	RGWGW	RGRGM
Nb17	479: Puyallup	Sa	W	O	I	I	.	O	P	RGWGW	RGMSW
Nb18	480: Quileute	Cm	D	O	H	P	.	.	.	RSWGM	————
Nb19	481: Chinook	OpC	D	O	H	P	.	.	.	RGWGW	————
Nb21	483: Coos	Xy	W	O	S	I	O	Qe*	.	RSWGW	RGGGG
Nb22	505: Tlingit	Xy	D	O	H	M	*	Mp	P	RSWGW	CGRCB
Nb23	506: Bellabella	Wa	D	O	H	N	.	Np	.	RGWGW	RGRCB
Nb24	507: Makah	Wa	D	O	H	P	O	Ce	.	RGWSW	————
Nb25	508: Quinault	Sa	D	O	H	I	O	Pe	A	RGWGW	RGBGB
Nb26	509: Cowichan	Sa	W	O	H	O	.	Pe	V	RGRSW	————
Nb27	510: Stalo	Sa	D	O	H	C	O	O	V	CSRHE	RGWSW
Nb28	511: Alsea	Ya	W	O	H	I	.	.	.	RSWGW	RGGGG
Nb31	514: Tututni	AtP	W	O	I	I	.	Pe	P	RSWGW	————
Nb32	515: Shasta	HoS	W	O	I	Q	Qp	Pe	.	RSEGW	————
Nb33	516: Chimariko	HoC	W	O	O	P	O	O	P	CSBGB	————
Nb34	517: Karok	HoK	W	O	I	O	.	.	P	RGWGW	————
Nb35	518: Hupa	AtP	W	O	I	P	.	.	P	RGWGW	————
Nb36	519: Wiyot	Ri	W	O	I	O	.	.	V	RGWGW	————
Nb39	522: Sinkyone	AtP	W	O	O	P	O	O	A	CSBHB	————
Nc1	72: Nomlaki	PeW	W	O	O	P	.	O	P	CGRCG	CS.CG
Nc2	173: Tubatulabal	Ss	O	O	O	P	O	O	P	CSRDM	RGGFG
Nc3	174: Yokuts	PeY	W	O	O	Q	O	O	.	CGRDG	CSRDE
Nc4	272: Atsugewi	HoS	W	O	O	P	Pp	Pe	V	RSRHE	CSRCE
Nc5	273: Miwok	PeN	O	O	O	P	O	O	.	CSRDB	————
Nc6	339: Diegueno	HoY	O	O	O	P	O	O	.	CGRDE	————
Nc7	375: Yuki	Yu	W	O	O	P	O	O	P	CSRCE	CGRCG
Nc8	523: Klamath	ShL	W	O	I	C	O	O	V	CSRHE	CGRDM
Nc9	524: Modoc	ShL	W	O	I	E	O	Pp	P	CSRHE	RGMFM
Nc10	525: Achomawi	HoS	W	O	O	P	.	O	A	RSRCB	CGRDM
Nc11	526: Yana	HoZ	W	O	O	P	Pe	Pe	V	CSRCB	CSRCE
Nc12	527: Maidu	PeM	W	O	O	C	O	O	.	CSRCE	CGRCB
Nc13	528: Nisenan	PeM	W	O	O	P	.	O	V	CSRCE	CGRCB
Nc14	529: Wintu	PeW	W	O	O	P	O	O	.	CSRCE	CGRCB
Nc15	530: Coast Yuki	Yu	O	O	O	C	O	O	P	CGRCB	CGRCG
Nc17	532: Northern Pomo	HoP	.	O	O	P	O	O	P	CSRCE	————
Nc18	533: Eastern Pomo	HoP	W	O	O	C	O	Pe	.	CGRDG	————
Nc19	534: Southern Pomo	HoP	W	O	O	M	O	O	.	CGRDG	————
Nc20	535: Wappo	Yu	.	O	I	C	O	O	F	CGRDG	————
Nc22	537: Patwin	PeW	W	O	O	P	.	O	.	CSRDE	RGOFG
Nc23	538: Monachi	Ss	W	O	O	P	O	O	.	CSRCG	CGRCB
Nc24	539: Lake Yokuts	PeY	W	O	O	.	O	.	.	EGRRM	————
Nc25	540: Wukchumni	PeY	W	O	O	Q	.	.	.	CSRCG	SGREB
Nc27	542: Kawaiisu	Ss	W	O	O	I	.	O	.	CGRDM	————
Nc29	544: Gabrielino	Ss	W	O	O	P	.	Pe.	.	CGRDG	————
Nc30	545: Serrano	Ss	O	O	O	P	.	Pe	.	CGRCG	————
Nc31	546: Cahuilla	Ss	O	O	O	P	.	O	.	RGGGG	————
Nc32	547: Cupeno	Ss	O	O	O	P	.	O	.	CGRCG	————
Nc33	548: Luiseno	Ss	O	O	O	P	.	O	.	CGRCG	RGGGG
Nc34	549: Kiliwa	HoY	O	O	O	P	.	Pp*	.	EGRGG	————
Nd1	73: Tenino	ShS	W	O	If	P	O	O	V	ESRHE	CGRCM
Nd2	74: Southern Ute	Ss	O	O	O	P	O	O	F	CGRCB	CGRDG

TABLE A. *Continued*

1	3	7	12	14	16	19	20	22	24	25	27
Nd3	175: Havasupai	32005	T	En	uV	D	O	O	Q	N	I
Nd4	176: Sanpoil	32500	T	Gp	V	A	O	O	B	N	H
Nd5	274: Hukundika	53200	O	Fr	B	D	O	O	B	N	H
Nd6	340: Washo	43300	O	N	uBn	A	O*	O	B	N	H
Nd7	380: Kutenai	33400	O	N*	uVu	A	O	O	B	N	H
Nd8	550: Chilcotin	23500	Gs	Fn	Vu	A	O	O	K	N	H
Nd9	551: Lillooet	23500	O	Fr	Vu	E	O	O	K	N	H
Nd10	552: Thompson	23500	O	Fp	Vu	E	O	O	B	N	H
Nd11	553: Shuswap	33400	G	Fp	V	A	O	O	B	N	H
Nd12	554: Flathead	34300	O	R*	Vu	A	O	O	K	N	H
Nd14	556: Coeur d'Alene	34300	O	Fr	V	A	O	O	B	S	.
Nd15	557: Sinkaietk	33400	G	R*	vBn	D	O	O	K	N	H
Nd18	560: Wishram	32500	G	Fp	Vu	A	O	O	B	N	H
Nd19	561: Umatilla	33400	G	N	V	E	O	O	B	N	H
Nd20	562: Nez Perce	33400	B	En	Vu	E	O	O	K	N	H
Nd22	564: Wadadokado	53200	O	N	uUv	A	O	O	B	N	H
Nd24	566: Kidutokado	44200	S	R	uB	A	O	O	B	N	H
Nd27	569: Kuyuidokado	52300	O	N	U	A	O	O	B	N	H
Nd30	572: Eastern Mono	54100	T	Fn	uVu	E	O	O	B	N	H
Nd32	574: Panamint	64000	O	N	Un	A	O	O	B	N	H
Nd43	585: White Knife	54100	O	N	Uv	A	O	O	B	C*	H*
Nd45	587: Bohogue	35200	S	N	B	A	O	O	B	O	H
Nd46	588: Agaiduka	33400	S	N	uV	A	O	O	B	N	H
Nd48	590: Gosiute	54100	O*	N	Uv	A	O	O	B	Cc	H
Nd49	591: Antarianunts	53200	O	N	U	.	O	O	B	N	H
Nd52	594: Shivwits	54001	O*	N	uB	A	O	O	B	N	H
Nd53	595: Kaibab	73000	O	N	uV	A	O	O	B	N	H
Nd54	596: Chemehuevi	63001	O	M	B	A	O	O	B	N	H
Nd56	598: San Juan	53101	O	N	Uv	.	O	O	B	N	H
Nd58	600: Uintah	34300	O	N	Uv	A	O	O	B	N	H
Nd62	604: Uncompahgre	45100	T	N	U	A	O	O	B	.	H
Nd63	605: Bannock	35200	O	N	Uv	E	O	O	B	O	H
Nd64	606: Wind River	35200	S	Fn	U	A	O	O	B	N	H
Nd65	607: Walapai	64000	O	Fn	uVu	A	O	O	B	C	I
Nd66	608: Yavapai	64000	Ts	N	uBn	A	O	O	B	N	I
Nd67	609: Tolkepaya	63001	B	R	uB	A	O	O	B	O	I
Ne1	75: Gros Ventre	28000	B	R	Vu	E	O	O	B	N	H
Ne2	76: Kiowa-Apache	28000	G	Er	Uv	A	O	O	K	N	H
Ne3	177: Comanche	19000	O	Er	B	D	O	O	B	O	H
Ne4	178: Crow	28000	T	R	V	E	O	Ps	O	O	C
Ne5	275: Cheyenne	28000	T	Er	Uv	E	O	O	K	N	H
Ne6	341: Mandan	03205	O	Fr	Mv	A	O	Ms	O	M	C
Ne7	381: Sarsi	28000	B	R	Vn	A	O	O	B	O	H
Ne8	382: Teton	19000	B	Fr	Vu	E	O	O	K	O	I
Ne9	616: Arapaho	28000	O	Er	U	E	O	O	B	N	H
Ne10	617: Arikara	03205	O	Fr	U	.	O	O	B	.	C
Ne11	618: Assiniboin	27100	Bs	R	Vu	E	O	O	B	N	I
Ne12	619: Blackfoot	28000	B	Er	Vu	E	O	O	B	N	H
Ne13	620: Blood	28000	Gb	R	Vn	E	O	O	B	O	H
Ne14	621: Bungi	26200	O	N	.	A	S	O	O	S	I
Ne15	622: Hidatsa	12106	O	Fr	M	A	O	Ms	O	O	C
Ne16	623: Karankawa	33400	S	N*	uB	.	O	O	B	.	.
Ne17	624: Kiowa	19000	O	R*	Vu	A	O	O	K	O	H
Ne18	625: Piegan	28000	Gb	R	Vn	E	O	O	B	O	H
Ne19	626: Plains Cree	26200	B	N	Vn	A	O	O	B	C	I

TABLE B. *Continued*

1	3	28	30	31	32	34	35	36	37	38	39
Nd3	175: Havasupai	Jc	T	3	30	O	C	.	0	A	O
Nd4	176: Sanpoil	O	S	2	20	B	C*	1	0	A	O
Nd5	274: Hukundika	O	S	.	20	O	C	.	0	A	O
Nd6	340: Washo	O	S	1	20	O	C	3	0	A	O
Nd7	380: Kutenai	O	S	.	21	A	C	2	0	A	Eo*
Nd8	550: Chilcotin	O	S	1	30	.	C	1	0	A	O
Nd9	551: Lillooet	O	S	.	30	O	C	2	0	A	O
Nd10	552: Thompson	O	S	.	31	.	C	2	0	.	O
Nd11	553: Shuswap	O	S	3	31	O	C	2	0	P	O
Nd12	554: Flathead	O	S	.	21	O	C	5*	0	A	Eo
Nd14	556: Coeur d'Alene	O	S	3	31	O	C	2	0	P	Eo
Nd15	557: Sinkaietk	O	S	2	20	A	C	.	0	A	Eo
Nd18	560: Wishram	O	T	2	30	O	C	.	0	A	O
Nd19	561: Umatilla	O	S	.	21	.	C	2	0	.	Eo
Nd20	562: Nez Perce	O	S	2	31	O	C	1	0	P	Eo
Nd22	564: Wadadokado	O	S	1	20	O	C	2	0	A	O
Nd24	566: Kidutokado	O	S	1	20	.	C	2	0	A	O
Nd27	569: Kuyuidokado	O	S	1	20	O	C	3	0	A	O
Nd30	572: Eastern Mono	O*	S	.	30	A	C	4	0	A	O
Nd32	574: Panamint	O	S	1	20	.	C	1	0	A	O
Nd43	585: White Knife	O	S	1	20	A	C	.	0	A	O
Nd45	587: Bohogue	O	S	2	20	.	C	.	0	A	Eo
Nd46	588: Agaiduka	O	S	2	20	.	C	2	0	A	O*
Nd48	590: Gosiute	O	S	1	20	.	C	4	0	A	O
Nd49	591: Antarianunts	O	S	1	20	.	C	4	0	A	O
Nd52	594: Shivwits	Jc	S	.	20	.	C	2	0	A	O
Nd53	595: Kaibab	Jc*	S	1	20	.	C	2	0	A	O
Nd54	596: Chemehuevi	Jc	S	.	20	O*	C	2	0	A	O
Nd56	598: San Juan	Jc	S	.	20	.	C	2	0	A	·Eo
Nd58	600: Uintah	O	S	.	20	.	C	4	0	.	Eo
Nd62	604: Uncompahgre	O	B	2	20	.	C	4	0	A	Eo
Nd63	605: Bannock	O	S	2	21	.	C	2	0	A	Eo
Nd64	606: Wind River	O	S	3	21	.	C	2	0	A	Eo
Nd65	607: Walapai	Cc	S	1	30	O	C	2	0	A	Eo
Nd66	608: Yavapai	Cc	S	.	20	O	C	2	0	A	O
Nd67	609: Tolkepaya	Ec	S	2	20	O	C	.	0	A	O
Ne1	75: Gros Ventre	O	B	.	21	C	C	2	0	.	Eo
Ne2	76: Kiowa-Apache	O	B	.	30*	.	.	.	0	A	Eo
Ne3	177: Comanche	O	B	.	30	.	.	.	0	.	Eo
Ne4	178: Crow	Cn	S	.	21	O	C	1	0	.	Eo
Ne5	275: Cheyenne	Cc	B	.	31	O	C	5	0	A	Eo
Ne6	341: Mandan	Ic	T	.	31	.	.	.	0	A	Eo
Ne7	381: Sarsi	O	S	.	21	.	.	2	0	A	Eo
Ne8	382: Teton	O	S	.	31	A	C	.	0	.	Eo
Ne9	616: Arapaho	O	S	4	31	O	C	5	0	A	Eo
Ne10	617: Arikara	Ic	V	5	32	.	C	.	0	.	Eo
Ne11	618: Assiniboin	O	B	4	20	A*	C	5*	0	.	Eo
Ne12	619: Blackfoot	O	B	4	30	A	C	1	0	A	Eo
Ne13	620: Blood	O	B	3	21	A	C	1	0	A	Eo
Ne14	621: Bungi	O	B	4	20	A	C	.	0	A	Eo
Ne15	622: Hidatsa	Ic	T	5	30	A	C	.	0	A	Eo
Ne16	623: Karankawa	O	B	.	21	.	A*	4	0	.	Eo
Ne17	624: Kiowa	O	S	3	31	.	.	.	0	A	Eo
Ne18	625: Piegan	O	B	4	21	A	C	.	0	A	Eo
Ne19	626: Plains Cree	O	B	.	20	A	C	4	0	A	Eo

TABLE C. *Continued*

1	3	42	44	46	48	50	52	54	56	58	60	62
Nd3	175: Havasupai	O	O	M	F	O	N	F	M	O	O	N
Nd4	176: Sanpoil	O	O	F	F	M	.	F	M	N	O	O
Nd5	274: Hukundika	O	O	P	O*	O	.	E	M	.	O	O
Nd6	340: Washo	O	O	M	O	O	E	G	M	E	O	O
Nd7	380: Kutenai	O	O	F	P*	M	D	F	M	M	M	O
Nd8	550: Chilcotin	O	O*	G	O	N	N	G	N	N	O	O
Nd9	551: Lillooet	O	O	E	O	P	.	.	M	N	O	O
Nd10	552: Thompson	O	P	G	O	P	.	.	N	N	O	O
Nd11	553: Shuswap	O	O	G	O	P	.	F	M	N	O	O
Nd12	554: Flathead	O	O	F	O	P	F	F	M	N	M	O
Nd14	556: Coeur d'Alene	O	O	F	O	P	F	G	M	N	.	O
Nd15	557: Sinkaietk	O	O	F	O	M	F	F	N	M	O	O
Nd18	560: Wishram	O	O	P	O	M	.	F	M	M	O	O
Nd19	561: Umatilla	O	O	F	O	P	.	F	M	M	.	O
Nd20	562: Nez Perce	O	O	F	O	P	.	F	M	M	M	O
Nd22	564: Wadadokado	O	O	F	O	O	M	F	M	M	O	O
Nd24	566: Kidutokado	O	O	G	O	O	E	G	M	M	O	O
Nd27	569: Kuyuidokado	O	O	N	O	O	D	G	M	M	O	O
Nd30	572: Eastern Mono	O	O	.	F	.	M	F	M	M	O	O
Nd32	574: Panamint	O	O	G	F	O	M	F	M	O	O	O
Nd43	585: White Knife	O	F	E	F	O	E	F	M	M	O	O
Nd45	587: Bohogue	O	O	F	P	O	F	F	M	M	M	O
Nd46	588: Agaiduka	O	M*	F	P	O	.	F	M	M	O	O
Nd48	590: Gosiute	O	F	F	P	M	G	M	.	O	O	O
Nd49	591: Antarianunts	O	G	F	O	M	G	M	.	O	O	O
Nd52	594: Shivwits	O	G	F	F	O	M	F	M	O	O	N
Nd53	595: Kaibab	O	O	F	M	O	D	G	M	O	O	D
Nd54	596: Chemehuevi	O	O	M	F	O	.	G	M	O	O	.
Nd56	598: San Juan	O	F	M	O	O	E	E	M	P	P	.
Nd58	600: Uintah	O	F	F	F	O	F	G	M	M	.	O
Nd62	604: Uncompahgre	O	O	F	O	O	.	F	M	N	M	O
Nd63	605: Bannock	O	O	F	O*	O	.	F	M	M	.	O
Nd64	606: Wind River	O	O	F	O	P	F	G	M	M	M	O
Nd65	607: Walapai	O	E	M	F	O	M	F	M	O	O	N
Nd66	608: Yavapai	O	O	M	F	O	F	G	M	O	O	E
Nd67	609: Tolkepaya	O	.	M	F	O	F	.	M	O	O	E
Ne1	75: Gros Ventre	O	O	F	F	O	F	F	M	O	M	O
Ne2	76: Kiowa-Apache	O	O	F	O	.	F	F	M	O	M	O
Ne3	177: Comanche	O	O	F	O	O	.	F	M	O	M	O
Ne4	178: Crow	O	O	F	O	O	F	F	M	O	M	.
Ne5	275: Cheyenne	O	O	F	F*	.	F	F	M	O	M	F
Ne6	341: Mandan	O	O	.	P	.	.	O	M	M	M	F
Ne7	381: Sarsi	O	O	F	O	O	F	F	M	O	M	O
Ne8	382: Teton	O	O	F	O	.	F	G	M	M	O	O
Ne9	616: Arapaho	O	O	F	O*	.	F	F	M	O	M	O
Ne10	617: Arikara	O	O	F	F	F*	.	.	M	M	.	F
Ne11	618: Assiniboin	O	O	F	O	P	F	F	M	M	M	O
Ne12	619: Blackfoot	O	O	F	O	O	F	F	M	O	M	O
Ne13	620: Blood	O	O	F	O	O	F	F	M	O	M	O
Ne14	621: Bungi	O	O	F	O	P	F	G	M	M	M	O
Ne15	622: Hidatsa	O	O	F	F	F*	G	F	M	.	N	F
Ne16	623: Karankawa	O	O	P	P	P	F	G	M	O	M	O
Ne17	624: Kiowa	O	O	P	.	.	F	.	M	O	.	O
Ne18	625: Piegan	O	O	F	O	O	F	F	M	O	M	O
Ne19	626: Plains Cree	O	O	F	O	P	F	F	M	M	M	O

TABLE D. *Continued*

1	3	64	67	69	71	73	74	76	78	80–84	85–89
Nd3	175: Havasupai	HoY	O	O	O	Q	Pe	O	.	CGRDG	————
Nd4	176: Sanpoil	Sa	O	O	O	P	O	Q*	P	EGRGM	CGRCM
Nd5	274: Hukundika	Ss	O	O	O	P	O	Pe	.	CGRCG	CGRDG
Nd6	340: Washo	Xy*	O	O	O	P	O	O	.	CGRCW	CGRDG
Nd7	380: Kutenai	Xx	O	O	If	I	O	Pe*	P	RSRGM	CGRCM
Nd8	550: Chilcotin	AtN	W	O	If	P	Pe	Pe	F	RSRGW	CSRCW
Nd9	551: Lillooet	Sa	W	O	I	P	O	Pe	V	CSRHE	RSRGM
Nd10	552: Thompson	Sa	W	O	H	C	.	.	P	CSRHE	RSMGM
Nd11	553: Shuswap	Sa	O	O	I	P	O	*	V	CSRHE	CSRCW*
Nd12	554: Flathead	Sa	O	O	I	P	O	.	P	ESRGM	CGRCH
Nd14	556: Coeur d'Alene	Sa	W	O	I	E	O	*	V	CSRCM	ESRGM*
Nd15	557: Sinkaietk	Sa	O	O	O	P	O	*	P	EGRCM	CGRCM
Nd18	560: Wishram	OpC	W	O	H	P	.	.	.	CS.DE	RGMGM
Nd19	561: Umatilla	ShS	O	O	I	C	.	.	V	ESRGM	————
Nd20	562: Nez Perce	ShS	W	O	I	E	O	O	A	ESRGM	CGRCG
Nd22	564: Wadadokado	Ss	O	O	O	C	O	O	P	CGRDM	CGRCG
Nd24	566: Kidutokado	Ss	O	O	O	C	O	O	E	CGRCG	————
Nd27	569: Kuyuidokado	Ss	O	O	O	C	O	O	.	CGRDM	————
Nd30	572: Eastern Mono	Ss	O	O	O	P	O	O	P	RGRGG	CSRCM
Nd32	574: Panamint	Ss	O	O	O	P	O	O	.	CSRCG	CGRDG
Nd43	585: White Knife	Ss	O	O	O	O	O	O	F	CGRDG	CGRCG
Nd45	587: Bohogue	Ss	W	O	O	C	O	O	A	CGRCG	CGRDG
Nd46	588: Agaiduka	Ss	O	O	O	C	O	O	P	CGRCG	CGRCM
Nd48	590: Gosiute	Ss	O	O	O	O	O	O	P	*	————
Nd49	591: Antarianunts	Ss	O	O	O	C	O	O	P	CSRGG	————
Nd52	594: Shivwits	Ss	O	O	O	S	Ce	O	.	CGRCG	————
Nd53	595: Kaibab	Ss	O	O	O	C	Pe	O	F	CGRCG	————
Nd54	596: Chemehuevi	Ss	O	O	O	P	.	O	.	CSRHE	————
Nd56	598: San Juan	Ss	O	O	O	C	Ce	O	P	RGGGG	CGRCB
Nd58	600: Uintah	Ss	O	O	O	P	O	O	.	CGRDG	CGRCG
Nd62	604: Uncompahgre	Ss	O	O	O	.	O	O	.	CGRCH	CGRCG
Nd63	605: Bannock	Ss	O	O	O	C	O	O	P	CGRCH	CGRCG
Nd64	606: Wind River	Ss	O	O	O	C	O	O	F	CGRCG	CGRCH
Nd65	607: Walapai	HoY	O	O	O	P	.	O	P	CGRDG	————
Nd66	608: Yavapai	HoY	O	O	O	I	O	O	.	CGRDG	————
Nd67	609: Tolkepaya	HoY	O	O	O	C	O	O	P	CGRDG	RSGFE
Ne1	75: Gros Ventre	Ag	O	O	O	I	O	O	E	CGRCH	————
Ne2	76: Kiowa-Apache	AtS	O	O	O	.	O	O	P	CGRCH	————
Ne3	177: Comanche	Ss	O	O	If	C	O	O	.	CGRCH	————
Ne4	178: Crow	Sx	O	O	O	I	O	Ne	.	CGRCH	————
Ne5	275: Cheyenne	Ag	O	O	O	O	O	O	V	CGRCH	————
Ne6	341: Mandan	Sx	O	O	O	.	*	M.	.	CSRDE	CGRCH
Ne7	381: Sarsi	AtN	O	O	O	I	O	Ce	V	CGRCH	————
Ne8	382: Teton	Sx	O	O	I	O	O	.	P	CGRCH	————
Ne9	616: Arapaho	Ag	O	O	O	I	O	O	V	CGRCH	————
Ne10	617: Arikara	Cd	.	O	O	P	*	.	.	CSWDE	CGRCH
Ne11	618: Assiniboin	Sx	O	O	O	C	O	O	P	CGRCH	————
Ne12	619: Blackfoot	Ag	W	O	O	C	O	D.	V	CGRCH	————
Ne13	620: Blood	Ag	W	O	O	C	O	Pe	A	CGRCH	————
Ne14	621: Bungi	Ag	O	O	O	P	O	.	P	CGRCH	CGRCB
Ne15	622: Hidatsa	Sx	O	O	O	C	*	P.	.	CSWDE	CGRCH
Ne16	623: Karankawa	Xy*	O	O	O	P	O	O	.	CGRDH	————
Ne17	624: Kiowa	Xy*	O	O	O	I	O	O	.	CGRCH	————
Ne18	625: Piegan	Ag	W	O	O	C	O	Pe	A	CGRCH	————
Ne19	626: Plains Cree	Ag	O	O	O	P	O	.	F	CGRCH	————

TABLE A. *Continued*

1	3	7	12	14	16	19	20	22	24	25	27
Ne20	627: Santee	17101	B	P	uVu	.	O	O	B	O	I
Nf2	78: Winnebago	23203	S	Fn	uPn	S	M	O	O	C	O
Nf3	179: Omaha	14104	G	N	uP*	S	Ms	O	O	N	O
Nf4	276: Miami	23104	G	R	Pn	.	S	O	O	O	O
Nf5	277: Wichita	14005	S	Fr	Uv	A	O	O	K	O	H
Nf6	342: Pawnee	14005	O	Er	M	D	O	L*	O*	Ss	C
Nf7	383: Fox	14104	S	Er	uB	A	S	O	K	N	O
Nf8	384: Hasinai	13105	O	En	Uv	A	O	O	B	N	H
Nf9	661: Menomini	42202	O	Fp	P	C	M	O	O	O	O
Nf10	695: Iowa	05005	O	N	uP	.	Ms	O	O	.	O
Nf11	696: Oto	05104	Bs	N	uPu	.	S	O	O	O	O
Nf12	1104: Ponca	24103	T	N	Pu	.	S	O	O	O	O
Nf13	1158: Shawnee	14203	T	Fn	P	A	S	O	O	N	O
Ng1	79: Huron	11305	O	Em	M	S	O	S	O	N	I
Ng3	180: Creek	22204	T	En	M	S	O	Ms	O	N	C
Ng5	278: Cherokee	12205	O	Fn	M	S	O	S	O	S	C
Ng6	279: Delaware	22204	O	En	Mv	S	O	S	O	.	H
Ng7	385: Natchez	03205	O	Fr	V	A	O	O*	B	N	Z*
Ng8	386: Timucua	22204	.	En	M	S	O	P	O	.	C
Ng10	663: Iroquois	13204	O	Em	M	S	O	M	K	.	I
Ng11	664: Yuchi	11206	O	N	Nu*	A	O	S	O	.	C*
Ng12	1159: Choctaw	22204	O	N	Mn	A	O	M	O	N	C
Nh1	81: Chiricahua	64000	O	Fr	Uv	A	O	O	B	N	H
Nh2	82: Hano	00037	O	Fm	M	S	O	L	O	N	C
Nh3	182: Navaho	21034	T	Fs	Mv	A	O	Ps	O	N	I
Nh4	183: Zuni	11008	O	Em	M	S	O	Pl	O	N	C
Nh5	280: Maricopa	41203	O	N	P	A	S	O	O	N	I*
Nh6	281: Taos	02017	O	M	N	D	O	O	B	N	E
Nh7	343: Cochiti	02107	O	Fm	Mn	D	O	S	O	N	H
Nh8	387: Jemez	12007	O	M	bN	D	O	L	O	N	E
Nh9	433: Picuris	02017	O	M	N	D	O*	O	B	O	E
Nh10	434: Isleta	11017	O	M	N	D	O	O	B	N	H
Nh11	435: Tewa	01018	O	M	N	D	O	O	B	N	E
Nh12	436: Santa Ana	11026	O	Fm	Bn	D	O	L	O	O	H
Nh13	437: Acoma	11017	O	Em	Bn	D	O	L	O	O	C
Nh15	439: Mescalero	44101	O	Fr	U	A	O	O	B	N	H
Nh16	440: Jicarilla	34102	O	Fr	U	A	O	O	B	N	I
Nh17	441: W. Apache	34003	T	Fn	Mv	S	O	Ps	O	N	I
Nh18	442: Hopi	11017	O	Em	M	A	O	S	O	N	C
Nh19	443: Cocopa	22204	S	N	uP	A	S	O	O	N	I
Nh20	444: Kamia	22204	O	N	uP	A	S	O	O	N	I
Nh21	445: Mohave	32104	O	N	B	A	S	O	O	N	H
Nh22	446: Yuma	21205	O	M	Pu	C	S	O	O	N	I
Nh23	628: Keweyipaya	63001	O	N	B	A	S	O	O	N	I
Nh24	697: Lipan	64000	O	Em	U	A	O	O	B	O	H
Nh25	716: Sia	01027	O	M	N	D	O	S	O	O	C
Ni1	83: Tarahumara	11035	S	N	uNb	D	O	O	K	S	H
Ni2	184: Papago	32005	O	Fr	V	A	O*	O	B	N	H
Ni3	282: Huichol	12115	O	Fn	uB	D	O	O	K	Q	H
Ni4	283: Seri	22600	B	Fm	V	A	O	O	B	O	H
Ni5	717: Chichimec	54100	O	M	Uv	A	O	O	B	O	H*
Ni6	1160: Pima	31105	O	Fn	V	A	O*	O	B	N	I
Ni7	1161: Yaqui	21106	O	Fn	V	A	O	O	B	N	H
Nj1	84: Chinantec	00028	O	Gm	V	D	O	O	B	N	H
Nj2	185: Aztec	01207	T	N	V	S	O	O	R*	O	H

TABLE B. *Continued*

1	3	28	30	31	32	34	35	36	37	38	39
Ne20	627: Santee	Cc	S	.	20	.	C	.	0	.	Eo
Nf2	78: Winnebago	Ec	T	.	41	.	.	.	0	P	O
Nf3	179: Omaha	Ec	T	2	31	O	C	1	0	A	Eo
Nf4	276: Miami	Ec	T	5	31	B	C	.	0	.	O
Nf5	277: Wichita	Ec	T	.	31	A	.	5	0	A	Eo
Nf6	342: Pawnee	Ec	T	4	31	A	C	1	0	R	Eo
Nf7	383: Fox	Ec	S	.	41	C*	.	.	0	A	Eo
Nf8	384: Hasinai	Ec	H	.	32	C	C	.	0	A	O
Nf9	661: Menomini	Ec	T	.	31	.	C	.	0	.	O
Nf10	695: Iowa	Ec	T	.	31	.	C	.	0	A	Eo
Nf11	696: Oto	Ec	T	.	30	.	C	.	0	A	Eo
Nf12	1104: Ponca	Ec	T	.	31	.	C	.	0	A	Eo
Nf13	1158: Shawnee	Ec	T	.	31	C	C	.	0	A	O
Ng1	79: Huron	Ec	T	5	31	A	C	5	0	A	O
Ng3	180: Creek	Ec	V	5	42	A	C	2	0	.	O
Ng5	278: Cherokee	Ec	V	4	32	.	C	.	0	A	O
Ng6	279: Delaware	Ec	T	4	30	B	.	.	0	A	O
Ng7	385: Natchez	Ec	V	4	31	A	A	.	0	.	O
Ng8	386: Timucua	Ec	T	.	31	O	.	.	0	.	O
Ng10	663: Iroquois	Ec	V	4	32	A	C	4*	0	P*	O
Ng11	664: Yuchi	Ec	V	.	31	.	C	.	0	.	O
Ng12	1159: Choctaw	Ec	N	.	21	.	.	.	0	A	O
Nh1	81: Chiricahua	Cc	B	.	30	O	C	5	0	A	Eo
Nh2	82: Hano	Jc	V	5	40	.	.	.	0	A	Bo*
Nh3	182: Navaho	Jc	T	4	30	O	C	2	0	A	So*
Nh4	183: Zuni	Jc	V	6	40	O	S	.	0	A	So
Nh5	280: Maricopa	Jc	V	2	31	O	C	.	0	A	O
Nh6	281: Taos	Ic	V	5	20	.	C	.	0	A	qEo*
Nh7	343: Cochiti	Jc	V	5	30	O	.	1	0	A	qEo*
Nh8	387: Jemez	Jc	V	5	30	.	C	.	0	A	Eo
Nh9	433: Picuris	Jc	V	3	20	O	C	.	0	.	.
Nh10	434: Isleta	Jc	V	6	20	O	C	.	0	A	So
Nh11	435: Tewa	Jc	V	4*	20	O	.	.	0	.	qEo*
Nh12	436: Santa Ana	Jc	V	4	30	O	.	2	0	A	qBo*
Nh13	437: Acoma	Ic	V	6	30	.	.	.	0	A	So
Nh15	439: Mescalero	Cc	S	.	30	.	C	.	0	A	O
Nh16	440: Jicarilla	Ec	S	.	30	O	C	4	0	A	Eo
Nh17	441: W. Apache	Ec	T	1	30	.	C	.	0	A	Eo
Nh18	442: Hopi	Jc	V	4	40	O	.	2	0	P	So
Nh19	443: Cocopa	Ic	N	.	30	O	C	3	0	A	Eo
Nh20	444: Kamia	Ic	N	.	31	O	C	.	0	.	O
Nh21	445: Mohave	Ic	N	.	31	O	C	.	0	.	O
Nh22	446: Yuma	Ic	V	1	20	.	C	1	0	A	O
Nh23	628: Keweyipaya	Cc	S	.	20	.	.	.	0	A	O
Nh24	697: Lipan	O	S	.	31	.	C	.	0	A	Eo
Nh25	716: Sia	Jc	V	4	30	A	.	2	0	A	Bo*
Ni1	83: Tarahumara	Ic	N	.	20	C	S	1	0	A	Bo*
Ni2	184: Papago	Jc	T	.	30	C	C	1	0	A	O
Ni3	282: Huichol	Ec	H	5	30	.	O*	.	0	A	Bm
Ni4	283: Seri	O	S	.	30	.	.	.	0	A	O
Ni5	717: Chichimec	O	B	.	20	O	C	2*	0*	A*	O
Ni6	1160: Pima	Jc	V	.	30	.	C	.	0	A	O*
Ni7	1161: Yaqui	Jc	V	.	30	.	C	.	0	A	O*
Nj1	84: Chinantec	Ec	V	5	30	C	.	.	0	A	So
Nj2	185: Aztec	Jc	V	8	32	B	S	.	0	.	O

TABLE C.   *Continued*

1	3	42	44	46	48	50	52	54	56	58	60	62
Ne20	627: Santee	O	O	P	O	.	.	.	M	M	.	F
Nf2	78: Winnebago	O	.	F	F	P	F	G	M	N	O	G
Nf3	179: Omaha	O	O	F	F	M	D	F	M	E	M	G
Nf4	276: Miami	O	F	F	F	P	F	F	M	.	O	F
Nf5	277: Wichita	O	O	.	.	.	N	F	M	O	M	F
Nf6	342: Pawnee	O	O	F	F	.	D	.	M	.	M	F
Nf7	383: Fox	O	O	F	F	M	F	.	M	.	M	F
Nf8	384: Hasinai	O	O	G	F	.	M	F	M	.	O	G
Nf9	661: Menomini	O	.	F	F	P	F	G	M	M	O	F
Nf10	696: Iowa	O	O	F	F	.	M	.	M	.	M	.
Nf11	696: Oto	O	O	F	F	.	M	.	M	M	M	G
Nf12	1104: Ponca	O	O	F	F	.	M	F	M	M	M	F
Nf13	1158: Shawnee	O	O	F	F	P	F	.	M	.	O	F
Ng1	79: Huron	O	O	F	F	M	M	F	M	M	O	F
Ng3	180: Creek	O*	F	F	F	M	M	F	M	N	O	G
Ng5	278: Cherokee	O	.	.	F	M	.	F	M	M	O	G
Ng6	279: Delaware	O	.	F	F	M	M	G	M	M	O	G
Ng7	385: Natchez	O	F	F	F	M	M	.	M	M	O	G
Ng8	386: Timucua	O	O	.	F	P	M	.	M	.	O	G
Ng10	663: Iroquois	O	O	P	F	M	M	F	M	M	O	F
Ng11	664: Yuchi	O	.	P	F	P	.	.	M	E	O	E
Ng12	1159: Choctaw	O	O	F	F	P	M	.	M	.	O	G
Nh1	81: Chiricahua	O	O	F	F	O	F	F	M	O	M	E
Nh2	82: Hano	O	M	.	F	O	.	.	M	O	M	M
Nh3	182: Navaho	Mc*	F	M	F	O	M	F	M	O	E	N
Nh4	183: Zuni	O	M	.	F	O	.	O	M	O	.	N
Nh5	280: Maricopa	O	M	M	F	O	M	F	M	M	O	N
Nh6	281: Taos	O	O	.	F	O	.	.	M	O	N	N
Nh7	343: Cochiti	O	.	.	F	O	.	.	M	M	.	N
Nh8	387: Jemez	O	M	.	F	O	.	E	M	O	.	M
Nh9	433: Picuris	O	.	.	F	.	.	.	M	O	.	M
Nh10	434: Isleta	O	D	.	F	.	.	.	M	O	.	.
Nh11	435: Tewa	O	M	M	F	.	N	.	M	.	.	M
Nh12	436: Santa Ana	O	O	P	F*	O	.	.	M	O	.	N
Nh13	437: Acoma	O	.	.	F	O	.	.	M	O	.	N
Nh15	439: Mescalero	O	O	F	F	O	E	F	M	.	O	G
Nh16	440: Jicarilla	O	O	F	F	O	F	F	M	.	.	E
Nh17	441: W. Apache	O	O	F*	F	O	G	F	M	O	Mb	G
Nh18	442: Hopi	O*	M	M	F	O	N	F	M	O	M	M
Nh19	443: Cocopa	O	N	M	F	O	.	G	M	.	O	E
Nh20	444: Kamia	O	G	.	F	O	M	.	M	.	O	E
Nh21	445: Mohave	O	M	E	F	O	M	.	M	.	O	E
Nh22	446: Yuma	O	M	M	F	O	.	.	M	.	O	E
Nh23	628: Keweyipaya	O	M	O	F	M	M	G	M	M	F	G
Nh24	697: Lipan	O	O	F	.	O	.	F	M	O	.	O
Nh25	716: Sia	O	O*	P	F	O	.	.	M	O	.	M
Ni1	83: Tarahumara	O*	F	D	F	.	M	F	M	O	D	M
Ni2	184: Papago	O	M	M	F	O	.	F	M	O	O	N
Ni3	282: Huichol	O	F	P	F	.	M	Nb	M	M	D	N
Ni4	283: Seri	O	O	.	F	O	M	.	M	.	O	O
Ni5	717: Chichimec	O	O	M*	O	O	M*	F	M	.	O	O
Ni6	1160: Pima	O	M	M	F	O	M	D	M	.	O	N
Ni7	1161: Yaqui	O	P	M	F	P	.	.	M	N	O	M
Nj1	84: Chinante	O	F	.	F	.	.	F	M	O	F	M
Nj2	185: Aztec	Mc	F	Mc	Mc	P	Mc	O	M	Mc	O	N

TABLE D. *Continued*

1	3	64	67	69	71	73	74	76	78	80–84	85–89
Ne20	627: Santee	Sx	O	O	O	.	.	O	.	CGRCH	————
Nf2	87: Winnebago	Sx	O	O	O	P	.	Pe	.	RGBGB	CGRDM
Nf3	179: Omaha	Sx	O	O	If	I	Pe	Pe	P	CSWDE	CGRCH
Nf4	276: Miami	Ag	O	O	Sf	P	.	.	.	RGM.M	————
Nf5	277: Wichita	Cd	O	O	O	P	.	O	.	CGRBG	————
Nf6	342: Pawnee	Cd	D	O	If	P	O	Np	.	CSRDE	CGRCH
Nf7	383: Fox	Ag	O	O	Sf	P	.	O	.	RGB.B	CGRDM
Nf8	384: Hasinai	Cd	D	O	I	P	.	.	.	CGRBG	————
Nf9	661: Menomini	Ag	O	O	Sf	.	.	.	.	RG...	————
Nf10	695: Iowa	Sx	D	O	O	Q	.	.	.	CSWDE	CGRCH
Nf11	696: Oto	Sx	D	O	O	.	.	Pe	.	CSWDE	CGRCH
Nf12	1104: Ponca	Sx	D	O	O	P	.	O	F	CGRDE	CGRCH
Nf13	1158: Shawnee	Ag	O	O	I	P	O	Pe	F	CGRDB	RG...
Ng1	79: Huron	Ir	W	O	O	N	.	.	F	RGSRB	————
Ng3	180: Creek	Nm	O	O	O	N	.	Pe	E	RGPGB	CGPCG
Ng5	278: Cherokee	Ir	O	O	O	.	.	.	.	RGPGW	CGRCE
Ng6	279: Delaware	Ag	O	O	O	N	N*	.	F	CGRDB	RGB.B
Ng7	385: Natchez	Nm	E*	C*	.	M	.	.	F	RGPDG	————
Ng8	386: Timucua	Nm	D	O	.	M	Me	Me	.	CGPCG	RGP.G
Ng10	663: Iroquois	Ir	O	O	O	N	.	Me	F	RGBRB	————
Ng11	664: Yuchi	Xx	O	O	O	E	.	.	.	RGPGE	————
Ng12	1159: Choctaw	Nm	O	O	O	.	.	.	.	CGPCB	RG.GG
Nh1	81: Chiricahua	AtS	O	O	O	C	O	O	V	CGRDG	————
Nh2	82: Hano	TaE	O	O	O	.	N	.	A	RGAFE	————
Nh3	182: Navaho	AtS	O	O	If	C	.	Me*	P	CGRDE	————
Nh4	183: Zuni	Xx	O	O	O	E	N*	Ce	.	RGAFE	————
Nh5	280: Maricopa	HoY	O	O	O	.	Ce	O	.	CGRDE	RGEFE
Nh6	281: Taos	TaI	O	O	O	E	.	.	A	RGAFE	————
Nh7	343: Cochiti	Kr	O	O	O	E	.	Ce	.	RGAFE	————
Nh8	387: Jemez	TaO	O	O	O	E	.	Qe	.	RGAFE	————
Nh9	433: Picuris	TaI	O	O	O	E	.	.	.	RGSFE	————
Nh10	434: Isleta	TaI	O	O	O	E	Ce	Ce	.	RGAFE	————
Nh11	435: Tewa	TaE	O	O	O	E	Ce	Ce	F	RGAFE	————
Nh12	436: Santa Ana	Kr	W	O	O	E	Ce	Ce	F	RGAFE	————
Nh13	437: Acoma	Kr	O	O	O	.	Ce	Ce	.	RGAFE	————
Nh15	439: Mescalero	AtS	O	O	I	.	.	O	.	CGRDG	————
Nh16	440: Jicarilla	AtS	O	O	O	P	Ce	Ce	P	CGRDG	CGRCH
Nh17	441: W. Apache	StS	O	O	O	N*	Ce	Ce	P	CGRDG	————
Nh18	442: Hopi	Ss	O	O	O	N	N*	Pe	F	RGAFE	————
Nh19	443: Cocopa	HoY	O	O	I	C	O	O	P	RSRRE	RGAFG
Nh20	444: Kamia	HoY	O	O	.	C	O	O	.	RGRDE	————
Nh21	445: Mohave	HoY	O	O	I	P	.	O	F	RSRRE	————
Nh22	446: Yuma	HoY	O	O	.	C	O	O	.	CSRDE	RGAGG
Nh23	628: Keweyipaya	HoY	O	O	O	O	O	Pe	F	EGWHG	————
Nh24	697: Lipan	AtS	O	O	O	C	O	.	.	CGRDG	————
Nh25	716: Sia	Kr	O	O	O	E	Pe	Ce	.	RGAFE	————
Ni1	83: Tarahumara	Tc	W	O	O	E	Ce	Ce	F	RGWHW	————
Ni2	184: Papago	Pi	O	O	O	O	Pe	O	.	CSG.E	RGOFE
Ni3	282: Huichol	Na	W	O	O	E	Qp	Ce	.	RGSHG	————
Ni4	283: Seri	Xy	O	O	O	.	O	O	.	RGRRG	————
Ni5	717: Chichimec	Om	O	O	O	C	O	O	V	RG.GG*	————
Ni6	1160: Pima	Pi	O	O	O	P	Pe	O	.	CGRDE	————
Ni7	1161: Yaqui	Tc	O	O	O	E	.	.	.	RGGGG	————
Nj1	84: Chinantec	Xx	.	O	O	E	Pu	Pu	.	RGAGG	————
Nj2	185: Aztec	Na	C	O	I	P	Pp	Pp	P	REAFG	QGSF.

TABLE A. *Continued*

1	3	7	12	14	16	19	20	22	24	25	27
Nj3	284: Popoluca	01108	O	R	V	.	O	O	B	O		H
Nj4	285: Totonac	11116	O	.	V	.	O	O	B	O		H
Nj7	1162: Mixe	01018	O	Fm	V	S	O	O	B		.	H
Nj8	1163: Tarasco	01207	O	Fn	V	S	O	O	B	Q		D
Nj9	1164: Tlaxcalans	00028	O	Fn	V	C	S	O	O	Õ		H
Nj10	1165: Zapotec	00118	O	M	Vn	D	O	O	B	O		H
Sa1	85: Cuna	01306	S	En	U	D	O	O	B	S		H
Sa3	186: Chorti	01126	S	Fm	B	E	O	O	B	S		H
Sa4	286: Choco	12106	O	M	uNv	D	O	O	K	S		H
Sa5	287: Bribri	11215	S	M	uNv	A	O	S*	O	M		H
Sa6	345: Yucatec Maya	01207	St	M	uVn	A	L	O	O	E		H
Sa7	388: Black Carib	01306	O	N	No	A	O	O	R*	C		I
Sa8	389: Mam	00019	T	Fm	P	S	L	O	O	N		H
Sa9	390: Miskito	32212	Ts	En	Un	A	O	O	B*	Cc		I
Sa10	665: Lacandon	02206	T	Fp	P	C	L	O	O	.		.
Sa12	1129: Lenca	11107	O	P	uN	D	O	O	B		.	.
Sa13	1166: Quiche	00019	T	N	P	S	L	O	O	O		H
Sb1	87: Callinago	01504	S	En	M	S	O	L	O	Cp		I
Sb2	187: Cagaba	00028	S	N	U	A	O	O	B	S		H
Sb5	289: Paraujano	31600	B	N	Bn	D	O	O	B	O		H
Sb6	391: Goajiro	01171	B	Fq	uA	A	O	Sl	O	T		C
Sb7	718: Yupa	31105	O	N	Un	A	O	O	B*	Cc		I
Sb8	1130: Taino	11206	B	Fn	V	.	O	*			.	.
Sc1	88: Warrau	43201	S	Er	U	D	O	O	B		.	H
Sc2	89: Yaruro	22114	S	Gn	Ua	D	O	O	B	Cc		H
Sc3	189: Barama Carib	22204	S	N	uBn	A	O	O	Q*	Cc		I
Sc4	290: Guahibo	13204	S	Fn	U	A	O	O	B	Cc		I
Sc5	291: Wapishana	22204	S	P*	uV	E	O	O	B*	Cc		I
Sc6	392: Saramacca	12205	Bs	Q	Au	S	O	S	O	T		H
Sc7	393: Yabarana	13204	S	N	uUv	E	O	O	B*	Cc		I
Sc8	447: Piaroa	24301	O	N	U	E	O	O	B*	Cc		I
Sc9	448: Curipaco	02305	.	M	V	D	O	O	B	O		H
Sc10	449: Locono	11305	S	N	M	A	O	S	O	Cm		.
Sc11	450: Camaracoto	02206	S*	P	Vn	A	O	O	B	C		I
Sc12	451: Macusi	12205	S	N	uUn	A	O	O	B	Cc		I
Sc13	452: Panare	03205	O	R*	Uv	D	O	O	B*	Cc		I
Sc15	454: Taulipang	12304	S	N	U	.	O	O	B	.		I
Sc16	455: Makitare	23203	O	Fr*	U	E	O	O	B*	Cc		I
Sc17	719: Piapoco	02206	O	Fq	uV	E	O	O	B	Cc		I
Sd1	90: Mundurucu	13204	S	En	Uv*	A	M	O	O	Cc		Z*
Sd2	190: Tapirape	11305	O	Em	U	D	O	O	B	O		H
Sd3	292: Palikur	02305	O	M	bPu	.	Ms	O	O	.		.
Sd5	720: Maue	12106	S	Fn	Pn	.	S	O	O	.		.
Sd6	721: Shiriana	34300	St	En	U	D	O	O	B	C		I
Sd7	722: Waiwai	12205	S	N*	uB	A	O	O	B	C		I
Sd8	723: Sanema	34102	S	Ep	uB	S	O	O	B	O		H
Se1	91: Siriono	35101	O	Er	U	S	O	O*	B*	Mm		C
Se2	92: Tucuna	11404	X	N	uPu	C	M	O	O	C		I
Se3	191: Jivaro	12106	S	P	uN	A	O	O	K	Cc		I
Se4	192: Yagua	05104	S	M*	uP	C	L	O	O	O		.
Se5	293: Cubeo	11305	X	N*	Pu	C	P	O	O	Cm		I
Se6	347: Witoto	22204	S	N*	P	C	L	O	O	C		.
Se8	634: Amahuaca	04105	Sx	Gn	Vn	E	O	O	B	Cc		I
Se9	666: Conibo	12403	S	Fr	U	E	O	O*	B	*		.
Se10	1131: Cocama	01504	S	En	uV	.	L*	O	O	*		.

TABLE B. *Continued*

1	3	28	30	31	32	34	35	36	37	38	39
Nj3	284: Popoluca	Ec	V	.	20	C	A	.	0	.	P*
Nj4	285: Totonac	Ec*	V	7	31	.	.	.	0*	A	Eo
Nj7	1162: Mixe	Ec	V	.	41	C	.	2	0	A	qBo
Nj8	1163: Tarasco	Ic	V	.	42	.	.	.	0	.	O
Nj9	1164: Tlaxcalans	Ec	X	7	4*	C	O	3	0	A	qBm
Nj10	1165: Zapotec	Ec	V	7	3*	C	.	.	0	A	.
Sa1	85: Cuna	Ec	V	2	31	C	O*	.	0	A	P
Sa3	186: Chorti	Ec	X	.	41	A	O	.	0	A	P*
Sa4	286: Choco	Et	N	2	20	A	.	.	0	A	O
Sa5	287: Bribri	Ec	N	.	20	B	O*	2	0	A	P
Sa6	345: Yucatec Maya	Ec	X	7	31	.	C	.	0	T	O
Sa7	388: Black Carib	Hr	V	6	20	C	.	2	0	A	O
Sa8	389: Mam	Ec	V	6	4*	C	.	.	0	A	Eo
Sa9	390: Miskito	Er	V	3	31	C	A	1	0	A	Bm
Sa10	665: Lacandon	Ec	N	.	3*	A	.	.	0	A	.
Sa12	1129: Lenca	Ec	V	.	20	C	.	.	0	A	P
Sa13	1166: Quiche	Ec	V	.	31	C	.	.	0	A	Sm
Sb1	87: Callinago	Ir	H	.	30	A	.	2	0	T	O
Sb2	187: Cagaba	Er	T	.	30	A	O	.	0	.	P*
Sb5	289: Paraujano	O	V	.	20	A	.	.	0	A	O
Sb6	391: Goajiro	Cc	B	1	30	B	A	2	0	.	Bm
Sb7	718: Yupa	Ec	V	1	20	A	.	.	0	A	O
Sb8	1130: Taino	Jr	V	.	22	A	A	.	0	.	O
Sc1	88: Warrau	Cr	T	2	30	C	A	2	0	A	O
Sc2	89: Yaruro	Er	V	.	20	.	O	1	0	.	P
Sc3	189: Barama Carib	Er	N	1	20	A	A	1	0	A	O
Sc4	290: Guahibo	Er	T	2	30	O	A	2	0	A	O
Sc5	291: Wapishana	Er	V	.	30	.	A	.	0	A	O
Sc6	392: Saramacca	Er	V	.	32	.	.	.	0	.	O
Sc7	393: Yabarana	Er	V	1	20	O	.	2	0	.	O
Sc8	447: Piaroa	Er	S	.	20	O*	.	.	0	.	O
Sc9	448: Curipaco	Er	V	1	20	.	.	.	0	.	O
Sc10	449: Locono	Er	V	1	30	A	.	.	0	.	O
Sc11	450: Camaracoto	Er	V	.	20	.	.	.	0	.	O
Sc12	451: Macusi	Er	V	.	20	.	.	.	0	.	O
Sc13	452: Panare	Er	S	1	20	.	.	.	0	.	O
Sc15	454: Taulipang	Er	V	.	20	.	.	.	0	.	O
Sc16	455: Makitare	Er	V	.	30	.	.	.	0	P	O
Sc17	719: Piapoco	Er	V	1	30	.	.	.	0	.	O
Sd1	90: Mundurucu	Er	V	2	30	O	.	.	0	T	O
Sd2	190: Tapirape	Er	V	3	30	O	A	3	0	T	O
Sd3	292: Palikur	Er	V	.	20	.	.	.	0	.	O
Sd5	720: Maue	Er	V	2	30	.	.	2	0	.	O*
Sd6	721: Shiriana	O*	S	2	30	.	.	.	0	A	O
Sd7	722: Waiwai	Er	V	.	20	O*	.	.	0	A	O
Sd8	723: Sanema	Cr	S	1	30	O	.	.	0	.	O
Se1	91: Siriono	Ec	S	1	30	A	A	1	0	A	O
Se2	92: Tucuna	Er	V	3	20	A	A	3	0	P	O
Se3	191: Jivaro	Er	N	1	20	O	O	5	0	A	P
Se4	192: Yagua	Er	V	1	20	O	A	3	0	A	O
Se5	293: Cubeo	Er	W	1	20	A	O	4	0	A	O
Se6	347: Witoto	Er	V	.	20	A	A	5	0	A	O
Se8	634: Amahuaca	Ec	N	1	20	O	A	1	0	A	O
Se9	666: Conibo	Er	V	1	20	O	O	.	0	T	O
Se10	1131: Cocama	Er	V	5	30	A	.	.	0	A	P

TABLE C. *Continued*

1	3	42	44	46	48	50	52	54	56	58	60	62
Nj3	284: Popoluca	O	F	.	P	.	.	O	M	M	.	M
Nj4	285: Totonac	O*	F	.	F	.	M	F	M	M	D	N
Nj7	1162: Mixe	O	F	F	F	O	M	O	M	M	M	N
Nj8	1163: Tarasco	P*	F	.	P	P	M	.	M	.	O	M
Nj9	1164: Tlaxcalans	Mc	Mc	O	F	O	M	O	O	O	Eb	M
Nj10	1165: Zapotec	.	F	.	Mc	O	M	.	M	M	E	M
Sa1	85: Cuna	O	F*	.	G	Mc	M	N	M	M	M	M
Sa3	186: Chorti	O	O	M	G	.	M	G	M	N	D	M
Sa4	286: Choco	O	O	.	Fa	M	.	.	M	M	O	E
Sa5	287: Bribri	O	F	O	F	O	.	G	M	M	.	E
Sa6	345: Yucatec Maya	P	F	.	P	P	.	O	M	M	O	M
Sa7	388: Black Carib	O	O	O	O	M	M	.	M	D	O	G
Sa8	389: Mam	.	F	.	P*	.	.	.	.	.	M	M
Sa9	390: Miskito	O	F	P	F	M	E	E	M	N	.	F
Sa10	665: Lacandon	O	F	O	P	.	M	.	M	M	.	M
Sa12	1129: Lenca	O	O*	P	F	.	.	.	M	M	.	M
Sa13	1166: Quiche	O	D	.	F	O	Mc	.	M	M	Eb	M
Sb1	87: Callinago	O	F	.	F	M	M	F	M	N	O	G
Sb2	187: Cagaba	O	M	.	M	M	N	F	M	E	.	E
Sb5	289: Paraujano	O	.	.	P	P	.	.	.	.	O	O
Sb6	391: Goajiro	O	F	M	F	O	M	F	M	M	D	F
Sb7	718: Yupa	O	F	O	M	.	.	B	M	N	O	D
Sb8	1130: Taino	O	O	O	P	M	.	.	M	M	O	G
Sc1	88: Warrau	O	M	.	F	P	.	.	M	M	O	G
Sc2	89: Yaruro	O	O	.	F	M	M	F	M	M	M	N
Sc3	189: Barama Carib	O	F	O	F	M	M	G	M	N	O	D
Sc4	290: Guahibo	O	O	O	F	M	M	G	M	M	O	N
Sc5	291: Wapishana	O	F	.	F	M	.	F	M	N	O	G
Sc6	392: Saramacca	O	.	.	.	P	.	E	M	M	O	G
Sc7	393: Yabarana	O	O	O	F	M	M	F	M	N	O	G
Sc8	447: Piaroa	O	F	.	P	P	.	F	M	M	O	G
Sc9	448: Curipaco	O	P	O	P	.	M	F	M	M	O	G
Sc10	449: Locono	O	P	O	P	P	M	.	M	.	O	N
Sc11	450: Camaracoto	O	.	O	.	.	M	F	M	M	O	G
Sc12	451: Macusi	O	F	O	P	.	M	.	M	M	O	G
Sc13	452: Panare	O	.	O	.	O	E	.	M	N	O	G
Sc15	454: Taulipang	O	F	O	F	M	M	.	M	.	O	G
Sc16	455: Makitare	O	M	O	M	M	M	.	M	N	O	G
Sc17	719: Piapoco	O	F	O	.	.	.	.	M	M	O	G
Sd1	90: Mundurucu	O	O	.	F	O	N	E	M	N	O	D
Sd2	190: Tapirape	O	O	O	F	O	M	E	M	N	O	N
Sd3	292: Palikur	O	P	O	P	M	M	.	M	M	O	E
Sd5	720: Maue	O	O	.	O*	P	.	M	M	M	O	D
Sd6	721: Shiriana	O	.	O	F	M	M	F	M	M	O	G
Sd7	722: Waiwai	O	D	.	F	M	M	G	M	N	O	G
Sd8	723: Sanema	O	F	O	P	O	.	.	M	.	O	.
Se1	91: Siriono	O	O	.	F	O	M	E	M	M	O	E
Se2	92: Tucuna	O	F	.	G	M	M	E	M	M	O	G
Se3	191: Jivaro	O	M	O	F	M	M	G	M	M	F	G
Se4	192: Yagua	O	O	P	Fa	M	N	.	M	N	O	G
Se5	293: Cubeo	O	O	O	F	M	M	G	M	M	O	G
Se6	347: Witoto	O	O	O	F	M	M	M	M	M	O	G
Se8	634: Amahuaca	O	F	O	F	O	M	E	M	M	O	D
Se9	666: Conibo	O	F	O	F	P	.	.	M	M	O	F
Se10	1131: Cocama	O	F	.	F	M	.	.	.	.	O	.

TABLE D. *Continued*

1	3	64	67	69	71	73	74	76	78	80–84	85–89
Nj3	284: Popoluca	Mz	O	O	O	E	Pe	Pe	.	RGWHG	————
Nj4	285: Totonac	Xx	.	O	Sf	.	.	.	.	RGWHG	————
Nj7	1162: Mixe	Mz	O	O	O	E	Ce	Ce	P	RGAHG	————
Nj8	1163: Tarasco	Xx	D	O	.	P	P.	P.	.	REWHW	RGAGG
Nj9	1164: Tlaxcalans	Na	O	O	O	S	Pe	Pe	P	RGAGT	————
Nj10	1165: Zapotec	Za	.	O	O	E	Ce	Ce	.	RGAGG	————
Sa1	85: Cuna	Ch	W	O	Sf	E	.	.	V	RGWGG	————
Sa3	186: Chorti	Ma	C*	O	O	E	Ce	Ce	.	REGGG	————
Sa4	286: Choco	Xy*	O	O	O	.	Pp	.	.	CPOCG	————
Sa5	287: Bribri	Ch	O	O	O	.	O	Ce	A	CGRCG	RPBGG
Sa6	345: Yucatec Maya	Ma	C	O	H	.	Qe	Qe	.	RG.GG	————
Sa7	388: Black Carib	Ca	O	O*	O	A	.	.	.	RGGGG	————
Sa8	389: Mam	Ma	W	O	O	A	Pe	Pe	V	RGAGG	RGAGT
Sa9	390: Miskito	Ms	O	O	O	.	.	.	E	RPMGG	RGWGG
Sa10	665: Lacandon	Ma	O	O	O	.	.	.	V	RGOGG	————
Sa12	1129: Lenca	Xx	D	O	O	P	.	.	.	RGAHG	————
Sa13	1166: Quiche	Ma	W	E*	Hf	C	Pe	Pe	V	RGAGT	————
Sb1	87: Callinago	Ca	O	O	H	C	*	*	T	RGWGG	————
Sb2	187: Cagaba	Ch	W	O	O	P	Pe	Pe	.	CGMCG	CGACG
Sb5	289: Paraujano	Ar	O	O	O	.	.	.	F	RPMGG	————
Sb6	391: Goajiro	Ar	W	O	H	M	.	Me	P	RGRGG	————
Sb7	718: Yupa	Ca	O	O	O	S	.	.	.	R....	————
Sb8	1130: Taino	Ar	D	O	S	M	.	M.	F	CGWCG	RGWGG
Sc1	88: Warrau	Xx	O	O	O	C	.	.	.	RPOGG	————
Sc2	89: Yaruro	Xx	O	O	O	Q	Ce	Pe	.	CGRDG	————
Sc3	189: Barama Carib	Ca	O	O	O	C	.	.	F	RGOGG	————
Sc4	290: Guahibo	Xx	O	O	O	C	O	Pp	P	RGGGG	————
Sc5	291: Wapishana	Ar	O	O	O	.	.	.	.	EGGHG	RGPGG
Sc6	392: Saramacca	IeR*	O	O	O	N	.	Ne	.	RGMGG	————
Sc7	393: Yabarana	Ca	O	O	O	.	.	.	F	RGOGG	————
Sc8	447: Piaroa	Xx	O	O	O	.	.	.	.	CGRBG	RGRGG
Sc9	448: Curipaco	Ar	O	O	O	.	.	.	.	RGA..	————
Sc10	449: Locono	Ar	O	O	S	.	.	.	.	.....	————
Sc11	450: Camaracoto	Ca	O	O	.	.	.	.	.	RG.CG	————
Sc12	451: Macusi	Ca	O	O	.	P	.	.	.	RGPHG	————
Sc13	452: Panare	Ca	O	O	O	.	.	.	.	CGRBG	————
Sc15	454: Taulipang	Ca	O	O	S	P	.	.	.	CGPCG	————
Sc16	455: Makitare	Ca	O	O	O	.	.	.	.	CGACG	————
Sc17	719: Piapoco	Ar	O	O	O	.	.	P.	P	RGWHG	————
Sd1	90: Mundurucu	Tg	O	O	O	P	O	O	T	RGPGG	RGOHG
Sd2	190: Tapirape	Tg	O	O	O	.	.	.	E	RGRRG	————
Sd3	292: Palikur	Ar	O	O	O	E	.	.	.	CP..G	————
Sd5	720: Maue	Tg	O	O	O	P	.	.	.	RGOGG	————
Sd6	721: Shiriana	Xx	O	O	O	C	.	.	.	RGRSG	————
Sd7	722: Waiwai	Ca	O	O	O	P	.	Pe	F	CGGCG	RGGGG
Sd8	723: Sanema	Xx	O	O	O	Q	.	.	F	RGWHG	————
Se1	91: Siriono	Tg	O	O	O	P	O	O	F	RGRHG	RGRSG
Se2	92: Tucuna	Xy*	O	O	O	.	O	Pe	P	EGGHG	RPGGG
Se3	191: Jivaro	Xx	O	O	O	O	O	Pe	P	EGWHG	————
Se4	192: Yagua	Pb	O	O	O	E	O	.	O	EGRHG	————
Se5	293: Cubeo	Be	O	O	Hf	P*	O	Pe	.	RGWHG	————
Se6	347: Witoto	Wi	O	O	I	P	.	.	P	RGGGG	————
Se8	634: Amahuaca	Pn	O	O	O	O	O	O	F	RGOGG	EGWHG
Se9	666: Conibo	Pn	O	O	I	.	O	P.	F	EGOHG	————
Se10	1131: Cocama	Tg	W	O	I	.	.	.	.	RGWGG	————

TABLE A. *Continued*

1	3	7	12	14	16	19	20	22	24	25	27
Se11	1167: Chacobo	22204	O	N	uV	A	O	O	B	Cc	I
Sf1	93: Inca	01027	O	M	Vn	D	O	O	B	Q	H
Sf2	193: Aymara	00136	O	Em	P	D	L	O	O	Ō	H
Sf3	194: Cayapa	11215	O	Fm	Vu	D	O	O	K	O	H
Sf4	294: Tunebo	11206	Ts	P	uVu	D	O	O	B	O	H
Sf5	348: Paez	11026	O	P	N	.	O	O	B	.	.
Sf6	395: Chibcha	01108	B	P	V	.	O	O*	B*	.	E
Sf7	667: Campa	03205	O	N	Vu	A	O	O	B	Q	.
Sg1	94: Yahgan	12700	St	N	V	E	O	O	B	Ñ	E
Sg2	195: Mapuche	10126	B	Fq	Pn	T	L	O	O	Mm	O*
Sg3	295: Ona	16300	O	N	Vn	E	O*	O	B	N	E
Sg4	349: Tehuelche	27100	Gb	Fn	V	A	O	O	B	Q	.
Sg5	396: Alacaluf	12700	O	N	uBn	A	O	O	B	Q	.
Sh1	95: Mataco	22411	S	Fn*	uUv	E	O	O	B	O	H
Sh2	96: Terena	21313	O	En	uBn	D	O	O	A	O	H
Sh3	196: Abipon	26110	B	N	uN	A	O	O	B	N	E
Sh4	296: Caduveo	04312	O	Fn	U	.	O	O	B	O	H
Sh5	297: Choroti	43201	S	M	U	E	O	O	B	O	E
Sh6	397: Chamacoco	64000	S	M	Uv	A	O	O	B	.	.
Sh7	398: Chiriguano	11215	S	Fn	uVn	A	O	O	B	Q	.
Sh8	724: Toba	23113	O	Fn	B	A	O	O	B	S	H
Sh9	1168: Lengua	25201	O	En	Uv	A	O	O	B	.	.
Si1	97: Bororo	45100	O	Fn	M	S	O	M	O	C	C
Si2	98: Trumai	21304	T	En	V	A	O	O	Q*	Cc	I
Si3	197: Bacairi	02305	O	Fn	uVn	D	O	O	Q*	C	I
Si4	198: Nambicuara	43102	O	N	Vu	A	O	O	B	Cc	I
Si5	298: Camayura	21304	S	En	uV	A	O	O	B*	Cc	I
Si6	350: Guato	42301	.	R	N	.	O	O	B	.	I
Si7	1131: Paressi	22105	O	Er	Uv	.	O	O	B	.	I
Si8	1169: Umotina	22105	O	.	uV	D	O	O	B	S	H
Sj1	99: Caraja	22402	O	Fn	Un	D	O*	O	K	Q	H
Sj2	100: Sherente	23104	O	N	uP	S	M	O	O	P	O
Sj3	199: Aweikoma	46000	O	P	B	D	O	O	B	Q	H
Sj4	200: Ramcocamecra	23104	S	Fm	M	S	O	M	O	O	C
Sj5	299: Botocudo	54100	O	Er	.	E	O	O	B	Q	H
Sj6	300: Tenetehara	12115	S	En	U	D	O	O	B	O	H
Sj7	399: Apinaye	22105	T	Em	M	S	*	*	O	R	C
Sj8	400: Tupinamba	22204	S	Eq	uUv	A	O	O	B*	Cc	.
Sj9	725: Coroa	12106	O	M	U	D	O*	O	B	O	O
Sj10	1170: Cayua	22105	O	M*	Vn	A	O	O	B	.	H

TABLE B. *Continued*

1	3	28	30	31	32	34	35	36	37	38	39
Se11	1167: Chacobo	Er	V	.	20	.	.	5	0	T	O
Sf1	93: Inca	Jc	V	7	24	A	S	.	0	A	Co
Sf2	193: Aymara	Er	V	5	3*	C	C	1	0	A	qBm*
Sf3	194: Cayapa	Ht	N	5	30	O	O	.	0	A	P
Sf4	294: Tunebo	Ec	V	3	20	A	.	.	0	A	O
Sf5	348: Paez	Ir	N	.	21	.	O	1	0	.	Bm*
Sf6	395: Chibcha	Jr	V	7	32	O*	.	.	0	.	O
Sf7	667: Campa	Er	V	1	20	A	A	.	0	T	O
Sg1	94: Yahgan	O	B	1	20	C	A	2	0	.	O
Sg2	195: Mapuche	Ic	H	2	40	B	C	3	0	A	Bm*
Sg3	295: Ona	O	B	2	20	A	A	.	0	A	O
Sg4	349: Tehuelche	O	B	2	30	A	C*	3	0	A	Eo*
Sg5	396: Alacaluf	O	B	1	20	O	A	1	0	.	O
Sh1	95: Mataco	Cv	S	2	30	O	C	3	0	A	So
Sh2	96: Terena	Er	S	.	40	A	.	.	0	A	Bo
Sh3	196: Abipon	O	B	.	20	O	A	5	0	.	Eo
Sh4	296: Caduveo	Er	B	.	31	.	A	4	0	A	Eo
Sh5	297: Choroti	Cv	W	1	20	O	C*	.	0	A	O*
Sh6	397: Chamacoco	Cn	B	.	21	B	.	4	0	.	O
Sh7	398: Chiriguano	Ec	V	.	31	.	C*	.	0	.	O*
Sh8	724: Toba	Hr	T	4	21	C*	C	3	0	A	Eo
Sh9	1168: Lengua	Cr	B	.	30	A	A*	.	0	A	O*
Si1	97: Bororo	O	S	.	41	O	A	.	0	.	O
Si2	98: Trumai	Er	V	1	30	O	A	4	0	.	O
Si3	197: Bacairi	Er	V	1	40	O	A	.	0	*	O
Si4	198: Nambicuara	Er	S	1	30	O	.	4	0	A	O
Si5	298: Camayura	Er	W	3	30	A	A	.	0	P	O
Si6	350: Guato	Ct	S	.	20	.	.	.	0	R	O
Si7	1131: Paressi	Er	V	1	30	O	A	.	0	A	O*
Si8	1169: Umotina	Er	V	2	30	O	.	.	0	A	O
Sj1	99: Caraja	Er	T	.	30	O	A	.	0	T	O
Sj2	100: Sherente	Er	V	.	30	O	A	.	0	T	O
Sj3	199: Aweikoma	O	B	1	20	O	.	.	0	A	O
Sj4	200: Ramcocamecra	Er	S	3	40	O	A	2	0	P	P
Sj5	299: Botocudo	O	B	2	30	.	.	.	0	.	O
Sj6	300: Tenetehara	Er	V	.	30	O	O	2	0	A	So*
Sj7	399: Apinaye	Er	V	2	30	A	A	2	0	A	O
Sj8	400: Tupinamba	Er	V	4	31	A	O*	.	0	.	O
Sj9	725: Coroa	Er	S	3	30	.	.	4	0	T	O
Sj10	1170: Cayua	Er	V	.	20	.	.	.	0	.	O*

TABLE C. *Continued*

1	3	42	44	46	48	50	52	54	56	58	60	62
Se11	1167: Chacobo	O	O	O	F	M	M	G	M	M	O	G
Sf1	93: Inca	Mc	F	O	F	P	M	O	M	O	OMG	
Sf2	193: Aymara	M	D	M	N	M	M	O	M	M	G	E
Sf3	194: Cayapa	O	F	.	F	M	.	F	M	M	.	G
Sf4	294: Tunebo	O	F	.	F	.	.	G	M	M	O	D
Sf5	348: Paez	P	F	.	F	O	M	.	M	O	M	E
Sf6	395: Chibcha	P	P	.	P	.	.	.	M	.	O	E
Sf7	667: Campa	O	P	.	P	P	.	M	M	O		F
Sg1	94: Yahgan	O	O	F	O	M	D	F	M	D	O	N
Sg2	195: Mapuche	M*	F	G	F	M	N	F	M	M	N	O
Sg3	295: Ona	O	O	F	O	.	.	F	M	N	O	O
Sg4	349: Tehuelche	M*	F*	F	P	O	F	E	M	.	M	O
Sg5	396: Alacaluf	O	O	O	O	M	M	.	M	D	O	O
Sh1	95: Mataco	O	F	F	F	O	F	G	M	M	F	G
Sh2	96: Terena	O	F	M	F	.	M	E	M	M	.	D
Sh3	196: Abipon	O	F	F	F	M	.	G	M	M	E	G
Sh4	296: Caduveo	O	F	M	F	.	.	E	M	N	M	O
Sh5	297: Choroti	O	F	F	F	O	E	G	M	M	G	D
Sh6	397: Chamacoco	O	P	O	P	O	.	E	M	.	O	F
Sh7	398: Chiriguano	O	F	M*	F	O	M	.	M	D	E	N
Sh8	724: Toba	O	F	O	F	O*	M	F	M	M	.	D
Sh9	1168: Lengua	O	F	O	F	M	D	F	M	M	O	M
Si1	97: Bororo	O	O	.	F	O	M	F	M	M	O	O
Si2	98: Trumai	O	O		O	M	M	G	M	M	O	D
Si3	197: Bacairi	O	O	O	E	M	M	.	M	M	O	D
Si4	198: Nambicuara	O	P	O	O*	O	M	G	M	N	O	N
Si5	298: Camayura	O	O	.	F	M	M	F	M	M	O	N
Si6	350: Guato	O	F	.	F	M	.	N	M	M	O	.
Si7	1131: Paressi	O	P	.	P	O	M	.	M	.		
Si8	1169: Umotina	O	F	.	F	.	.	F	M	E	O	M
Sj1	99: Caraja	O	F*	.	P	.	.	D	M	.	O	N
Sj2	100: Sherente	O	O	.	O	.	N	F	M	N	O	G
Sj3	199: Aweikoma	O	O	.	F	O	G	G	M	O	O	G
Sj4	200: Ramcocamecra	O	O	O	O	O	N	G	M	N	F	G
Sj5	299: Botocudo	O	O	.	O*	O	.	F	M	M	O	O
Sj6	300: Tenetehara	O	O	.	O*	.	.	M	.	N		E
Sj7	399: Apinaye	O	O	.	O	M	.	F	M	N	O	G
Sj8	400: Tupinamba	O	O	O	F	M	M	F	M	M	O	D
Sj9	725: Coroa	O	O	.	O	O	N*	F	M	M	O	N
Sj10	1170: Cayua	O	F	O	F	O	.	G	M	M	O	N

TABLE D. *Continued*

1	3	64	67	69	71	73	74	76	78	80–84	85–89
Se11	1167: Chacobo	Pn	O	O	O	.	.	.	P	RGBGG	————
Sf1	93: Inca	Ke	Ce	O	O	.	O	Pe	V	RGSGG	RGAHG
Sf2	193: Aymara	Ke	W	O*	O	.	Pe	Pe	A	RGEGG	————
Sf3	194: Cayapa	Ch	O	O	O	P	.	.	.	RPOHG	————
Sf4	294: Tunebo	Ch	O	O	.	C	.	Ce	.	RGWCG	RGWGG
Sf5	384: Paez	Ch	.	O	O	E	O	Pe	.	RGMHG	RGSHG
Sf6	395: Chibcha	Ch	Dc	O	S	M	Pe	Pe	F	RPPGG	CPPCG
Sf7	667: Campa	Ar	O	O	O	P	.	.	.	CGRDG	————
Sg1	94: Yahgan	Xx	O	O	O	O	O	O	P	CSRDG	CSRCG
Sg2	195: Mapuche	Ac	W	O	If	P	Pe	Pe	A	RGMHG	RGPGG
Sg3	295: Ona	Th	O	O	O	C	O	O	V	SGREH	CGRCG
Sg4	349: Tehuelche	Th	O	O	I	P	O	.	P	SGREH	————
Sg5	396: Alacaluf	Xx	O	O	O	O	O	.	.	CGRDH	————
Sh1	95: Mataco	Mm	O	O	O	.	O	O	F	CGRBG	————
Sh2	96: Terena	Ar	D	O	H	P	.	.	E	RGRRG	————
Sh3	196: Abipon	Gu	D	O	H	P	O	.	V	RGRSM	————
Sh4	296: Caduveo	Gu	D	O	S	.	.	Pp	F	RGPGG	————
Sh5	297: Choroti	Mm	O	O	O	.	O	O	F	CGRCG	————
Sh6	397: Chamacoco	Zm	D	O	S	.	.	.	.	RGRSM	————
Sh7	398: Chiriguano	Tg	.	O	.	P	Pe	.	.	RGPGG	————
Sh8	724: Toba	Gu	O	O	O	P	O	O	F	RGPGP	RGPSG
Sh9	1168: Lengua	Mn	O	O	O	P	O	.	.	*	————
Si1	97: Bororo	Bo	O	O	O	N	.	.	F	RGGGG	CGRCG
Si2	98: Trumai	Xx	O	O	If	P	O	.	F	EGGGG	————
Si3	197: Bacairi	Ca	O	O	O	C	.	.	.	EGRHG	————
Si4	198: Nambicuara	Xx	O	O	O	C	O	O	E	CGRBG	SGREG
Si5	298: Camayura	Tg	O	O	O	P	O	O	.	RGRHG	————
Si6	350: Guato	Xx	O	O	O	P	.	.	.	RGRGG	————
Si7	1131: Paressi	Ar	O	O	I	P	.	.	.	EGRRG	————
Si8	1169: Umotina	Bo	O	O	O	P	.	.	.	RGRGG	————
Sj1	99: Caraja	Xx	O	O	I	Q	.	.	.	RGRHG	————
Sj2	100: Sherente	Ge	O	O	O	P	.	.	.	RG.GG	————
Sj3	199: Aweikoma	Cg	O	O	O	O	O	O	F	RGRRG	————
Sj4	200: Ramcocamecra	Ge	O	O	O	.	O	Ce	P	RGGHG	————
Sj5	299: Botocudo	Xy*	O	O	O	C	O	.	E	CGRDG	RGRSG
Sj6	300: Tenetehara	Tg	O	O	O	A	O	Pe	.	RGGHG	————
Sj7	399: Apinaye	Ge	O	O	O	N	.	.	E	RGGGG	————
Sj8	400: Tupinamba	Tg	W	O	I	P	.	.	F	RGRRG	————
Sj9	725: Coroa	Ge	O	O	O	M	.	.	E	EGRRG	RGAHG
Sj10	1170: Cayua	Tg	O	O	.	.	.	.	.	RGRGG	————

Additional Bibliography

Masa (Ai9)
    Garine, I. de. 1964. Les Massa du Cameroun. Paris.
French Canadians (Cf5)
    Miner, H. 1939. St. Denis. Chicago.
Lithuanians (Ch9)
    Maciuika, B. V., ed. 1955. Lithuania. New Haven.
Sindhi (Ea1)
    Wilber, D. N. 1964. Pakistan. New Haven.
Iranians (Ea9)
    Vreeland, H. H., ed. 1957. Iran. New Haven.
Gujarati (Ef9)
    Karve, I. 1942-43. Kinship Terminology and Kinship Usages in Gujarat and Kathiawab. Bull. Deccan Coll. Res. Inst. 4: 208-226. Poona.
    Mukhtyar, G. C. 1930. Life and Labour in a Southern Gujarat Village. Studies in Indian Economics, ed. C. N. Vakil, 3: 1-304. Calcutta.
Muria Gond (Eg12)
    Elwin, V. 1947. The Muria and Their Ghotul. Bombay.
Senoi (Ej14)
    Dentan, R. H. 1967. The Semai of West Malaysia. New York (in press).
Kalinga (Ia16)
    Barton, R. F. 1949. The Kalingas. Chicago.
Ambonese (Ic11)
    Cooley, F. L. 1962. Ambonese Kin Groups. Ethnology 1: 102-112.
    ——— 1962. Ambonese Adat. Yale Univ. Southeast Asia Studies, Cult. Rep. Ser., 10: 1-94.
Tasmanians (Id8)
    Roth, H. L. 1890. The Aborigines of Tasmania. London.
Wongaibon (Id9)
    Howitt, A. E. 1904. The Native Tribes of South-East Australia. London.
    Radcliffe-Brown, A. R. 1923. Notes on the Social Organization of Australian Tribes. Journ. Roy. Anth. Inst. 53: 424-446.
Koita (Ie20)
    Seligmann, C. G. 1910. The Melanesians of British New Guinea. Cambridge.
Mailu (Ie21)
    Malinowski, B. 1916. The Natives of Mailu. Trans. Proc. Roy. Soc. South Australia 39: 494-706.
Mekeo (Ie22)
    Williamson, R. W. 1913. Some Unrecorded Customs of the Mekeo People. Journ. Roy. Anth. Inst. 43: 268-290.
    Belshaw, C. S. 1951. Recent History of Mekeo Society. Oceania 22: 1-23.
    Seligmann, C. G. 1910. The Melanesians of British New Guinea. Cambridge.
Muju (Ie23)
    Schoorl, J. W. 1957. Kultuur en kulturveranderingen in het Moejoe-gebied. Leiden.
Koiari (Ie24)
    Chalmers, J. 1890. Toaripi and Koiari Tribes. Rep. Austr. Assoc. Adv. Sci. 2: ii, 311-323.
    Lawes, W. G. 1879. Ethnological Notes on the Motu, Koitapu, and Koiari Tribes. Journ. Roy. Anth. Inst. 8: 369-377.
Mafulu (Ie25)
    Williamson, R. W. 1912. The Mafulu. London.

Ngarawapum (Ie26)
Read, K. E. 1946. Social Organization in the Markham Valley. Oceania 17: 93-118.
——— 1950. The Political System of the Ngarawapum. Oceania 20: 183-223.
Banaro (Ie27)
Thurnwald, R. 1916. Banaro Society. Mem. Amer. Anth. Assoc. 3: 251-391.
Busama (Ie28)
Hogbin, H. I. 1946. Local Government for New Guinea. Oceania 17: 38-66.
——— 1946-47. Sex and Marriage in Busama. Oceania 17-18.
Manam Islanders (Ie29)
Wedgwood, C. 1934. Report on Research in Manam Island. Oceania 373-403.
——— 1937. Women in Manam. Oceania 7: 401-428; 8: 170-192.
Mimika (Ie30)
Pouwer, J. 1955. Enkele aspecten van de Mimika-cultuur. 's-Gravenhage.
Aua (Ig13)
Hambruch, P. 1907. Wuvulu und Aua. Mitt. Mus. Völkerkunde Hamburg 21: 1-156.
Pitt-Rivers, G. L. F. 1925. Aua Island. Journ. Roy. Anth. Inst. 55: 425-438.
Dahuni (Ig14)
Seligmann, C. G. The Melanesians of British New Guinea. Cambridge.
Belshaw, C. S. 1955. In Search of Wealth. Mem. Amer. Anth. Assoc. 80: 1-84.
Santa Cruz Islanders (Ih9)
Davenport, W. 1964. Social Structure of Santa Cruz Island. Explorations in Cultural Anthropology, ed. W. H. Goodenough, pp. 57-93. New York.
Tannese (Ih10)
Humphreys, C. B. 1926. The Southern New Hebrides. Cambridge.
Bungi (Ne14)
Howard, J. H. 1965. The Plains-Ojibwa or Bungi. Anth. Pap. South Dakota Mus. 1: 1-165.
Shawnee (Nf13)
Trowbridge, C. C. 1939. Shawnese Traditions, ed. V. Kinietz and E. W. Voegelin. Occas. Contr. Mus. Anth. Univ. Michigan 9: 1-71.
Choctaw (Ng12)
Eggan, F. 1937. Historical Changes in the Choctaw Kinship System. Amer. Anth. 39: 34-52.
Swanton, J. R. 1931. Source Material for the Social and Ceremonial Life of the Choctaw Indians. Bull. Bur. Amer. Ethnol. 103: 1-282.
——— 1946. Indians of the Southeastern United States. Bull. Bur. Amer. Ethnol. 137: 1-943.
Pima (Ni6)
Russell, F. 1908. The Pima Indians. Ann. Rep. Bur. Amer. Ethnol. 26: 3-390.
Parsons, E. C. 1928. Notes on the Pima. Amer. Anth. 30: 445-464.
Drucker, P. 1941. Yuman-Piman. Anth. Rec. 3: 91-230.
Castetter, E. F., and W. H. Bell. 1942. Pima and Papago Indian Agriculture. Albuquerque.
Yaqui (Ni7)
Beals, R. L. 1943. Aboriginal Culture of the Cáhita Indians. Ibero-Americana 19: 1-86.
Drucker, P. 1941. Yuman-Piman. Anth. Rec. 3: 91-230.
Mixe (Nj7)
Beals, R. L. 1945. Ethnology of the Western Mixe. Univ. Calif. Publ. Amer. Arch. Ethnol. 42: 1-176.
Tarasco (Nj8)
Foster, G. M. 1948. Empire's Children. Publ. Inst. Soc. Anth., Smithsonian Inst. 6: 1-297.

Tlaxcalans (Nj9)
Nutini, H. G. 1962. Marriage and the Family in a Nahuatl-speaking Village. Unpublished doctoral dissertation, University of California at Los Angeles.
——— 1965. Polygyny in a Tlaxcalan Community. Ethnology 4: 123-147.
Zapotec (Nj10)
Fuente, J. de la. 1949. Yalagag: Una villa zapoteca serrana. Mexico.
Nader, L. 1964. Talea and Juquila: A Comparison of Zapotec Social Organization. Univ. Calif. Publ. Amer. Arch. Ethnol. 48: 195-296.
Parsons, E. C. 1936. Mitla. Chicago.
Quiche (Sa13)
Bunzel, R. 1952. Chichicastenango. Publ. Amer. Ethnol. Soc. 22: 1-438.
Schultze, L. 1933. Indiana, I: Leben Glaube und Sprache der Quiché von Guatemala. Jena.
Guahibo (Sc4)
Morey, R. 1966. Personal communication.
Chacobo (Se11)
Prost, M. D. 1965. Material Culture and Life Cycle of the Chacobo. Ms.
Lengua (Sh9)
Grubb, W. B. 1911. An Unknown People in an Unknown Land. London.
Hawtrey, S. H. C. 1901. The Lengua Indians. Journ. Roy. Anth. Inst. 31: 280-299.
Umotina (Si8)
Oberg, K. 1953. Indian Tribes of Northern Mato Grosso. Publ. Inst. Soc. Anth., Smithsonian Inst. 15: 1-144.
Cayua (Sj10)
Watson, J. B. 1952. Cayuá Culture Change. Mem. Amer. Anth. Assoc. 73: 1-144.